BECOMING WHOLE

THE ART OF INNER
TRANSFORMATION

KARIMA ANDREA EAMES

Cover design by Stephanie Wicker
Internal design by Post Pre-press Group
Edited by Shelley Kenigsberg
Typeset in 11.5/14.5 pt Minion Pro by Post Pre-press Group

 A catalogue record for this
book is available from the
National Library of Australia

ISBN: 978-0-6450113-7-1
ISBN: 978-0-6450113-6-4 (ebook)

CONTENTS

PART 6 - DEEP HEALING

PART 7 - INNER GUIDANCE

PART 8 - FROM BECOMING TO BEING WHOLE

FOREWORD

I HAVE KNOWN KARIMA since 1987, when I invited her into my Counselling Course in Pune as I knew she had studied psychology. We had an immediate loving connection. In these past 34 years, I have seen her grow and expand tremendously to become a healer, counsellor and therapist in her own right and her own capacity.

From my reading of Becoming Whole: The Art of Inner Transformation, I am impressed by her expertise and her knowledge of the different ways of dealing with people's problems and traumas.

Karima has a wide range of understanding of psychological tools and of profound methods of transformation. At the same time, she's found her unique way of growing and healing herself as well as the thousands of people that she has worked with. I find it, also, very touching how she exposes her own inner journey of maturing and awakening.

The book offers very mature and comprehensive guidance and I can highly recommend it – it is sure to be a gift to all healers, therapists, parents, teachers and everybody who is working with people.

Turiya Hanover, Cofounder of Path of Love; Founder of School of Counselling – Working with People trainings; working with people since 1975; www.turiyahanover.net

ACKNOWLEDGMENTS

THE THANKS ARE OFFERED to those who guided me as my path unfolded.

My first big thank you is to Osho. Meeting him changed my life forever. I am grateful for having spent 20 years in his communes in India and Germany. Everything I learnt during that time is the foundation of the teachings in this book. There are so many great teachers I met during those 20 years that naming all of them would fill too many pages. You know who you are. I learnt so much from living together with all my friends in the ashram and Mystery School. It was an incredibly rich time and built the foundations of who I am now.

Special thanks to Turiya Hanover and Rafia Morgan, my original teachers in my first counselling training and many trainings since, including trauma healing skills. I have the deepest respect for both of you and all the transformative work you have shared with so many. Turiya and Rafia have since created the powerful transformative process called Path of Love that I have been involved in for many years and highly recommend to anybody interested in transformation.

Thank you to Brandon Bays and the brilliant journey process that she has created. I feel proud to share these highly transformative tools as a Journey Practitioner. They have influenced and shaped the way I work. Many of them are part of this book.

Thank you to Volker Krohn and the team at Hoffmann Process which provided crucial healing when I needed it in 2004.

I would like to thank all the teachers of the Diamond Approach Australia, (DAA) a modern spiritual path based on self-understanding.

I have been studying with them since 2013 and my understanding continues to evolve and deepen. What I share in this book in relation to the DA teaching is based on what I have currently experienced and how I understand the application of the teachings at this point. I need the community of like-minded souls. It is nourishment that I wouldn't want to live without. Thank you to all my fellow lovers of truth in our group.

I am grateful to all my clients for their ongoing trust and allowing me to share my love for truth with them. Without them this book would not exist. They have contributed through participating in my original research at the start of writing this book. Thank you to all of them who have given me permission to use session transcripts, quotes or examples to demonstrate the teachings. (*Many of them appear directly and indirectly in the pages of this book*).

A heartfelt thank you to Joanne Fedler, my writing mentor. Her courses helped me to finally start writing – instead of thinking about it – and to develop my first draft.

Special thanks to my editor and 'midwife' Shelley Kenigsberg, who believed in the material when I first showed it to her and helped to shape it into the book that it is now.

I would like to thank my test readers and their feedback when my manuscript moved into its final stages.

I am very grateful to Natasha Gilmour and her team at the Kind Press. Her vision makes my heart sing, and I am proud to publish with her.

The deepest gratitude to my close friends for believing in me, propping me up when I needed it and cheering me on, especially Lisa, Pramada, Taruno, Raji and Kate.

Thank you to my beloved mother, Elfriede Hinterleitner, who keeps saying, 'I know the book will be brilliant'. I am glad the book includes a love letter to her.

Last, I am forever grateful to my husband, Terry Eames, for his unwavering support and love. He has seen me through all the ups and downs in the creation of this book and has always believed in me. Terry, I could not have done it without you!

NOTE TO THE READER

THIS IS NOT A 'read-through' and then 'put-away' kind of book. It offers the integration of theory I've gained from decades of experience as a holistic therapist. I offer my methods and, here, suggest there's an optimal way to digest and integrate the material in this book.

- When you come across an exercise or meditation within the text, take a few minutes, and, if you can, find time to do the exercise or meditation.
- It's useful to digest and integrate one chapter at a time. It's particularly relevant for Chapters 2 to 7.
- Pay attention to your body, feelings and energy as you read. If you feel restless or memories and emotions are triggered, stop and take a break.
- I mention different modalities and teachers whose work I recommend through the book and have provided details in the Further resources chapter.
- If a chapter interests you deeply, let it be an inspiration to do more research on the topic.

This is a book to come back to when you need it and to deepen your understanding of inner transformation, in time. A friend has called it a 'therapist in your pocket'.

Disclaimer

This book is written for generally healthy, well functioning individuals. It's for people with an undefined sense, or some knowing, that there is something missing in their life; for people who are seekers of a full life, of truth. This book is not suitable for those with difficult psychiatric conditions or people with heavy addictions.

PROLOGUE

'*Create your path while walking,*' said Osho, the enlightened Master under whom I studied for more than two decades. It is from that, and other, sage advice that my life philosophy has evolved. I believe that, wherever we have a choice, we can all learn to do more of what works and less of what doesn't.

There is a treasure chest deep in the core of every person. That treasure is called true nature and with our discovery of true nature we are freed from suffering. Finding it feels like coming home.

Becoming Whole: The Art of Inner Transformation is the book I would have loved to have read when, at 21, I took my first wobbly steps onto the path that was unfolding for me then; the path which I am now firmly on.

These pages contain a map to this treasure chest. They hold clues to finding the treasure; laws that can be learnt and understood. I am thrilled to share with you the toolkit I've gathered over the past four decades of inner exploration. The treasure chest that exists within can be opened using all the tools in the toolkit. And I will reveal the profound steps I have taken and continue to take on my journey. It has been a journey from a place of disconnection to a place of deep connection with myself.

There are such riches to be found in the core of your being – beauty, peace, freedom, love or whatever you are searching for. I hope this book shows you the entry points to your true nature; that these pages touch hearts and souls through sharing and understanding common challenges.

With these steps as your guide, you'll find a deep, calm place of self-acceptance. Understand and practise all the steps and connection to true nature and the feeling of being safely home, is guaranteed.

Finally, may I offer this as my wish for your journey with this book. That it is:

- a compassionate and wise tour guide on your search for truth and the meaning of life
- a friend who doesn't let you down, understands, inspires and supports you and your curious spirit
- a roadmap, helping you understand the elements of the inner world and showing you how to navigate your inner world safely
- a part of a new consciousness on this planet, a new paradigm where living in harmony, with heart and compassion – for ourselves and each other – becomes normal
- a whisper saying, 'You can do this; you can heal and find amazing treasures in the core of your being'.

Finding my way

I had arranged to meet a good friend in a nearby park for a morning walk. The drive usually takes about 10 mins and that morning, I was distracted, thinking about my book; what it's about and how to communicate it all in as good a way as possible.

Suddenly I realised I was driving the wrong route. My inner GPS had called up my friend's name and, on autopilot, I drove towards her home, not remembering that we were meeting in the park.

After I realised my mistake, I tried to get into the park through a gate I don't normally use. It's on the opposite end of my usual entry and, with traffic holdups and a closed gate, I had to turn around. This took me through yet another busy area with yet more waiting at traffic lights. Eventually, I found an open gate.

What struck me as I drove through was the exceptional beauty of this park. I was very relieved to find my friend at our agreed meeting spot. It could have been so easy to get to the right place if I hadn't taken that first wrong turn, which sent me on a maze-like journey. But

I missed it, because I was on automatic, wasn't present while driving that morning.

There are so many teachings in this.

Travelling through the inner world can feel like walking through a labyrinth. You encounter lots of roadblocks and don't know where the opening is. Yet, it can feel automatic to keep going, driving in circles, finding lots of old grooves that make us act and react in preprogramed ways. With all that activity, we're not able to get into the beautiful inner garden.

How often have I been in that same groove? How many years have I wasted stuck in a misunderstanding or by simply not knowing better?

With this book I'd like to help you travel skilfully and safely. To not waste time; to know what to avoid. Feel safe to go deeper. To find the real entrance to the inner garden.

Most of all, to get in touch with the wonder of your inner landscape, with true nature itself.

There is a great richness, beauty, and wisdom in true nature. It has everything we need, if we dare to search for, and find it.

The first step is being hungry for it, having a longing for something more in your life, something real inside your being.

True nature is at the core of every human. And it's possible for everybody to find it.

You can activate your inner compass for truth and it can guide you for the rest of your life.

My wish is that this book helps you to venture with courage, love and safety.

Developing a toolkit

I've been on a long and truly interesting journey to find what works to make me love my life. At different points of the journey, I had a lot of tools for inner transformation, but wasn't always sure which tool to use, or, when to use it.

Just as a skilled handyman can identify which tool to use for a specific job – a drill to make a hole or a spatula to fill a hole – we need to understand which tools work for us in each situation. I also present different 'recipes' for inner transformation throughout the book. They are steps to achieve results: just as a good cooking recipe can guide us to cook a delicious meal.

Let's start filling up your toolkit. I've made it as easy as possible to identify what to use when. You'll find a summary of my 'golden tools' at the end of the book, alongside more explanation where each tool first appears.

Some practical tips

At the end of Chapters 2 to 7 you'll find 'Tips for my 21-year-old self' which is a summary of the essential teachings from each chapter, that I would have loved to know at the beginning of my journey.

From Chapter 2 onwards, I've included session transcripts, presented with permission from my clients, to demonstrate the application of specific tools.

Interviews with clients was a part of the creation of this book, who generously answered questions about what process or technique worked for them and what would make the book relevant. You will find their comments or feedback throughout the book and the first one comes from Aline.

When I think about inner transformation, it comes to me that I used to think it is so mystical and unachievable, something that only the Dalai Lama or highly spiritual people do. But what you do is very very easy, accessible, and inside us all the time. If the book could express that, that anyone can easily transform, that would be the most relevant. —ALINE

PART 1

OPENING THE STORY

FINDING MY TRUE PATH

I LOOK FORWARD TO sharing with you the tools that I have gathered, tried and tested that can lead to transformation. I also want to share those moments on my path that led me to where I am now. An unusual path for a young girl born in a remote, tiny village in Northern Germany and chooses to move to live in an ashram in India. Then, 20 years later, moves to Australia. It's a journey from north to east, from east to south and it has been a fortunate and most transformative journey.

Who is Karima?

Let me tell you a bit about myself. The other night, I was invited to a party where all the guests were women. They were of all ages and I so enjoyed meeting and finding out as much as possible about them.

One, a woman in her early twenties and studying psychology in Germany shared stories about her adventures particularly travelling to Portugal and Greece in a VW Bus with her boyfriend. 'I read a tour guide,' she said, 'but we went to places not in the guidebook – one massive beach had not another soul on it. We'd drive, find a good spot and park; our home was right there. A mattress in the back was our bedroom and our kitchen had only a tiny camping gas cooker and a simple pot. We bought food at local markets. Life was easy.' I felt jealous of the simplicity of her life.

She'd also hitchhiked alone to Greece. Without fear; without anything dangerous happening to her. I couldn't believe her courage. Or stupidity? Or was it luck?

Another woman went to India at 22 and lived in an ashram for 20 years. She said it was as if she'd lived 50 lives during that time. I could have spent hours listening to her amazing experiences.

One woman from Europe immigrated to Australia when she was 42 and told me about the pain of being away from her family. She also, though, spoke about her joy at finding love.

A 60-year-old described building her own very successful business from scratch, sharing her passion, helping people. She jokingly said, 'I have lived the American dream in Australia. I arrived with $100 to my name ... hardly any possessions. Now, I'm financially secure.'

One woman stood out – she was so confident, the life of the party. Everybody gathered around her and she was radiant. Engaging, friendly, inclusive. Another woman, standing in the corner, was very shy, and I could sense her anxiety.

I wondered how all these different women ended up in one space together. Two of the women were particularly interesting and I sensed I could learn so much from them.

The first had had a chronic illness, for more than six years, and in the beginning it had reduced her energy levels by half or more. She'd been a ball of energy years before that – jumping out of bed and heading into her day with enthusiasm. When her illness started she felt like an old phone battery unable to recharge more than 40 percent at any given time. She had to relearn how to live every facet of her life. I felt sorry for her, but she didn't want pity. The illness was a life lesson, she said, and in the third year of being sick she began discovering more about the gifts of her disease.

The second was happily married late in life. She'd had lots of heart-breaks before but now, she wanted to tell anybody still looking for love to never give up. At 49, she'd found the love of her life. I laughed when she said, 'Just before I met my husband, I was considering turning gay or just accepting being alone for the rest of my life'. I was so encouraged by listening to her, by seeing her.

So, dear readers, welcome to a glimpse of my inner world!

The hunger for truth

These last 42 years of my inner work and journey have had one singular focus; they have been all about searching for truth. I was born with the longing to find out how we tick and explore the true answers to the questions: Who am I, really? What, actually, is truth? What is the meaning of life? What is true nature? What are universal laws? What are the laws of transformation? What is real?

Of course, these are not small questions! Yet, I have a passion to make transformation and metaphysics simple and understandable.

I am a human whale

I feel most at home in the depths of my inner ocean. The ocean represents feelings, sensitivity, depth. So, the deeper I go inside myself the better I feel, like a fish in water.

If I happen to be exposed to superficiality for a long stretch, it's one of my worst experiences. I feel as if I'm a fish on the beach, grilling in the sun.

Being present with a client or a friend in the depth of their inner world – whether they are dealing with shadows or inner beauty – I come alive. I feel energised in a conversation that is real and authentic. I love truth.

Twenty-one years growing up, unconsciously

I was born and grew up in Germany post World War II and lived in a small town called Borken from age three to 19. My parents and grandparents went through very difficult times during the War. Later in the book I will talk more about how that affected me. In *Chapter 6 Healing the inner child* I will show more of my childhood but the most relevant information about my first two decades is that I had no idea of an inner world, I was only oriented towards the outside.

I was 19 when I started my journey – the journey I have now come to appreciate as my path to consciousness. In the 1970s I was studying psychology and, while the study was somewhat interesting, I still had a yearning for something more – something 'out there' that I wasn't being taught. That 'something more' was in me but I didn't know it then.

My budding search led me to learn meditation. I tried a few techniques, one of which, Transcendental Meditation, wasn't a good fit for me. I kept searching and experimenting with different alternative therapy methods and joined my first experiential therapy group. It would turn out to be a most noteworthy event.

A seed falling onto fertile earth

I shared a house with 11 other students in their 20s when I was at university – a large, three-storey house where I had a simple room with a balcony, maroon and brown walls and boxes painted in the same colours served as shelves.

It was a precious time with lots of connection, laughter around the dinner table and community. The most significant feeling of that time was an intuitive understanding – from a then unknown place inside myself – that I was a seed finally falling onto fertile earth. Now, I'd call that place my soul, or being, or deeper knowing. My soul knew that I could and would grow.

Studying and boredom

I finished my half diploma in psychology but can't remember anything useful from it other than too much about rats and statistics. It certainly didn't satisfy my quest for meaning or the search for something more.

However, I read one intensely satisfying book at that time – Thomas Anthony Harris' *I'm OK—You're OK* on transactional analysis. It touched me deeply; resonated with my heart which was still very closed at that time. The book made me aware of my longing for acceptance.

Opening the door to my inner world

My back is against the wall, my knees are bent and my arms are outstretched in front of me. The longer I'm in this chair position, the more unbearable it gets. I can't hold the pose and start screaming, no idea where the screams are coming from or what they're about. A dam's breaking. From unknown places, deep inside, unidentifiable emotions surface and tears roll. I am in chaos and turmoil. Then, eventually things start settling and I lie down. A deep relaxation spreads in my body. I'm filled with a sense of peace and all the noise dissolves into silence.

I heard about the experiential psychotherapy group through a friend in my share house. The group was very intense and lasted five days. I learnt different breathing and emotional release techniques through it and at the end of that group I felt, for the first time, what energy was, that there were many unfelt feelings in me, and, importantly, that I had a centre deep in my belly that could support me and had wisdom.

I couldn't have known how powerful it would be; that it would be one of the major turning points in my life. It was, what one of my teachers calls a 'core crystallising event'. It was the first of many such groups to come.

After this group I decided to go to India and learn from the source – an Indian mystic who had been the teacher of the people running this group.

I'm going to India

I'd been so intrigued by that first experiential therapy group that I wanted to understand where the people who ran it had learned their skills.

They were disciples of an Indian guru – Bhagwan Shree Rajneesh – who lived in an ashram in India. Disciples showed their devotion by wearing orange clothes or robes and around their neck, a mala, a locket with the picture of the guru. I wanted none of that. It was weird, spooky and terribly foreign to someone who'd grown up in a small German town. More than that, I'd never been in contact with the Indian tradition of devotion to a master till then.

I was in some conflict by even going to learn from the guru. I prided myself on being a student who used their mind to study and think. It was through my mind that I understood the world and had, till then, received much praise and admiration for my intellect and ability to think. Naturally I held all that dear and feared that in learning from a guru I would have to give up my autonomous thinking. I wasn't interested in that.

Nonetheless, what I'd experienced in the group I attended was an aliveness, energy flow, feelings I hadn't even known existed. There was an inner world that I had no understanding of and I had also always wanted to find out 'how we tick'.

Also, nothing I'd studied until that time answered my deeper questions about life and I was halfway through my studies. I was disillusioned and there'd been an argument inside myself for about six months.

Heart We need to go to India! Let's check it out!

Head No way! Are you crazy? You don't want a guru. It's ridiculous to run around in orange with a necklace and a picture of a strange guy with a long beard! Do not go!

My heart won. My decision was made. I know, now, that this was the longing of my deeper self, taking me on my next important step.

I had to tell my mum. On the afternoon of a summer's day in 1979, she was standing at the sink washing dishes and I announced to her that I was going to India for my term break. I said I'd be away from mid-November for about two months.

I don't remember the detail of what I said, but it was a shock for her. In the last few years we've talked a good deal about how it was for her to be the mother of a daughter with an unusual path, a drop-out. Yet, in talking to her years later, she said, 'Nothing would have stopped you. You'd made up your mind'.

At the time I decided to leave I had two paths that my life could have taken and they could not have been more different. One (which my mother so wanted) was marriage, children, expected outcomes; the other, the life of a seeker far away from where I was born.

Those who knew me before I left, imagined I was destined for a great career, marriage, children and that I would be both rich and successful. Yet, I ended up in India for 20 years, living in a spiritual commune, an alternative society.

My friends thought I'd thrown away my chances at success. In truth, I'd just taken a different fork in my road.

Twenty years in an ashram

I am sitting on the plane to India. It is early November 1979, my first long flight, about nine hrs, and I'm nervous. Yet, halfway into the flight a deep sense of peace descends, the anxiety settles and I'm excited, looking forward to the adventure. My heart knows I'm flying in the right direction.

We land in what was then called Bombay and as the plane door opens a wall of moist shit hits my Western nose. I had been warned of the Indian smells, but nothing truly prepares you for this sensation.

I cover my nose with a tissue doused with eucalyptus oil, manage to exit a crazy chaotic airport and get into an Indian taxi for the first time.

The chaos on Indian streets is unbelievable, particularly compared with orderly German traffic. Rickshaws honk their horns and drive as if it's a slalom race. Each car, rickshaw, bicycle, moped navigates gaps and ignores normal lanes. As we leave Bombay it gets quieter. We have a four-hour ride to my destination – Pune.

Entering the gateless gate

We've navigated hundreds of potholes, and I've made sure the driver stayed awake (Indian taxi drivers are usually overworked, drive through the night and risk falling asleep at the wheel), and about four hrs later, we arrive in Pune. Sounds of early morning prayers in mosques fill the air. We pass a large number of beggars living under the bridge in Koregaon Park, a wealthy part of the city.

The smells, sounds, colours, faces create a strong set of impressions and my first night, spent in a hotel close to the ashram, is wakeful and disturbed.

The next morning, a rickshaw driver takes me to 'the gateless gate' as the entrance to the ashram was called. I have made it!

Going through feels like entering another world. There are lots of people walking around, all in long robes in a wide range of orange shades and each wears a long locket on their chest inset with a picture of Bhagwan (as he was called at that time). The guru would later change his name to Osho but for now, it's Bhagwan that we are all here to see and listen to.

As new and unfamiliar as it all is, I feel at home. Something inside me recognises I'm in the right place. Seekers from all over the planet, people like me searching for meaning, are gathered here. Within days, I feel like I've found my tribe; I am not alone anymore. The deep loneliness I felt throughout my teenage years – despite being fully involved in life, school, sports and friendships – is dissolving. I feel elated and head to the front office where I find a program of groups to join and techniques I can learn.

Taking sannyas

In the six months leading up to my trip, I'd found out about the community and the option, for those in it, to become a disciple of Bhagwan or a 'sannyasin'. I'd repeated my declaration that I was only going to, 'check this place out and learn a few things' but not commit to being a disciple. Every day of being in this invigorating energy field which Bhagwan and his devotees called 'The Buddha field' lessened that solid resolve.

It is my second week in the ashram and I stride towards the front office. 'I want to take sannyas!' I say and Arup, a female sannyasin, takes my name down and gives me a date for my initiation. It will be 17 December and will take place during the regular evening darshan (Sanskrit for being in the presence of the divine. Simply put, it means, 'seeing the master').

Darshan with the Master is a devotional event with strict rules and is no different on 17 December. I arrive, wearing a long flowing orange dress, and my long black hair is washed and neat. We're not allowed to use scented shampoo – no fragrances are allowed in the auditorium as Bhagwan has allergies and it is respectful to everybody else to not impose strong smells, fragrances like perfume or even nicotine on others.

About 30 of us sit in rows on the floor. Soft meditative music is playing.

The only conditions attached to taking sannyas in 1979 were to wear orange and have a mala with the picture of the master. Devotional rituals are part of the Indian culture but the robes symbolised an outer ritual of an inner shift, to demonstrate our interest in waking up, a commitment to finding out who we truly are.

When my name is called, I walk up to the Master and am seated right in front of him. I look into his eyes and he looks right at me. It feels as if the world around me disappears and all I can see are two light beams shooting at me. Bhagwan talks to me and I am entranced; the only sentence that penetrates my stupor is 'dawn is not far'.

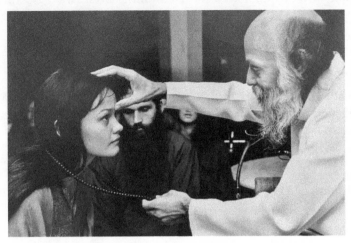

I feel like a deer caught in a car's head lights.

My well trained literal German mind thinks that is very likely a good thing! I don't know what he means by dawn, but if it is not far, that can only mean weeks before I reach full understanding, right? It sounds promising.

If I'd known then that the dawn he was talking about would take decades, I would probably not have felt so positive about the statement. I don't remember what else he said, but it was being transcribed and, years later, I managed to read what he'd said in one of his books.

'Dawn is not far'
A few years ago, watching an actual sunrise after a night of very little sleep on a meditation retreat, I reflected on what Osho's statement means to me now, 40 years later. It resonates as an awakening to who I really am; a deep and real connection to myself; a trust in the goodness of the universe and a knowing that everything I ever searched for, is right inside of me.

Thirteen groups in five months
There were two distinct timelines for the life of the ashram and the disciples in Pune – Pune 1 and 2. I was there at some point in both:

during Pune 1, from the mid 1970s to 1981 and in Pune 2 from 1986 onwards.

On my first trip, I stayed for five months from Nov 1979 till April 1980 and took part in 13 personal growth workshops of three to seven days each. I wanted to grow and was hungry to learn.

The encounter group

What am I doing here? We're on mattresses, sitting in a circle. Teertha, the leader and his assistants sit in front. Everybody is invited to express and release whatever is there.

This is pure chaos, people screaming at each other, attacking each other. All I did in that group was try to survive. I don't have any recollection of a good moment or a breakthrough. I think I was mostly in shock and overwhelm.

I know now that the program was designed to break down layers of thick protection.

Now, I call that style of therapeutic work 'the dinosaur times of therapy'. Just as they died out, so did this kind of work. And for good reason. It was rough, raw and maybe suited some people. It was definitely not for sensitive souls like me and it was, by far, the worst therapeutic experience I ever had.

Still, I'm proud I tried it. My motto has always been that you never know where gold can be found.

Art groups

All I remember is that I did them and they were fun. They didn't stick with me and though for some people art, painting and creative expression is a pathway, it wasn't mine.

Who is in?

I remember this group was hard. For three days we would work in pairs and ask each other, 'Who are you?'

It was the opposite of the Encounter group. This one was very disciplined and totally structured.

That was my first deeper interaction with myself and it was too much, I got sick on the second day. Meeting myself was hard work and there was lots of resistance and fear. I also have no memory of a breakthrough.

Somendra's energy group

This softer finer energy work resonated with me and here my heart started to sing. I don't have a clue how or why it worked but I started feeling some interesting states of openness and flow. I even had my first glimpses of inner ecstatic states.

Somendra, who led the group, was a very skilled energy worker; a magician. Through his techniques I was opened up to dimensions inside myself that I didn't even know existed. I loved his work.

The other courses? I don't remember anything else in detail. But I do remember that after five months of groups, tasting it all, meditating every night with the Master, I wanted more. I started experiencing exhilarating states of inner freedom, silence, the first glimpses of letting go, relaxation and inner peace. I was hooked.

This was my tribe, my people, my true home and I decided to live in Pune forever. But to be able to live in India for good, I needed to fly back to Germany and settle things there.

I was young and naive and had no idea what a crazy, interesting rollercoaster journey lay ahead of me.

India forever

In April 1980, I flew back to Germany having decided to leave it for good and believed, at the time, that I would never come back. Now, when I think of my 23-year-old self, I'd like to tell her something. 'Never make a decision for the rest of your life at a young age.'

What did I leave behind?

There were many future paths for me, in Germany. A career as a licensed psychologist. Marriage to my first boyfriend and life as a lawyer's wife. I'd be living a 35-minute drive from where I grew up.

Yet, my determination to leave was solid and I made sure that the past was erased in quite dramatic ways. I burnt my photographs, sold everything I owned. I kept nothing except for my orange clothes and a small backpack.

I didn't have much money to take with me, the equivalent of AU $3000, but living and travelling in India was very cheap at the time. A month's rental was about $50 and a basic Indian meal cost around 50 cents.

I can't even remember how I communicated with my parents about this decision; I must have blocked those conversations out. In talking to my Mum about it recently it's clear that she, too, remembers very little from that time. But she remembers it was very hard to have her child go to a foreign country, for good. Had I known how difficult it was going to be for her, I don't think I could have left. Now that I'm able to put myself in her shoes, I apologised for the hurt or confusion I must have caused.

And, in the end, neither could I have known that my 'forever' would last for only eight months.

Back in Pune

So, back in India, I think, I am here for good. I laugh, now, at my naivete. My 23-year-old self might have heard someone saying, 'We plan, and God laughs'.

I started working in the ashram and with my worker pass, I had free entrance and food passes. My only living expense was a very low rent. My money could last quite a long time.

On meditation

The day's activities included many hours of meditation. Each morning, a Bhagwan-designed technique called Dynamic meditation. Most afternoons, there would be Kundalini meditation. I will be grateful for the rest of my life to know and practise these meditations. Each evening included a two-hour meditation with the Master in our Buddha Hall – later called Osho discourses. Most of these discourses have been transcribed and have filled hundreds of books. Many are in India's state libraries.

Bhagwan's vision for all of us in the ashram was that we look at what separates us from each other and work to erode it. Equality was the ideal. Our origins, possessions and status outside the ashram did not matter here. We all wore orange robes and didn't pay attention to the external (and typical) symbols of status – fancy clothes and accessories, jewellery, cars, posh houses or certificates on the wall.

The next step on the journey for many was to become an ashram worker. The different jobs – all unpaid and voluntary – were assigned by staff in the front office. Our work – a commitment to living consciously, in the present – might be domestic, or administrative. An academic might be cleaning toilets or scrubbing pots in the kitchen. We were put in situations where we could question our beliefs about our superiority, or entitlement. The intention was that, in time, our sense of separation from each other would fade.

I was ready to take that next step yet dreaded to hear what work I'd be assigned.

So, when I was given the role of kids' mama, I felt very lucky. For the next few months, I'd be spending my days with the two- to four-year-old children of those in the ashram in our ashram kindergarten or play school.

I learnt so much from the children. I had, until then, lived completely in my head, with no understanding of living in the moment, living in what is also called presence. The children were great barometers to keep me present.

If I wasn't, they'd be demanding and difficult. When I was present with them, we'd have a great time – splashing water in the warm Indian weather, paint, telling stories or just goofing around. It was meditation in action, and I grew more and more aware of when I was present or when I was drifting off in thought.

However, I started to feel more intensely. Being in the ashram allowed me to be more open and that, in turn, meant repressed emotions – pain and hurt – began to surface. Sometimes, they were triggered through romantic relationships. I had thought, hoped, that the previous five months of being in Pune and doing all the groups would help me feel better.

I believed in doing the inner work and had memorable openings, but one day when I felt rejected by a lover, I was deeply disappointed. I thought the sense of freedom, love and peace would continue, get better. This was, I discovered, my expectation of a linear progression on the journey.

But the real work of going within to discover your truth is slow, fluctuating – definitely not linear. There were times when old memories, old wounds surfaced. These, too, wanted to be healed or met with consciousness. But I had no roadmap to navigate the inner world safely. And I certainly had no lasting understanding of healing or inner transformation yet.

Throwing the mala

On my second time in Pune, one unforgettable day, I was in my room, heartbroken, challenged because I was confronting my hurt. I was so frustrated that I threw my mala into the corner; threw away the locket with 108 beads and Bhagwan's picture – the symbol of my commitment to being a sannyasin. I hadn't signed up to hurt or to feeling so deeply challenged. The spiritual honeymoon was over.

Fortunately, I didn't leave the ashram. The hurt passed and I continued. The desire to run away from pain was, I learned, completely normal. Probably even expected. Had I left, I would've missed out on so many formative and powerful experiences. I would not have understood how inner transformation happens.

My intellectual framework had me believe that transformation happens in the mind, from study. Yet, I came to see that real transformation happens through the body, through directly experiencing our pain or joy, all our emotions, and being able to heal past wounding.

Sexuality and spirituality

In the eight months of my second stay, I dated a lot. I felt free to experience different sexual relationships and this was, also, something – perhaps radical and certainly commented on by those outside the ashram – that Bhagwan encouraged. He wanted us to understand the mental divisions that most people have between spirituality and sexuality. To become whole and dissolve all separations, we needed to reconsider some of the traditional religious precepts that a lot of us had been brought up with. One of those, for many religions and spiritual traditions, is the concept of celibacy. Bhagwan encouraged us to ignore that restrictive thinking; we didn't need to commit to that. He wanted us to be free and natural, to experiment and find out what our natural sexuality was. I definitely enjoyed the sexual freedom.

Looking back at that time now, I feel grateful for having had that freedom. It led eventually to wanting a committed lasting relationship and prepared me for now being happily married without feeling I had missed out.

Bad press and misinterpretations

I want to mention too, that Osho was, often, a controversial figure. There were many things other than an encouragement for sexual freedom or other ways of being that led people to see Osho, throughout his life, as deserving of criticism. One particular spur for these observations was the fact that Osho owned 96 luxurious Rolls-Royces. The cars – given to him as gifts by his disciples – led to him earning the long-lasting name 'The Rolls-Royce Guru'. It was an issue that triggered a lot of discussion, particularly in US media and communities. Many people within families, particularly families of members of the ashram, speculated about what they represented.

I needed to find my own understanding of it, of all the bad press around Osho because it went on for decades. I eventually decided to only go with my own personal experience in the ashram and in his presence. Anything else, for me, was guess work. My personal experience was truly positive. Nothing weird happened to me, I wasn't brainwashed or forced into anything I didn't want to do. On the contrary, I felt liberated.

The simplicity and beauty of our daily life was not much talked about when comments were made about life in the ashram. One of the outstanding elements was that we were real; we didn't pretend to be anything we weren't. If we were sad, we would show sadness when merely walking around or at a meal together.

There were other ways that we let others know how we were feeling. For example, if we wanted to be alone and have space, we would wear an 'In Silence' button. All of this, was part of our conscious agreement, part of the 'Buddhafield' as Osho called it. He was referring to the energetic field of consciousness that was created by all of us being there for the same reason: to wake up.

Nowadays, thinking back to my time in Pune, I often feel like I lived on another planet. A good planet – a conscious planet.

I lived in a world with values that reflected a higher idea about life's purpose, living consciously and with integrity. It's a way of thinking and living that I hope will eventually become a wider reality on this planet. I got a glimpse of what is possible. Osho called this possibility for being different, the 'new man'.

Illness and return to Germany

One challenge for me, and one for which I had no knowledge or real understanding, was hygiene and health around food. When I first arrived in India, I ate and enjoyed Indian street food. I didn't understand that there might be problems with the hygiene of the food. I certainly wasn't the only one who got sick with a gut bug.

Parasites are commonly found where sanitation isn't necessarily of very high standards and this was the case where we were.

I have a memory of an awful day lying on my bed not being able to hold anything down – diarrhoea, vomiting; nausea and fever combined. When these symptoms eventually passed, I was very weak.

The medication for what was probably amoebic dysentery, was a strong antibiotic (Flagyl which was used then is now considered unsafe). I had three rounds of the medication, but relapsed each time. After the third round it was clear that I couldn't recover in India.

'Forever' lasts eight months

I was deeply disappointed to have to go back to Germany for treatment. When I arrived in Frankfurt in May 1981, I was physically exhausted and for the first few months recovered in my parents' home. I had no idea where I would go from there; I had never imagined I'd be coming back to Germany.

Bhagwan left the ashram in Pune shortly after I left in May 1981 and went to America, where he lived till 1985, in Rajneeshpuram, a community in Oregon built and run by sannyasins. So, Pune 1 was finished and, with that, there was no incentive to go back to India.

Once I had healed, I explored different options in Germany and Switzerland and found a commune of sannyasins in Belgium where I stayed for six months. My next big chapter unfolded when I went to Cologne.

A decade in Cologne

From 1982–1991, I lived as an ashramite in the Osho commune in Cologne that was modelled on the ashram in Pune; Bhagwan had officially changed his name to Osho in 1989. The ashram – my community of like-minded people – was located in the middle of the city and, just as it had operated in Pune, our jobs were assigned to us.

We lived in shared rooms and I didn't need any money. Every material need was taken care of.

My work included being a waitress, a seamstress, a kids' mama, handywoman and, even, a cocktail shaker in our disco. Our disco, called 'Zorba the Buddha', was famous – a place of celebration in the centre of Cologne where all of us, guests and crew alike would regularly dance the roof off.

Towards the end of my decade in Cologne, I lived in another share house that had the same warmth and camaraderie of my house at university. We were all friends, connected to each other, spending time, sharing meals. It was deeply comforting, uplifting, nourishing.

Pune 2

Pune 2 started when Osho came back to India in the mid 80s. Though I was living in Cologne I travelled to Pune regularly. Sometimes, for long stays. In 1986, I was back in Pune for eighteen months as Osho had returned to India by then.

Being invited to train as a counsellor, 1987

In 1987, at the age of 30, I did a six-week counselling training in Pune. It was these six weeks that set the path for the career I have now had for 33 years. I had wanted to be a therapist; and had studied psychology but as I was given different jobs when I first went to the commune, I didn't use that training.

When I was invited by two of the counselling trainers to join the training, I couldn't believe my luck. One needed to pay for the training, but I had no money, and wasn't earning anything. Some of my friends who did have money gave me some and, whatever I got together, I paid. Essentially, however, I was given the training for almost free and my dream had come true.

Once I'd finished the course I was invited to give sessions in the ashram. I have not stopped doing this kind of work, since. I often prayed to know if I was meant to do anything else or if this was the job I was meant to do.

I was lucky to get enough confirmation on the way that I eventually understood, deeply, that this is my destiny. I am passionate about my job – I'll be working for as long as my physical body allows me to do so.

Finland and spooky experiences

The first time I realised how much I love space and time and rest was in 1991 when I moved to Finland with a partner.

From April–Oct 1991 I lived in Finland and started working in a healing centre in Helsinki. I was a holistic therapist and fortunate to have flexibility with my work times.

I was free every morning and, as we lived close to a large forest, I walked through the Finnish forests most mornings – often for up to two hours. I was overwhelmed by its beauty.

Until then, I'd loved being in nature and found German forests were beautiful, rich and green. Having lived in India for a long period, I'd seen the brown barren stretches of nature that were called forest there. So, German forests stood out as very lush.

Yet, when I walked in a Finnish forest, for the first time, I was astounded by the aliveness of the trees. The tones of green were more radiant than anything I had ever seen.

During that time, I also began studying Native American Indian shamanism and, in this tradition, trees were considered 'standing people'. That description made so much sense to me as I could feel their energy, feel how alive they were. In that time, I started experimenting with different concepts that resonated with me from those teachings.

I started to call my daily walks medicine walks; I'd walk through the forest noticing everything around me. I'd pay attention to a leaf falling, the sounds of the wind, the chirping of a bird, the colours around me, the light filtering through the trees. I would walk and feel different energies in the ground. I would lie on big granite rocks. On each walk, I experienced a strong sense of relaxation and grounding.

Called by a rock

I became more and more attuned to the nature around me and walked wherever I felt drawn. One day I heard a call, followed it and came to a beautiful reddish rock, lying in the shade of a massive granite rock. It was one of a kind in that area.

In the Native American Indian tradition, stones are known as stone people and, that made sense to me. The stone told me to take it home. I listened and picked it up. I was probably two or three kilograms, so, not easy. But I had no doubt that this was meant to happen. I'd never had a rock call me, or even speak to me, before.

So, to be clear, I was not on any drugs or under the influence of anything mind altering. This was experienced with full consciousness. Until now, at some point in my metaphysics training – a training to understand subtle or finer energies and energy flow – I had learnt to feel stones but I had never learnt to listen to them. So I picked it up and took it home.

At home, I put the rock on my lower belly just below the belly button. It became a habit that I called a 'stone bath'. Often, I would leave it on my body for an hour or more and relax deeply.

By that time, I had begun working in the spiritual healing centre in Finland and had the wonderful opportunity of beginning to facilitate groups. I had led groups before, had participated in many and assisted in quite a few.

I started a women's group, one evening a week. After the ideas came to me during my 'stone bath' I would try them out in the evenings with great results.

This happened over the course of many weeks and months and, eventually, became a weekend women's group put together from the different pieces I had experimented with.

Sometimes it felt like my rock was the embodiment of an old Native American shaman woman, teaching me step-by-step. During that time someone gave me a book on native teachings called 'Sacred Path cards' by Jamie Sams. I still have it. The book came with tarot cards and I studied them and read the book. Each time the outer teachings confirmed what was revealed on the inner.

Many of the native American teachings made sense to me. The 'Great Spirit' as the universe, trees as 'Standing People', rocks as carriers of ancient wisdom, 'Mother' Earth, 'Father' Sky.

I often used that concept to feel held, loved, supported and protected by energies much bigger than my family, my personal parents with all their conditions and limitations.

Another massive fork in the road

By February 1994, I had been in India since October 1993, and had worked in the Mystery School – one of the faculties in our 'multiversity', a university within the ashram offering different modalities around healing and inner transformation. I had done the Energy Reading training, assisted in Heart Groups, and given Energy Reading sessions and Energy Balancing massages.

I had no idea that my decision to stay in India at the beginning of 1994 would change my life forever. Could I have known then that I would receive an amazing education? Have outstanding opportunities to develop my skills as a group leader? Grow tremendously through all the challenges of co-leading a faculty of up to 200 people? That what would unfold would become the foundation of a successful business in Sydney? Definitely not.

I stayed because of one regular evening meditation session. One evening, sitting in meditation in Buddha Hall I was feeling disturbed. I was about to fly back to Germany after a few months in the ashram, having stayed for as long as my money stretched. The disturbance, like an inner fire alarm going off, was so strong that it forced me to listen. I decided to stay and this is how it unfolded.

Within a very short time of the decision to stay, my life changed dramatically. A group of directors at the ashram's Mystery School decided to leave, for good, and head to Sedona, US and set up a school there. Suddenly, the Pune school had no director team.

A team of four or five of us working in the school wanted the Mystery School to continue. So we decided to step up and keep the faculty from falling apart. I became an assistant director with a few others.

We had students year-round. In High Season (October to March) there were 200 workers; in Low Season about 50 of us lived and worked there. I was given free accommodation in the ashram – a studio apartment in a black marble pyramid. I already had free food (all of it tasty and nutritious) in our canteen. So, with these bonuses, I was able to sustain myself.

I started offering regular groups – various women's groups and one I particularly valued called Opening to the Heart. I was, also, running a faculty, except I had no previous training for the role. I grew into it by doing it. I stayed at Pune for four-and-a-half years and the whole experience was a remarkable training.

Everything I learnt at that time became the foundation of what I now do. When I first arrived in Sydney, I ran a women's group and an Energy Reading training and gave individual and couples sessions.

In Feb 1999, my life took another drastic turn, the next massive fork in the road. This time it played out through the encounter with two very different men, which culminated with the three of us meeting to jointly decide how to continue. Would I stay with Ray or leave him for George?

Truth is a higher value than love

Ray and I had been together for about two years by early 1999 and there was a deep love between us. However, despite years of learning and growth it was clear our needs were not aligned.

George had been expressing his interest to me for a while, but I didn't act on it as I was faithful to Ray. I would openly discuss George's attraction to me with Ray.

I had inner guidance that my next chapter was going to be a different path to the one I was on. The message said, 'Now settle and marry'.

Ray, who had come from a settled life in France, wanted to spread his wings and travel, be free and explore.

I was in a different phase. I wanted to settle in the world. I had, by then, lived in an alternative society, a spiritual community, for 20 years. I was at the beginning of my fourth decade and it was getting clearer that I needed to take care of myself and earn money. I couldn't imagine myself getting old in India. One of the reasons for me to leave India, was the fact that there was no structure that gave me security for old age. It was time to come out of the 'spiritual greenhouse' and reenter the world.

I had been hearing Osho stories for 20 years. Sometimes, I'd be listening for one or two hours a night as he spoke on topics related to truth and spirituality. Twenty years adds up to roughly 10,000 hours of deep listening to a Master's wisdom.

Osho could translate any existing spiritual tradition – the Indian Sutras or Chinese wisdom, Buddhist teachings, Sufi wisdom – into modern understandable language. All of his talks were informative and uplifting and we'd learn unusual pieces of information including, for example, the Bauls whose traditions were relatively unknown in the wider world.

One of Osho's stories had particular meaning for me. It was of a man who had meditated for many years in the Himalayas and thought he'd found peace and a specific state of enlightenment. The man came down from the mountains and, for the first time in many years, entered a busy marketplace. In no time, this seemingly enlightened peaceful person flew into a rage at someone blocking his way.

Osho didn't tell us what to think of that story but the teaching for me was plain. I understood that our level of consciousness is only real if tested in the wider world and, best, in a busy life with normal challenges. How would we respond to obstacles? Unexpected betrayals? Misunderstandings? Rejections? Projections? People not living from the heart, not feeling? People acting unconsciously and being disconnected?

I was, at that time, living in an environment where consciousness was the highest value. If anything went wrong between people or with the organisation, we would address it. We might work directly with each other or we get help from a third person, a friend or a therapist. We would not walk around with emotional baggage. I understood how to live with an open heart by that time and wanted to live according to that.

Yet it was time to get out of the protected environment and test my level of consciousness.

I had the challenge of my relationship and of where to go or be. So, I came into the meeting with a prayer. 'Osho, please guide this meeting and let the three of us come to a truth that is a win-win for all of us.' With no idea what the outcome would be, we were all open to find a truth that resonated with the three of us.

George offered for me to leave for Sydney with him, to get married, and reconnect with the world at large. He was a man who had lived in the world, was grounded, and financially free. He owned a beautiful apartment on one of Sydney's most beautiful beachside suburbs, Tamarama. He had done a powerful process in Australia – Path of Love – and was seeking more understanding of himself and his spiritual path. It was his first time in India and he was opening to the wonders of the inner world.

My relationship with Ray was the most beautiful I had experienced until then. Tremendous sexual healing, beautiful conscious lovemaking, similar values, great honesty in communication. Our connection was based on being truthful with each other, and, as Osho said, 'to rise in love'.

Ray was very good looking, and he was French (I love the French language).

The three of us spent a few hours together; shared what we were feeling, longing for, our needs and visions for the future. When the meeting came to a clear outcome, each of us was satisfied that it was the right decision. The decision was for me to take up George's offer to go to Sydney with him.

My Australian adventure

On 1 May 1999, I arrived in Sydney with an old suitcase, hardly any money, a few scrappy clothes from living in a commune, as most of my daily wear there was a maroon robe. After 20 years in a spiritual commune, where the focus was on meditation and consciousness, I had no outer possessions, yet I felt rich on the inner.

The relationship with George didn't last. But I will be forever grateful to him for having brought me to Australia. That was his role in the bigger play. I would never have come here on my own.

I had thought I would go back to Europe and be closer to my family again. But I was in Sydney and, though George and I had parted, my heart had fallen in love with Sydney and doors were opening easily around work and sharing my gifts. I knew I was meant to be here.

I didn't know that you could have a love affair with a city or a place yet that is what I eventually experienced. I remember one day flying in from Germany. As we were about to land my heart felt warm, excited and fuzzy – the way it can feel when we see a loved one. I knew then that my heart wanted me to live in this amazing, beautiful city.

Once I was on Australian ground I was hooked. When, in my early days there, I received my tax file number and, soon after, my ABN (Australian Business Number) my friends couldn't believe how thrilled I was. I danced with excitement because I was so ready to be part of society again.

I lived in a beautiful beachside suburb, the fulfilment of a childhood dream. I always wanted to live close to the ocean and now I was living near the sea on the biggest island in the world. What a great manifestation – to witness such beauty of nature, the water, the blue skies and bright sunshine. In my first month in Australia, May 1999, I remember noting 31 glorious days of sunshine.

Sydney had won my heart. I loved its vibrancy, beauty, possibilities. Here, I built my business, this is the soil on which I express my passion. Now I am happily married, own a property and have a successful practice in the heart of Sydney.

A German friend who tried to settle in Australia but wasn't successful, put it well. 'Australia either gobbles you up or spits you out.' I feel very blessed that Australia has allowed me to stay.

Then and now

When we talk about inner work, there are many ways to describe it. There are interchangeable terms – you might read about spiritual or personal growth, becoming more conscious or learning to be more present, start awakening or waking up.

So, an intensely useful thing to do, when venturing into becoming more conscious is to make notes about as much of your life as you can. Document different ages and phases and begin to understand your 'biography'.

I didn't do that in my early stages of my journey through life. My journey is, obviously, understood in hindsight. Those insights have helped me understand not only the trajectory, but also the tools I needed, and those I found along the way to now.

Age 19 – the beginning of my journey into consciousness

At 19, I was rather disconnected from my body and from my emotions. I felt lonely deep inside, empty, I didn't know my inner world at all. I had weird beliefs about myself and they included feelings that I was unlovable, never really enjoying my body or feeling attractive.

Yet, I *was* creative, good looking and best in school. I knitted, sewed, played guitar and flute, painted, danced, swam and did sports. From the outside, I was highly functional and admired. I had friends and a boyfriend. To others it would have seemed I had it all.

Yet, I was missing something crucial: my real self.

Age 63 – now

I can feel. I experience pretty much every emotion that's available to human beings. I know that feeling emotions is part of my – and everybody's – healthy nature.

I'm now a great friend to my physical body. I am very connected to it and can choose to sense every part of it. I live in and honour it as the vehicle of who I really am. I respect its present reality – that I live with a chronic illness and my body needs a lot of care and attention. Sometimes it's like I'm a mum with a young baby and I am ok with that. My body was the last aspect of myself to get the right attention. I can see now that I didn't honour it enough at certain times.

Now, I feel full on the inside and I know true nature. I know it, its goodness is in me. Even in times of momentary disconnection, I sense it is there and it's up to me to connect to it.

I love my life the way it is right now. With its simplicity. I can feel myself and I can feel others. I appreciate my mind and it's my friend. I love the little balcony where I live; it is small, lush and green and I'm proud of 'my little Bali,' which I have created. My little paradise.

I love my husband and our honest relationship that keeps deepening. Most importantly: my heart is happy.

There are times I recognise a spontaneous upwelling of love for life, of gratitude, and inner happiness for no specific outer reason. I often feel contentment, inner warmth and fullness. Satisfaction. A deep love for being human and all that it entails.

Compassion, stillness, peace, deep relaxation and letting go have become familiar.

The purpose of my life – to know who I truly am – is something I know in the present moment. And it's not a stagnant state; the discovery of the inner world, of true nature continues and deepens.

Life is never boring. I have found true inner richness. And some outer wealth has gathered around me and, as well as not feeling attached to it, I am very grateful.

I have a 'village' of clients and I care deeply for them. It is a joy that I can help, share with them what I know and what worked for me, and make their lives a little better. It is so satisfying when a client, having arrived in suffering, or struggle, leaves a session feeling better.

I feel real, human and, because of it, connected to other humans in large and small moments – walking down the street, smiling at a stranger and, having them smile back. I feel moments of heartbreak too, for example, when I see a homeless person in numb disconnection from things around them. All of this – the joy and the heartbreak – is part of understanding my humanity.

Would I trade my unusual path for another type of life? Should I have married my first boyfriend and have become a lawyer's wife, and probably had two to four children, and be working as a psychologist? I can't know for sure, but I don't for one minute, regret the path I chose.

I wish I knew then ...

My biography plots a path with many ups and downs. From all those, it has brought me to this place and still, there are many steps to take. They can each be thrilling; each be tough going. They will always be worth it. I am so glad to be able to offer the toolkit that I wish I had had with me, on the journey. These are things I wish I knew along the way...

I wish I knew about love

I wish I knew that the source of love is inside me. It's hidden under the layers of protection and heartbreaks, bad memories, failed attempts to find love by looking in the wrong places. Often, I would choose unavailable men, or start a sexual connection when, in truth, all I wanted was a hug.

I wish I truly knew that love conquers all

Keeping our hearts open doesn't mean we won't feel pain. And true love includes the fear of loss. It's this open heart that will feel joy and pain – they are inseparable and inescapable.

Yet inside each of us is a place that has never been wounded. And love has the power to transform us. We'll look at details of the transformative power of love in *Part 4 Opening to the heart.*

I wish I knew about faith

Having a faith – whether religious, spiritual or just a belief that love conquers all – keeps us going when life is joyous and, also, when life is at its darkest, its hardest. Faith creates a connection to something bigger than us and it can help us to find a way to take the next step even if it seems impossible to keep going.

For some faith may come from a particular religion or religious practice. My faith comes from knowing that true nature is in me. For a long time, being in Osho's presence gave me a sense of faith. When I saw him for the first time I felt a deep sense of trust and, over the years, he restored my faith in myself and humanity.

I wish I knew about loss

I understand that any loss can truly be overcome, and while grief is inevitable in some measure, all of it needs to be embraced, felt, allowed, in order to heal. There will most likely be times, when feeling grief in a given moment is too overwhelming. At those times, it's healthy to disconnect from it.

Yet coming back, to feel it, is the way to heal. Repressing grief in some way – perhaps by stopping ourselves weeping, or even forgetting that we have grief – can lengthen the grieving experience.

I wish I knew about success

Success doesn't give lasting fulfilment; success comes and goes. Success is, also, subjective. Though I was best in my class each year for 13 years it didn't make me happy. I definitely enjoyed school and learning and my success did give me security and a sense of worth, but it only went so far. It was, in the main, artificial. And it didn't give me inner happiness. All the years of studying were definitely not fulfilling. I knew there was something beyond outer success, and that I hadn't yet found it.

Now, I *know* that real success is not the position or status you have, the fame or the amount of money you earn. Real success is doing what you love.

I wish I knew about friendship

True friendship – a real connection between two people – is a precious gift. It is built on honesty, trust, vulnerability, shared experiences, understanding each other, having courage to expose difficult things, having fun together, being able to relax or being quiet together.

I wish I knew about money

Money was never a high priority in my life and I never chased it. So much so, that I lived for 20 years with almost no material possessions. Now, my relationship with money feels healthy, I treat money with respect and gratitude. I also know it's possible to live without material wealth and feel blessed. In the early days of being in the commune in Pune, I had a tiny part of an apartment, a mattress on the floor, a wooden shelf for my things, and a curtain for a wall. I was happy because I lived in a conscious environment. Now, though I enjoy my physical possessions, I don't take them for granted.

I wish I knew about health

I wish I knew when I was in my 20s and 30s how important the physical body is for any life of conscious understanding. I know that I can't take health and physical wellbeing for granted.

I didn't understand how important nutrition and healthy eating was; nor that sleep or supplements were important. When, after 10 years of sleep-deprivation, I became very ill with a chronic illness I understood all that.

My body also tells me how to treat it; it doesn't lie. What this means is that it's important to listen to physical symptoms and, often, they can emerge from emotional or physical issues. I say thank you to my body every day; it's the house I live in and I know health is a precious gift.

I wish I knew about beauty

I've understood that inner beauty is much more important than outer beauty. Beauty comes from the inside and radiates out. It is a feeling. If someone is fully present and loving towards themselves, they have a 'glow' that transcends physical features.

I wish I knew about happiness

When our heart is open, when we feel the real parts of ourselves, we can feel true happiness. Inner happiness allows us to be fully present to our outer life and to enjoy what it presents to us. When we are real and connected with ourselves, happiness can well up for no specific reason. For me, the source of that well includes my relationships, my work, my home, my stillness, my aloneness. It includes simple household activities, cleaning, watching TV, shopping. It includes creative pursuits, writing, gardening. So much. Inner happiness is the foundation for outer happiness.

Was the work worth it?

In what was to be my first counselling training in India, one of my influential teachers said to a group of us, 'You are all here to wake up. You've left your old life behind and travelled to India! Well, I promise you the moment real transformation happens, you will want to pack your suitcases and run'.

Was it all worth it? Yes. It has been worth navigating the perils of my unknown inner landscape. Being stretched to my limit particularly when old pain surfaced, and I learnt to feel again. Worth it when, in moments, I felt like an elastic rubber band pulled apart by two strong people, and I wondered, 'Can I bear this for another second?' You will find different examples through the book, of specific challenges I confronted on my journey and how I overcame them.

When we begin inner work and delve into the layers of the unconscious and true inner parts, it can be confronting. Yet, we feel driven to continue no matter what we are confronting Then, as we persevere, we reach 'the point beyond return'. A point where the awakening consciousness and the growing awareness don't allow us to stop delving. Perhaps, it is only in hindsight, that we can see the value and blessing of our new understanding. Yet I do know, and we can all know, that it really is, always, worth persevering.

I wish I'd known ...

I wish I'd known from the beginning of my journey, what to expect, where it would take me. I wish I'd been assured I could find amazing treasures and had the roadmap. In truth, I wish I had everything I am trying to transmit through this book – a solid tool kit. I hope it is a companion on the path to normalise the challenges; challenges that anyone on a path to find who they truly are, will face.

And so, I offer this book to you. It is the one I would have loved to have.

TRUE NATURE

EVERY RELIGIOUS OR SPIRITUAL tradition has its own term for the notion of true nature.

I have come across many different names for true nature during my search for truth: being, essence, source, the divine, higher self, the eternal in us. The concept of true nature is the state of being whole. It can also be experienced as a godliness, god in us, magic, mystery.

This book describes the journey each of us can make from becoming whole to being whole.

A beggar on a treasure box

Each day, on my way to the ashram I passed a beggar, a man in his late 30s, always very friendly. In India, begging is an accepted manner of earning a living and this road was his territory. He managed to gather a reasonable sum of money each day from the hundreds of Westerners passing him on their way to the 'gateless gate', the ashram entrance.

In one of Osho's daily discourses he told us a joke that I found rather funny.

Two beggars, Alex and Ben are sitting under a tree in a small town.

Alex turns towards Ben and says, 'What is going on, you look depressed today?'

'Aah,' says Ben. 'I am thinking of applying for a job.'

'What?' replies Alex. 'And admit you're a failure!'

One of Osho's many teaching stories involved a beggar and each time he told it, I visualised the beggar I saw each day on the ashram road, sitting on a box, his rags and face dirty. His state and clothing befitted his role.

> *One day a well dressed gentleman passed a beggar on the road and turned towards him.*
>
> *'Why don't you get up and open the box you are sitting on?' the gentleman asked.*
>
> *The beggar looked at him, perplexed, and thought, 'How stupid is that? Why would I look into the old, bashed box I've been sitting on for years?'*
>
> *But the gentleman had a commanding presence and the beggar got up. Perhaps if he did, the beggar thought, the gentleman might give him some money. He turned around, bent down and saw the box was easy to open. He'd never paid much attention to it and certainly not thought to open it.*
>
> *The beggar lifted the lid and looked inside the box. The beauty and riches that met his eyes were nearly blinding. He couldn't believe that within his old rusty, dusty box were unimaginable treasures – sparkling diamonds, gold and silver, bright-coloured gems. He'd never seen such treasure before.*
>
> *He turned around to thank the gentleman, but the stranger had already disappeared.*

Wouldn't it be grand to open the treasure chest you are sitting on?

Changing my idea of enlightenment

Decades ago, my idea of enlightenment was a most elevated and unreachable state. A state whose arrival was accompanied by a massive explosion of light, a magnificent display of fireworks and a big bang on one's insides. This state facilitated the transition inside to a permanent state of inner peace.

The overlays from my Christian conditioning dictated that enlightenment would be like 'heaven' or eternal peace. It was outside of myself, a state to achieve, a goal to move towards.

When, in the early days of my journey, I heard Osho say, 'Enlightenment is a state of deepest relaxation', I was somewhat confused. That sounded like the opposite of what I thought it would be. I was striving for enlightenment, not relaxing into myself.

I believed that when I achieved it, it would be permanent. I hadn't yet heard of or understood the term – true nature – that I later, and since, use to understand the truth of what happens. That what we are seeking is true nature – a state we can move into and away from for decades.

My pictures of enlightenment as an outlandish achievement, have changed drastically over the last four decades. I also no longer use the term 'enlightenment'. Though, when I think about how tough my inner journey was, at times, I'm glad I had such inspiring images to hold onto or I might not have persisted. Now, it is true nature that I understand. I know true nature exists in the core of me and in each and every person. My work consists of connecting to it. It is up to me to find the courage to do the work.

True nature – what is it?

After decades of inner exploration I found that the most effective way to understand true nature was to understand what it is not. True nature is not a place of suffering. When we are in our true nature we do not experience pain, there is no fear, no shame, no guilt, no sense of unworthiness, no greed, no jealousy, no loneliness and no isolation.

True nature is a state of beingness and pure presence; knowing, strong, boundless, relaxing, oneness. It is in all of us; accessible to anybody who wants to connect with it and has the courage to face obstacles on the way. Typical obstacles or challenges are uncovering old, repressed emotions, meeting our shadows or navigating places of inner deficiency. Having the robustness to face those challenges is a way to enable and awaken true nature.

True nature is kind, patient, compassionate, intelligent in a wise way, benevolent, peaceful. When we're in our true nature, we are intrinsically good. It is real, it is what religions call God.

Suffering does not exist in true nature

There is no hierarchy of achievements or a merit system necessary so that we can experience true nature. This differs dramatically from what I learned growing up Catholic where I was taught I had to work off the sin I'd inherited over a lifetime, to have a chance to sit on the right of God when I died. I've never liked or agreed with any precept that a life of suffering is rewarded with a promise of some good after death.

All we need to experience true nature is a commitment and, maybe, a trained travel guide to help with the challenging parts. Those challenges do exist; the **dark night of the soul** is real (see *Chapter 2.2* for more material).

Our inner journey is our movement towards true nature and it can be hard at times. If we don't give up the search for truth, and we keep going – into the core of true nature – it is always good. It can be many variations of good, but it's always good.

The good gets better once you know how to reach and rest in true nature.

If we look at the example of love as one of the more known qualities arising from true nature, it's easier to get a sense of how we might embrace our own true nature.

There are many flavours of love, from gentle love to intense love, unconditional love. There is, even, a dissolution into a state of love that's formless, where all that exists is love.

One of the resources I have in my continuing seeking of true nature and my truth is my study of The Diamond Approach, a path of inner realisation. The Diamond Approach describes true nature as consisting of substances called essences. Our essences appear in different colours, at different levels of solidity, temperatures and textures. Red essence, for example, describes the quality of strength, black essence denotes peace, yellow essence joy.

One of the universal qualities of true nature is harmony. Were we to examine the states of true nature we'd find the atmosphere to always be harmonious. It would be in a state opposite to the more 'normal' chaotic, fragmented, all-over-the-place mind.

Check for yourself. Anytime you feel a sense of peace, joy, strength, love or freedom, does that state feel harmonious or chaotic?

Knowing that true nature exists and is real has an encouraging effect on the idea of keeping going with our exploring. We will not always be connected to our true nature, but it is comforting when we are in a challenging place to know it's always there.

When I had my first encounter with black essence, the substance of peace, it slowly spread as if it were a tangible substance in my right leg – something I'd never felt before. It was so new and fascinating and I had no preconception of it at all, at that time.

True nature is God; God is true nature

When different religions define God many talk of something external to us. In the Western Judeo-Christian conception, God is male, has a beard, sits in heaven on a massive chair and consults like a king. If we've been good enough on earth, we'll get to sit to the right of God in heaven once we've died.

Many religions' explanations for nature and natural phenomenon are that they are the work, or consequences of the actions of God and those in his kingdom, for example, angels. When I was growing up, I was told that whenever I saw a pink sky it signified a time when the angels were baking.

Other concepts from my religious instruction frightened me when I was a child. I was terrified by the idea of an omniscient God. Someone who saw everything was a horrifying thought. So much so, that when I started meditating and became aware of my internal world, I'd imagine a set of judgmental eyes watching everything I did. These were certainly not kind or compassionate eyes.

Nowadays, I believe that the positive qualities ascribed to an omnipotent God do exist. But not in an external God. These aspects live, as aspects of true nature, inside all of us. We may not experience them if we are disconnected from true nature.

Within each of us, we can discover or, rediscover those qualities. The capacity for rediscovery is given different names. For example, the spiritual teacher Byron Katie, calls the work to reveal the qualities, the Great Undoing. Osho called the process deconditioning or clearing of layers so we remember who we truly are.

True self and conditioned self

Within each human being, there are qualities that are aligned with true nature. However, as we grow up and form personalities, we may lose touch with these original qualities and begin to identify with our conditioned self.

This conditioned self is a limited self, and develops from the need to find strategies, mechanisms and behaviours to survive within our families of origin. This is also called our personality (I'll describe this more in later chapters) and once we identify with it, we begin to believe that the personality is who we are. However, believing that can obscure or completely block access to the true self.

The personality is an effective mimic. Imitating the original qualities that it was disconnected from is part of its survival strategy. True strength is a fine quality to have, yet, when mimicked by the personality it can present as rigidity and toughness. Healthy will, when mimicked becomes stubbornness. Knowing yourself as love can get twisted by the personality into an enormous effort to win others' love. There are also many behaviours and strategies that the personality adopts to achieve a sense of peace or joy or happiness in our lives.

Living as our true self – connected to true nature – is our ultimate aim and if we are to do this, we'll need to slowly deconstruct the conditioned self and replace it with the truth of who we are. Through the book, I'll guide you as to how to recognise and reconnect with the true nature in ourselves.

True nature always gives us what we need

When I first discovered the idea that we can always get what we need from true nature, it felt like magic. I had experienced a process where I wanted to understand an issue I was having in life and, through a few attempts to uncover what lay beneath my fears and resistances, I found an answer. That answer, which was inside me, was perfect. Eventually I understood that finding the answer inside is a law of true nature. It always gives us what we truly need if we dare to do the work.

For me there is no deeper intelligence or wisdom available than what we find in true nature. In the case of one client – a woman feeling unworthy, constantly judging herself, pushing herself to be perfect – was able, after a specific aspect of true nature came through to deeply relax, and in that state, feel her intrinsic value. She knew, in that moment, that just being herself was enough.

I have seen thousands of examples of this healing and it still fascinates me when I witness true nature resolving a client's issue.

My experience of different states of true nature

There are different states of true nature; all different gemstones in my inner treasure chest. At different times and in a variety of circumstances, on my inner journey, I feel certain inner states as very real, and they are, often, accompanied by an image. These are direct experiences of subtle states of energy.

Those most common inner states for me are different expressions of love, kindness, compassion and empathy, inner joy and happiness for no outer reason, forgiveness, gratitude, stillness, and a deep sense of peace.

I want to encourage you to start trusting your own experience; to find your own description and vocabulary for inner states that feel real to you. So, I'm sharing the images and feelings I have when I experience these different states and hope they inspire you to discover your own inner gems.

These are just a few examples and in *Chapter 4.1 Meeting your heart* I will describe many different versions of love as an inner experience. Here are some gems from my personal experience:

White trust in the core of my being is like sitting on a solid white marble floor with nothing able to destabilise me.

Crystal clarity or brilliance arising in my mind which enables focussed, inspired thinking.

Fluffy white relaxing softness that looks and feels like a white cloud and can arise in any part of my body.

Milky white soothing love that feels as nourishing as a mother's milk for her baby.

Black peace as if I were sitting under a beautiful night sky with stars on a balmy summer's evening.

Red strength flowing through the body, as blood runs through my physical body bringing aliveness, vibrancy, self-assertiveness from which I can set healthy boundaries.

Melting, orange warmth with a sense of the cosiness of having a massage on my insides.

Yellow joy like sunshine warming me, or as if I were walking through a field of full-faced sunflowers.

Golden champagne with bubbling joy rising from my base like a fountain flowing upwards and spreading throughout my body.

Pink precious love that fills my heart as it does when I look at a baby smiling.

Green compassion so I can feel somebody else's pain as it if were mine.

Light blue stillness and spaciousness that allows me to feel I am a bird in my own inner sky.

Everybody will have their own way of describing their personal experience of true nature. Depending on the primary sense we are using, our history, ways we learnt to communicate.

These descriptions contain some pretty way out images ... almost psychedelic or hallucinatory. Yet these arise without any external assistance. What I describe here are just a few of the many possibilities for experiencing true nature. The next time you experience a sense of peace, joy or love, allow yourself to become more aware of it and ask yourself, 'How would I describe this to someone else?' The very practice of noticing and beginning to articulate it will allow the sense of it to grow and embed itself in your being.

Begin the journey to wholeness

Let's start the journey of becoming whole. True nature is a state of being whole, there is no becoming. The becoming whole part of the journey is what I am introducing in the following steps. Without them, it's very difficult to experience wholeness. Though there may be glimpses, or, in a few lucky moments, spontaneous openings.

The journey I'm describing allows us to cultivate the connection to being whole.

You will learn to make the mind your friend, attain the right attitude for inner exploration, connect to the wisdom of your body, open your heart, learn the art of feeling, heal the inner child and connect to inner guidance.

PART 2

MAKING THE MIND YOUR FRIEND

OPENING TO THE MENTAL TERRITORY

I LEARNT, THROUGH DIRECT experience, what the elements of true transformation are. Learnt to see what is working and what isn't. When these elements are applied correctly, transformation happens.

I'm very fortunate to do the work I do and it's an incredible pleasure to share it because I know it has worked for me, and it is universal. I am a scientist, my mind likes to understand. And I've learnt that I can, that you can, train the mind to allow transformation. I believe that if we commit to doing the work and turn towards it, we can come out the other side of big traumas and difficult experiences. Anything, everything can heal.

For any inner transformation, it is vital that we develop a healthy relationship with our mind; truly befriend it.

How do we do make a friend of our mind? We begin by understanding the nature of the mind.

What is the mind?

The mind has a job and that is to think. It sounds very simple and, on some level, it is. The mind lives in the past and the future, remembering things that happened and projecting outcomes into the future.

One of my teachers would say the mind is concerned with fear, doubt and judgment and it evaluates, compares, plans. When bad things have happened, the mind recalls those events and is concerned they might happen again. So, in order to anticipate and plan, it starts thinking in terms of the worst-scenarios. It might be that the loss of a job leads us to be fearful of losing our job at any time again.

At the end of this chapter I introduce a golden tool to reverse the kind of thinking that leads from: 'What's the worst that can happen?' to 'What's the best that can happen'.

Meditation and mindfulness

Mindfulness, a form of meditation, has entered the mainstream vocabulary and practice for working with the mind; it's used, globally, as a focusing and relaxing tool for hundreds of thousands of people. Resources to teach us or guide us in mindfulness are abundant – many apps to download, classes to join.

I am happy to say that meditation has become part of the evolution of consciousness in the human race – it was bound to happen. Those of us who learned and practised meditation in the 1970s were, it seems, pioneers, ahead of our time, yet, unfortunately, misunderstood. When I first discovered meditation in 1978, it was still a foreign and strange thing to do or think about doing for those of us from the western developed world.

Within the past decade or so, the term mindfulness has become synonymous with meditation practices – both are seen to offer techniques with the same aim – becoming aware of, and feeling peaceful in, the present moment.

Each process presents a way to disengage from the overactive mind; to disengage from the tendency towards fear and judgment. What they offer is an invitation to appreciate each moment of our lives. Meditation uses the practice of witnessing, or watching what is in our environment, without making judgments, without being critical. And, remaining neutral and accepting of what is.

Witnessing can be compared to looking in a mirror. A mirror never berates the person looking into it. A mirror doesn't criticise or say, 'Oh, you're so ugly and smelly, I won't reflect your image. Take a shower first. Comb your hair! Why are you dressed like this? Why do you look so grumpy?'

A mirror reflects whatever is in front of it and does so without evaluation. It doesn't reflect better or more sharply when anything beautiful is in front of it.

Remember the witness

When I lived in Pune, I went through a relationship break up. I was emotionally stressed, in intense pain and when my inner voice would remind me to, 'Remember the witness', I didn't understand exactly what the voice was telling me. Yet, just hearing it, and listening to it, made me more peaceful. It provided a break from the turmoil, a way of stepping back from being identified with the pain.

What I experienced and now know, deeply, is that when we start feeling or sensing the quality of witnessing itself, not the object of the witnessing, we can experience a still, peaceful and harmonious quality within ourselves. It is one of the many beautiful aspects of true nature.

When we start disengaging from what we're seeing and, instead, sense the quality of the witnessing, there is a transition, a process of getting to that stillness and harmony. Think about:

- riding a bicycle and, jumping off mid-journey. Despite no one pedalling, the bike still has some momentum before it falls flat.
- turning on a ceiling fan till it has some speed and then, turning it off. You'll see that it takes time to come to a complete stop.

The busy mind, once running, also doesn't stop quickly. But when the right mindfulness techniques are applied, it will eventually settle down. In time, we experience more beautiful experiences of peacefulness or stillness.

Blue monkeys everywhere

The mind works in interesting ways and has a somewhat contradictory response to the idea of resisting thinking in certain ways. This story, another of the many tales from Osho, illustrates the power of resistance and how it feeds the mind.

A disciple travelled a long way to a Master in ancient India to learn about enlightenment.

'It's very simple,' said the Master. 'Stop thinking about blue monkeys'.
The disciple thought, 'What a strange Master. I travelled all this way
to learn from this enlightened being. I heard he's helped many people
to find the truth of life. But that? Blue monkeys? That sounds utterly
stupid. I've never even thought about blue monkeys'.

He left feeling disappointed and started his arduous journey home.
As he travelled, however, he couldn't stop thinking about blue monkeys.
They were everywhere, coming from all directions. The more he tried to
stop thinking about them, the more they multiplied.

Resistance is the problem; acceptance is the key

It was from Osho that I first heard the notion – resistance to what is,
feeds the mind. It works counter to how most of us think. That is,
instead of being able to shut off from a thought, ignore it and not be
affected by it, we are more deeply affected by it, because of our resistance. This is a seemingly contradictory effect, but I know it to be true.

The effects of trying to resist are demonstrated in the blue monkey
tale. The principle applies to our thoughts, emotions, physical
challenges, life challenges, everything. It is one of the most important
teachings in this whole journey.

The antidote to resistance, and a principle that's a master key in
inner transformation, is the acceptance of what is. In *Part 4 Opening*
to the heart there is far more detail on this.

Still the mind: Misunderstandings

Despite the surge of interest in the idea of mindfulness and meditation
there are still many misunderstandings about how it works. Many of
my clients report challenges with meditation, often saying, 'I've tried
it, but it doesn't work for me'.

Meditation is hard in the beginning. The biggest misunderstanding
about it is that it's trying to calm the mind with the mind. The trick
to being calm is to stop interfering with the mind. When we first start
meditating, we start confronting the mind being in control, chaotic,
dominating, running the show.

I compare this idea to being in the city during rush hour and trying
to push the cars out of my way, even trying to stop them. Imagine the

mess if we ran into the middle of the street trying to stop the cars. It'd be difficult, and certainly not peaceful.

But move away from the city into a park, into a much quieter area, and that frantic traffic disappears. So too, the mind quietens down on its own once you move away from the noise and the busyness.

When you stop engaging with the thoughts in your mind, the ancient traditions call this, 'Being indifferent. Being neither for nor against'. The stillness of the mind is a by-product of moving deeper into your heart, more connected to your feeling sense and not turning attention to your mind.

Meditation to still the mind

Here is a meditation that is a relatively short practice but will enable you to feel the first shifts in the mind. As you move deeper into the meditation and incorporate the heart and what it's feeling, there is a side benefit: the mind quietens down.

Compare trying to disengage from the mind to the process of stirring a glass of water, with mud in it. Any stirring will make the water murky. Then, when you stop stirring, the mud begins to settle and the water at the top of the glass gets clearer. If you're not engaging with the mind, you'd no longer be stirring mud. Then, you can see the water more clearly.

Mediation: Making the shift to sensing/feeling

One of the easiest meditations to settle the mind is to shift from thinking to sensing/feeling. To do this, start by sensing the activity of the mind. Instead of listening to the thoughts and getting engaged with the details, start feeling the buzz as if it were an electric pulse or just noise. With that shift of focus, you stop putting attention on the content of the mind.

At times, the more you get centred in your heart the more the mind, or thoughts, can feel like clouds drifting by. You are so nicely snuggled into your heart, you don't even bother about the mind. Such is the long-term benefit of healthy meditation.

The mind has no grip anymore. Even nasty, judgmental thoughts will be in the background. As if a radio station is broadcasting, but it's not one you're listening to anymore.

HOW TO PRACTISE THIS SHIFT

*Sit comfortably wherever you are and bring attention to the mind
without changing anything. Notice and describe it to yourself.*

*Shift attention into the chest area. Feel the breath moving
in and out. Describe, to yourself, whatever is there.*

*Move back to the mind. Move back to the heart.
Do this back and forth, three times in your own time.*

Can you notice any change in the mind?

A vast amount of research has been done on the effectiveness of
meditation and shifts in the brain. I heartily recommend doing some
online research and particularly recommend the HeartMath Institute
in America. One link to it is: https://www.heartmath.org/science/

Presence is the biggest gift

One of the qualities that we cultivate through mindfulness and
meditation practices is called presence. Most people would have been
introduced to this term through Eckart Tolle's book *The Power of Now.*
Being present to this moment was one of the main practices that Osho
taught us.

TIME TO STOP: BE PRESENT NOW

Become aware of yourself right now reading the book.

*Stop, take a breath and turn your attention towards yourself
and whatever you are experiencing in this moment.*

Then, keep reading and stay present to the words you are reading.

*How often do we read something, think about something
else and don't remember any of what we just read?*

Learning to be present is an ongoing practice.

For me, being present when we are with another person is the biggest gift we can give to each other. In my experience, everybody responds well to another person being present.

In many sessions with couples, a typical scene might include the woman being emotional and distressed, while her male partner doesn't know what to do. I've seen a similar scenario played out and am always aware that asking each to become fully present, will alleviate the tension. Within moments of my teaching the male partner a simple way to become present, the woman settles. I've seen this repeatedly; it does appear miraculous.

One of the simple ways I learnt to help someone understand the idea of 'presence' is by asking them to tell me what their hobbies are – fishing, cooking, dancing, golf, surfing, and so on. Hobbies are things we choose because we like that specific activity. And when we like something, we relax, and we are naturally present.

In the couple situation, above, the man usually tries too hard to solve the problem or do the right thing. This effort means he gets stressed and tense – the antithesis to being present.

The same dynamic operates with children. When they feel we are absent, they start screaming for attention. Once we are present with them – giving them our undivided attention – they calm down. When I was a kids' mama in the ashram, I experienced this hundreds of times.

For me, this truth relates to any relationship: friends, work relationships. If I wasn't present in my job as a therapist, I don't think any of my clients would come back. Imagine sitting with a therapist who is off in their own thoughts, distracted, looking at their phone.

In my counselling training we were taught that being present with our client is the most important quality we can offer. The rest, all our skills and modalities, is secondary.

Right living

One of the concepts I'd like to introduce here is 'right living', which will get clearer throughout the book. In a way this book can be seen as a manual for right or conscious living.

Consciousness is the boss

I learned, from my teachings, that we are born conscious, then lose connection to it and, eventually, reclaim it through waking up or our spiritual search, longing for more. Through that we become conscious again.

In many spiritual teachings, there is a way to talk about these processes of the mind by drawing a 'real-life comparison' and in this case it is played out with a landowner and his servants. In the story, the landowner is the true boss, or someone who is conscious; has consciousness about how to live; how things need to be. The servants, who have overturned the natural order of things, became the false bosses.

The story symbolises the place of true and false bosses, or, right living and not-right living.

A landowner leaves his home for an indefinite period of travel. In his absence, the servants take care of the house and the land. He stays away for years, decades eventually. One day he returns home. The servants were, by then, used to running the household. Some of them slept in the master bedroom. They settled in as if it was their house. But what do you think happens when he comes back?

They don't like it; they want to keep their comforts, those in the master bedroom want to stay in the cosy big bed. They like being in control with nobody telling them what to do.

Suddenly, however, they need to listen to someone who has been away for decades. They need time to adjust and respect the new-yet-old returned authority. They resist and reject the idea that he's back. There are many questions and comments. 'Why has he come back? Why didn't he stay away? It was so much easier without him when we could do what we wanted.'

The right relationship for true consciousness is that the mind is the servant, consciousness is the boss. When that right inner relationship is restored, we start living the life that is right for us.

Consciousness is choice

I often replace the word consciousness with choice. More consciousness means more choice and we may begin to ask, 'Am I going to react in the old automatic way, or do I have a choice to respond in a new, appropriate, "true for me" way?'

Reaction versus responsibility

In our conditioned self or mind we learn how to behave. We may be taught this formally – in our family of origin – or at some point during our childhood. We may have an automatic, conditioned response to events. It's called 'reaction'.

When we are more conscious – have more choice – we can learn to respond after some reflection. We can be responsible; in fact, the word responsibility holds the meaning – **ability to respond**. It has the same function as taking healthy action, responding appropriately to our situation in the now.

Think of a conditioned or automatic pattern of behaviour that creates suffering like the feeling of rejection or unworthiness. Compare it to a train arriving at the train station. Imagine this is a train you regularly take and, if you get in, you know exactly where you will end up. You know the stations along the route and you know the end station.

If you were more conscious, however, you could choose to not buy a ticket and not board that train. You could stand at the platform, see it approaching and let it pass by.

When I experienced that moment of choice for the first time, it was an incredible moment of liberation.

Let's think about a possible scenario at work where you might choose a different response to your regular or conditioned one, and create some freedom for yourself. Let's say someone ignores you at work. They usually greet you or smile at you, but today, nothing. One possible reaction you have is to think, 'They don't like me. Did I do something wrong? Did I hurt them?'

Keep going long enough with this self-flagellation and you could end up feeling collapsed and hurt for the rest of the day. The next day, you might withdraw, feel insecure around that person and not greet them. This is unlikely to feel at all pleasant, either way.

Yet, a different way of responding could look like this. First, you could assume that it's not personal – something could have happened to them that has nothing to do with you. Perhaps they didn't sleep well, or had a fight with their partner; got bad news or have a family member who is sick.

You could ask, 'Are you ok?' You might even check with them if their silence has anything to do with you. This openness might even deepen the relationship because you are showing care.

Following impulses

Imagine being happy, very present to yourself and suddenly you notice something changing. You might have heard something in a conversation and, as it reminded you of the loss of someone, some sadness wells up.

Our deeper consciousness communicates with us through impulses. In this case, a healthy impulse would be to acknowledge the sadness and, as soon as possible, give yourself the space to allow it.

Following our impulses is a way to respond healthily to what we face in the world, in our relationships.

This example from a client illustrates it. She'd been away for the weekend with some friends. On her way back, she passed the cemetery where her Dad was buried twelve years earlier. She stopped, sat in her car and allowed her tears to flow till she felt the sadness was gone. Then, she followed her next impulse to keep driving and return home.

It's important to be aware of the shift from automatic reaction to healthy response. Impulses come from true nature and they guide us. The healthier we get, the more we follow them.

The conscious (CM) and unconscious mind (UM)

Each of us has a conscious mind and an unconscious mind. Part of making the mind a friend is understanding the unconscious mind and learning to develop a healthy relationship between the two parts – CM (conscious mind) and UM (unconscious mind).

Almost 95 percent of brain activity is beyond our conscious awareness. Numerous cognitive neuroscientists' studies have revealed that only five percent of our cognitive activities (decisions, emotions, actions, behaviour) are conscious; the remaining 95 percent is generated in a non-conscious manner.

The relationship between CM and UM is relevant in the inner work in many ways. One is the area of making decisions. We use both parts to make any decisions about our lives and the steps we take. If the conscious mind comes to a decision and the unconscious mind doesn't agree with it, it is unlikely that things will work out well for us.

One fun example that helped me understand this was the idea of planning a holiday. The CM wants to go to a sunny beach. The UM wants to go to a cold country. As the CM books the trip, the UM packs the suitcase. You'll probably end up on a beach in winter clothes.

It is important to learn how to communicate healthily with the UM. There are a lot of techniques in modern psychology that deal with that particular facility and can be very useful in helping to change behaviours.

Take a more serious example, like the idea of healing an addiction. The CM wants to stop smoking, drinking or gambling ... name any addiction. Yet, if the UM doesn't agree, you won't succeed. The CM might think, 'I won't drink', yet the UM will let you pour the next drink.

The UM is where our memories are stored. This is all of them, including painful ones, which get locked away as if there were a vault inside the unconscious mind. This vault is an essential element for the work of inner transformation.

Without access to the vault we're unable to heal and become whole again. When we learn how to speak with the unconscious mind, or understand it, we have a more integrated life. This integration is essential in inner transformation.

Piece-by-piece

The UM is not logical, linear or rational. It communicates through symbols or images, words, feelings, body sensations. It connects with us through puzzle pieces of information. These might be a word we hear, a sentence, a memory, a feeling, a picture we see, a smell. The messages can come on any sensory level.

Imagine putting a puzzle together piece-by-piece. The first piece you pick up may not instantly fit the puzzle but, by not rejecting what you find, you have a chance of revealing more of the puzzle and, eventually, the whole picture.

These different sensory messages are the unconscious mind offering a piece of information to the conscious mind. The UM is encouraged when we accept what has been offered and then, it reveals more. Conversely, when we reject a piece, the flow can stop. If we take the time and pay attention to what's happening in the mind, we will improve the way we decode what the unconscious mind says to us. These words from a client help clarify the picture.

> *My sessions really accelerated when I decided to speak/expose/tell you exactly what was going on in my mind. In the early days I swore less (didn't want to offend you) and didn't voice things that I felt ashamed about (I wanted you to like me) or I'd voice a diluted version.*
>
> *So, the insight and learning are that the more honest I am the faster transformation happens. No matter how weird or bad it seems, it needs to be exposed in its rawest form.* —DREW

Taming the superego: Working with judgment

Start exploring and understanding the mind and you'll discover one aspect of it that can create a lot of suffering. It is called the superego (SE) or inner judge and has a specific job in our lives. That role is to judge everything we do, and to do that all day long. The inner judge runs a relentless running commentary on our lives; some nickname it 'Radio Station Crazy'.

Like a computer chip, the superego stores all the messages we received throughout our childhood about how to behave, and what to do to become functional human beings. It includes all messages from parents, siblings, religious teachings, culture, place we grew up and how to behave, function and survive.

The superego is part of our conditioned self and influences how we perceive the world and ourselves. It creates self-images. While the superego is not a real person, it can still create a great deal of suffering, driving people into depression and, in worst-case scenarios, even to suicide. Even at its lightest, it can create a lot of misery and stress.

Maintain status quo

Despite this potential for pain, the superego is not malicious. In fact, its main function is to protect the status quo. No matter how mature we are, the superego still sees us as children and runs to a script it learned when we were children. We may have grown up, but the superego hasn't. It doesn't understand that, as adults, we have more capacity for moral decisions, self direction and positive habits than we had as children.

Think about the behaviour of a normal two-year-old who doesn't have a concept of cars and speed. If this child were unsupervised, it might run into a busy street with disastrous consequences. To safe-guard the child from harm parents probably say, 'Don't cross the street on your own, hold my hand and do what I tell you to'.

That is appropriate and caring when the child is young. But once we're older, we can decide for ourselves when and how to cross a street. However, by then we have internalised that parental voice that, originally, was our protector. So, we keep listening and not question-ing the voice that might now be very limiting. Many of my clients believe their superego is true, is right and trustworthy.

The above example demonstrates how appropriate the message was originally, but not all messages we are hearing are that harmless. Take the example of the seemingly innocuous, 'be a good boy, be a good girl'. It implies that certain behaviours are good and by contrast, other behaviours are bad.

Parents generally mean well, but the messages go into the UM of the child, turn into beliefs and may no longer serve them in the future. Anything that parents valued becomes an ideal that the child tries to live up to. If being busy and efficient was valued and being idle was judged, it can lead to someone later in life becoming a 'busy bee'. They will run around in circles, frantically preventing being idle, and never be able to relax.

Messages like. 'Don't shout so loud. All the neighbours will hear you?' or 'Girls are meant to be seen not heard!' can lead to someone never speaking up later in life and/or repressing their strength.

....

TIME TO STOP: REMEMBER A MESSAGE

*Can you remember some typical messages
you received in your childhood?*

....

Working with the superego

Every judgment from the superego is an attack.

This statement is powerful for a few reasons. One, because it is true, but also, it gives us permission to defend ourselves against a part that is, often, not the loving voice of truth. I love this statement because the judgement, in some people, can be very harsh and mean.

The main steps to countering the sting of the superego, are to identify the judgmental voice, listen to, and ensure you hear, its messages clearly. Then, give yourself time to examine the judgments and see whether they still make sense.

We can defend ourselves by identifying and reframing the messages. One of the main ways to defend is through anger – also called the 'Fuck off transmission'. When you recognise or identify the voice, learn to tell it to stop, to shut up, to leave you alone.

Another way to defend is through presence. When we are fully in our hearts, open, knowing who we are, it's unlikely the old voices have power over us anymore.

For a comprehensive view of the many ways to defend against a superego attack I highly recommend Byron Brown's *Soul Without Shame*. You will find ways to work with the superego throughout the book, and especially in *Chapters 5.6 to 5.8 Understanding and transforming guilt, shame and unworthiness.*

GOLDEN TOOL
WORST AND BEST EXERCISE

An important step in understanding the nature of the mind is to become more aware of all the fears we carry. A useful exercise for that begins with working through a situation happening in your life by asking questions – of yourself, your mind.

What's the worst?
Let's say you're confronted with making a decision; a situation where you need to consider what to do. For the purposes of this exercise stay with one decision, or way of acting and, having decided, ask, 'If that's the case, what's the *worst* that can happen?'

Once you've articulated that scenario, ask the question again. 'So, if *that's* the case, what's the *worst* that can happen?' After any given answer, ask again.

Repeat the question till your mind has gone through all possibilities and can't come up with anything worse. By the time you've repeated and answered the question, you might have confronted terrible illness, loneliness and isolation. You might even have died. Of course, imagining that you've died can seem frightening or depressing. Yet looking at it, perhaps confronting it – particularly if it's very scary – can help relax your mind and calm its fear-based thinking.

What's the best?
Having exhausted the bad outcomes, turn the question around and ask, 'What's the *best* that can happen?' Repeat the question till your mind has gone through all possibilities and can't come up with anything more that is favourable.

The exercise is a quick, and a remarkably successful way to uncover fears lurking in the background and, by articulating them, see them for what they are. It will also uncover answers in your mind that counter the disaster scenarios. Invariably, you will make yourself feel better.

In the early days of my inner work, I had an unconscious fear of ending up on the street as a homeless person. Perhaps it had to do with being born in Germany 12 years after WW2 when the country was recovering from the War. It doesn't matter where it came from, it was there.

Yet, once I did this 'Worst and Best' exercise often enough, I got very clear that the scenario would not happen. I have too many resources to let it happen. I now believe I'll always find my way somehow and provide for myself. The idea of being homeless, now feels utterly unrealistic. I am not scared of it anymore.

It is common, far more common than you might think, for the mind to create a disaster scenario when faced with a problem. Yet, with that same capacity of the mind to think things through, we can also think of the best that can happen.

THE RIGHT ATTITUDE FOR INNER EXPLORATION

THIS CHAPTER HAS INFORMATION for a vital part of your preparation for inner transformation. Using it is similar to getting all the right ingredients and recipe for a dish you want to make.

How healing works: A roadmap

There is a beauty in the idea of inner transformation. When I work with clients, I take four stages into consideration. The elements and the sequence make sense of identifying where one's at and how to move forward from struggle to a sense of freedom and true nature. The stages are:
1. Diagnosis
2. Creating your toolkit for life: Going in
3. Allowing and watching transformation happen
4. Integration

Diagnosis

In the previous chapter I spoke of the importance of turning towards what is truly happening within your being. Of the importance of doing that in the right way. Diagnosis is about determining the **status quo.**

When we can meet our reality as it is in this moment, the door to inner transformation opens. All suffering can be transformed. I know that's a strong declaration. I know it to be true.

Human beings have issues – mental, physical or emotional. We suffer. Something upsets us, stresses us, leaves us unhappy, concerned. And each of these issues can be used to start the exploration; the issue is the gateway in. Through the issue, you open the door to your inner world. One gateway is no more special than another. All issues are equally valid.

When we resist accepting and delving, in the right way, the gateway or door closes.

In the medical field, this exploration would be equivalent to having blood tests or an X-ray. In order to identify the ailment (inner or outer) we need to know what the issue or specific suffering is in this moment.

Creating your toolkit for life: Going in

Here are tools I've gathered in my own inner exploration and in my work with thousands of clients.

Allowing and watching transformation happen

When I witness transformation in action either in myself, or with clients during sessions, I'm grateful, moved and, still, amazed. Those changes reflect some resolution of an issue or problem or a state of suffering and, usually, in a significant way. Someone may start with a sense of unworthiness and end up feeling their intrinsic value. Someone else starts with loneliness and finds self-love, someone's confusion turns into clarity, a person's collapse or weakness becomes strength.

What I've learned, too, is that we don't *do* transformation; we learn to apply the right tools. Then, through an organic process, guided from a deep inner wisdom, the transformation happens. Of its own accord. I am an eternal fan of that process because we witness the transformation.

Integration

Integration is an important stage in healing. It can be experienced as energy streaming through the body, a sense of realignment happening, the mind getting clear, a decision forming, the body relaxing, peace arising. Sometimes it happens very quickly; a client can feel settled and integrated by the end of a session, having arrived in a very different state.

Sometimes – depending how strong, deep or old the issue is, or how much inner work has happened around the issue already – the integration can take days. When a lot of old energy has started moving, for example, old, stored anger discharging, you can feel muddy for days. Eventually, you will settle; the process will settle.

In my experience, the longest it took to feel a sense of integration, was three days. Along the way, there are different sensations that alert you to the change. One can feel as if a drain is being cleared; memories can surface. Emotions want to be released. Sometimes, there's discomfort – it's an unavoidable part of healing.

After strong sessions, I always advise clients, 'Give yourself three days for the integration. Support your body by drinking enough water, eating well, resting enough and being kind and respectful to yourself.' These simple steps are very important.

Clearing of charges

Any issue we have will present with some kind of 'charge'. A charge on the inner can show up on all levels: mind, body, emotion or energy. It is a strong sudden automatic reaction, also known as '**being triggered**' and it's something we don't have control over.

Sometimes, as the charges clear, we can be totally fine one moment, then chat with a friend and something is said that creates an automatic uncomfortable reaction. So, it's good that you understand the value of the clearing of charges.

Issue, problem, charge – all words describing the same thing: a state of dis-ease or lack of balance, out-of-balance-ness. The work allows us to find our way back to ease in ourselves.

We know when we feel a charge, are triggered by something. A **charge in the mind** can show up as confusion, blankness, racing thoughts, having the same thought spinning in circles.

A **charge in the body** can be anything from temperature changes, sudden heat or cold anywhere in the body like hot cheeks, cold hands, nausea, sudden headache, tightness, cramping or churning.

An **emotional charge** can be frustration or anger, sadness, hopelessness, despair, sense of unworthiness, jealousy – pretty much any emotion that we experience as challenging, out of proportion, not appropriate in the circumstances and where the trigger doesn't justify the reaction.

An **energetic charge** can show up as a sinking feeling, as standing beside yourself, frozen, not being able to speak or think, an impulse to run, the need to get away from a person or situation and suddenly feeling beaten down.

Why clear charges?

Charges create barriers that stop us from moving towards and opening the treasure chest in the core of our being. A charge can keep us trapped and feeling as if we can't find our way out of a maze. In these pages you'll find the skills to help in the process of clearing charges and returning to wholeness.

In later chapters, I'll cover the three most important tools for clearing charges – the art of feeling, the inner child work, and trauma work.

Knowing if a charge is cleared

How do we know a specific issue is healed? We know, when we think of the original trigger moment and are not still reacting the same way we always have. In the healed state we feel clear, have a calm mind, have no negative emotions arising, and a relaxation in our body. There's no contraction anywhere, our energy flows, and we're no longer triggered in the least. That's the state of ease that is restored through the work.

As you might expect, the lighter the issue, the quicker it clears. The deeper the issue, or the earlier it started, or the stronger the impact was, the longer it takes.

Simple rule: The stronger the reaction the older the trigger.

Issues and scarring

While issues can be healed, sometimes they leave an imprint, or a scar. When you burn yourself cooking, for example, it may not hurt after a while, but there will be a scar. In fact, some traumatic experiences create a sensitivity in that area that may last the rest of your life.

Let's say you were never scared of driving until you had a car accident. After that you might be worried about having another accident.

That's perfectly understandable and it's good to accept the sensitivity that remains from your experience. Still, it needn't limit or terrify you.

Wounds around parents

All main psychological and healing traditions talk about the importance of our parents or main caretakers in our early childhood. The importance of their effect on us.

The person most likely to have the deepest effect on us, is our mother or our primary caretaker. Yet if the relationship with either of our parents was very difficult or even abusive, there can be a stage when we need a clear separation.

You may even 'divorce' your parent, to give yourself space to heal, have time to feel your anger, frustration or, even, hatred. Then, it's possible to learn to develop healthy boundaries. Once you stay with the process and work through every reaction a parent brings up in you, any emotion, any hurt, there is a point where you emerge on the other side. Eventually, you'll be more whole in yourself and can relate to them from a new level of maturity.

Often, a sign you've reached that point is when you don't feel the need to change them, 'the other person' anymore. You might even have compassion for the parent who triggered you originally and come to see their limitations.

Even if a parent doesn't change their opinion, attitude, behaviour, you can still be liberated. You are growing beyond that old relationship; you are healed in yourself. Know that this is possible.

My recommendation – keep the process moving and don't stay stuck in any stage. The freedom on the other side is worth the work.

Healing and commitment

Many times, after a lot of processing and inner work in India, I'd go home to Germany. Many times, I thought I was healed; the work was done. Then, I would spend time with my parents and feel reactive again.

It was clear, I had more work to do.

As we resolve the charges, do the clearing, our reactivity lessens. It may take time to disappear entirely but the interval between reactions gets longer and the reaction lasts for less time. What might have taken days can resolve within a few hours.

Growing pains: Puzzle pieces up in the air

When we have a commitment to growth and are doing the work, it's inevitable that we will change. We transition from one state to another.

Osho shared many stories with us to awaken our own understanding regarding different spiritual concepts and I'll share those that were relevant for my growth.

This next story is about the in-built drive in true nature, also called 'divine discontent'. It's a drive that wants us to grow in spite of the habit, in the conditioned mind, to stay with what we know, stay scared of change, scared of the unknown or not-yet known. It is not about the part of the mind that believes the grass is greener on the other side. In that case, the drive comes from the mind, always wanting more or better.

> *A man was working in a coal mine. One day, a passing traveller said, 'If you leave this place behind you will find a silver mine further down the road. Your life will be better, and you will make more money'.*
>
> *The coal worker wasn't sure whether he wanted to leave behind the security he already had. His was an arduous life and he worked hard, but he earned enough to survive. Still, something in the traveller intrigued him and the miner decided to leave his old life behind and move on.*
>
> *He did find the silver mine and the traveller's prediction came true. He had a better life, worked less and got paid more. He settled into this new life quickly, happy for the improvement to his life and, soon, life at the silver mine became normal.*
>
> *One day, the same traveller came by again and the men started chatting. The working man thanked him. To his surprise the traveller suggested that the miner not stay where he was. There was a gold mine further down the road, the traveller said, and life would be even better, less strenuous work, more money.*
>
> *The worker wasn't sure what to do. His life had improved already. Why should he even bother to give up what he'd found in the silver mine?*
>
> *But something in the traveller persuaded him once again. He left the silver mine and found a gold mine.*

You can guess what happened next. Once the miner was settled in the gold mine, which had the improvements the traveller predicted, the traveller came by again and suggested the man keep moving on.

Well, the traveller can also be seen as your own consciousness that wants you to grow. We have an in-built drive to grow. Not everybody is listening to that calling. But if you do, life starts moving in the right direction for your intrinsic potential.

Transitions from one state to another might be compared to a puzzle. Let's call your present state or status quo the puzzle which, when it is put together, will show a certain picture. When you're in transition all the puzzle pieces are thrown up into the air. Nothing makes sense, reality can feel warped, upside down, chaotic, confused.

If you learn to keep going, the pieces will be rearranged again. Only the next time, they come together in a new way and a different picture emerges.

Another helpful image for the process of transition is that of renovation. When you renovate, there's always dust, noise, chaos. Often your old rooms are not available, you have no bed to sleep in, no kitchen to cook in. Then, once the renovation is complete, you have a better home.

'Hang in there'

When I first heard this instruction or saying, I didn't get its importance. Let's explore what it means.

There are times, during transition from one state to another, that can feel like … well, like undergoing a psychic colonic. If you've ever had a physical colonic, you will know that the process includes clearing old crusty body waste by filling the colon with water and, after a time, flushing it out. It is a great detox and generally you feel better after it.

This applies to psychic colonics too; the old, stored matter, those blockages, get flushed out.

GOLDEN TOOL
SMILING AT THE UNKNOWN

The easiest way to switch from being scared of changes, transitions, the unknown or not-yet known territory is to, very simply, **imagine smiling at it**. Try it. I couldn't believe the immediate change I experienced when I tried it for the first time. Also, it never fails to work with clients.

The unconscious storehouse

Our unconscious is our mind's protective mechanism and helps us to survive and function. Anything that is too much to handle or process, at any time in our lives, moves into the unconscious part of the mind.

Once it is stored in the unconscious, the matter waits till we are ready to deal with it consciously. The unconscious doesn't have a secret outlet or a delete button so, sometimes, issues can wait for decades to be cleared; sometimes, even a lifetime.

The unconscious is like a post office storage system; parcels are stored, waiting for a signal to be delivered. That signal comes from our deeper wisdom. It gives the thumbs up to bring them to the surface; our deeper wisdom signals that we are ready.

Consider, too, that transition means clearing old, stored pain. If we can't cope at the time of the hurt or weren't supported in the right way, we disconnect from the pain. But when we do the work, we learn to feel and are more able, more resourced to feel pain without collapsing or being overwhelmed.

One of my favourite ways to describe this process is the 'digestion' of old material. This term is taught in a system of self-inquiry called the Diamond Approach.

When the old, stored material first comes back into consciousness it usually is accompanied by old thought patterns. They could include, 'This is too much', 'It is endless', 'I won't survive this'.

So, given that it's healthy to look at and clear the old wounds and patterns that don't serve us, it's useful to recognise that you are in transition. When you are in transition, it's best to interfere as little as possible, deal well with the old material (get help if needed), and wait till the waste is flushed out and you feel cleaner and clearer again.

Back to basics: A great resource

In the commune, I listened to Osho's daily talks in which he translated ancient traditions into contemporary language. This teaching stayed with me more than others.

> *In Zen they say: Before you meditate, rivers are rivers, mountains are mountains; when you meditate, rivers are no more rivers and mountains are no more mountains; and when the meditation is completed, when you have attained it, rivers are again rivers, mountains are again mountains.*

In times of transition everything can feel topsy-turvy. Nothing feels normal, and you may not even know who you are. You don't know what's right and what's wrong, what to trust and what not to. In those states of confusion, it is crucial that you don't make major decisions.

When you are walking in nature or on a mountain, for example, and a thick fog comes over the trail, it may be safer to wait it out rather than pushing forward in a particular direction. During that time, it's crucial to support yourself as much as possible and do simple things. Use your body and go for a walk. Empty the dishwasher, answer email.

When you are doing inner work and a lot of old sadness resurfaces, it can feel close to unbearable. That's precisely when the wise saying, 'Hang in there' comes in handy. All you can do is breathe and remember **'this too shall pass'**.

Dark night of the soul

Sometimes on the path of truth, we experience the growing pains of real change. A number of traditions around the world refer to this in different ways. A common term is 'the dark night of the soul'. It is a very real experience and aptly describes how hard transitions can be.

What can trigger this complex and delicate process that is the dark night? I'll cover this in more detail throughout the book, but for starters:

- Old, stored emotions like pain, anger, fear or trauma surface
- We meet our shadows: repressed personality parts that we believe are unacceptable or unlovable
- Inner deficiencies, also called 'holes', become apparent (for more on that, see *Chapter 6.3*)
- We suffer an 'ego death'. This is a dissolving of the old ego structure that was there for our survival. This dissolution of old structures can bring up a lot of fear.

At different times of my journey I encountered all those challenges. During these times the following ideas and declarations helped me.

'**When the night is the darkest, the dawn is the closest.**' Before a breakthrough in life, relationships often get tough. We want to resist. Our learnt resistance or our decision to not go to these difficult places, wants to stop us.

Another favourite statement, learnt from Barbara Marx Hubbard is, '**Every crisis is an evolutionary driver**'.

Every difficult situation is an incredible opportunity for us to grow and evolve. The old mind is confident that you're moving in the wrong direction. You feel sad, for example, but try to not feel the sadness. Still, once you've had a full, deep releasing cry, you feel better. You might even wonder what the fuss was about?

Many people experience a dark night of the soul before they start any inner work. They feel the intensity of suffering and hitting rock bottom, either through the abuse of drugs, repeated failed relationships, loss of money, death of a loved one, breakdown of a business. Each suffering can become the right 'kick in the butt' to move towards change.

Whenever it gets tough remembering to 'hang in there' is the best mantra.

The biggest lesson for me is that the mind, body and soul are all intricately linked and that the inner transformation process is not a smooth, easy journey but one that is challenging, exciting and, ultimately, rewarding. And it can only get better! —JULIA

NEUROPLASTICITY: UPGRADE THE MIND

THE MIND CAN BE upgraded, just as a computer's software can be. Though, unlike computers, what's needed is not just a one-time upgrade. To change the mind takes time and application and enough repetition of certain processes. Think about it as wiring and rewiring to be able to develop new mindsets, new memories and skills.

Research in the latter half of the 20th century shows that the brain is a dynamic organ; it has the capacity to be flexible. Mental and behavioural patterns can be altered (are 'plastic') and – while the developing brain is more prone to this plasticity – the change can occur through adulthood. The brain's nerve cells (neurons) can form new neural connections and behaviour in response to new information, or sensory stimulation.

By developing healthier thinking patterns and habits and repeating the new behaviour often enough, we can change our brain. We can become more resilient. This obviously has significant implications for healthy development, learning, memory, and recovery from brain damage.

It is also tremendously helpful in healing past wounding and inner transformation. This capacity, known as neuroplasticity, means we can bounce back from setbacks; we can heal painful memories. We can rewrite our script by visualising the healed version of the painful memory till the upgraded version becomes familiar.

You'll find some of my favourite tools for upgrading the mind in this chapter. For further examples of how to apply these, see *Chapter 6.1 Healing the inner child* and *Chapter 6.2 Healing trauma: Restoring safety.*

NLP: what is it?

Neuro-linguistic programming (NLP) is one of the tools, the modalities that I use and love.

Neuro-linguistic programming (NLP) is, according to Wikipedia, 'an approach to communication, personal development, and psychotherapy created by Richard Bandler and John Grinder in California, United States in the 1970s'. NLP's creators claim there is a connection between neurological processes (*neuro-*), language (*linguistic*) and behavioural patterns learned through experience (*programming*), and that these can be changed to achieve specific goals in life.

How NLP works

It works with the understanding that every word we hear, no matter who from or in which circumstance, gets filed in our minds in a unique way. We attach pictures, memories, emotions, stories to those words, which gives them a function and a power.

In one of my trainings in NLP, I did an exercise where the five people in my group wrote 'Love' on a sheet of paper and listed 10 associations with the word. What was interesting, inspiring, too was that when we compared lists, we had very few similarities. My association with love was not the same as anyone else's in the group.

Each of us has associations – memories and emotions – for concepts we assume are commonly understood. Love, freedom, change, thousands more. But our associations are individual. For one person, love might be loaded with pain and they may have given up on finding it. For another, love is an achievable and romantic ideal.

For those reasons, it's important to not assume we share a definition when we are talking about concepts or deeply personal issues; vital to communicate well with one another and listen to the meaning behind the words that are used.

Asking, '**What do you mean?**' can be a powerful way to build a bridge of understanding from one person to another.

The gifts of NLP

NLP is a brilliant tool for transformation. It's so powerfully persuasive that it's one of the tools used in advertising and marketing to link products with desired emotions.

When I was growing up, smoking was cool. When we see old movies today, it's common to see people smoking and there's an accompanying atmosphere of ease and sophistication. Growing up, I was exposed to Camel cigarettes' image of a rugged, smoking cowboy on a horse, in the fresh US countryside. This represented freedom. I smoked to be part of that cool club, to be free. Nowadays, there are very different images associated with cigarettes. Pictures of people desperately ill from smoking-related illness create very different emotions.

Every experience we have gets associated with and filed under a word or bunch of words. Knowing this we can reframe our experiences. We can retrain and rewire our brains to evoke healthier emotions. See *Chapter 6.1 Healing the inner child* for examples.

The positive intention of every part

Every part in any part of our mind – CM or UM – has a positive intention. What that means is we always do the best we can in any given moment with the resources we have at the time. I use that understanding in all my sessions and my own inner explorations.

NLP in the right hands is gold, in the wrong hands, disastrous. It can be used to manipulate thought to sell, to influence, to overpower. I'm sharing techniques designed to be helpful for your inner work towards transformation. I value this modality so highly that I recommend researching NLP. You'll find a wealth of resources – books, courses, teachers – available.

How NLP helped me

I want to share how my relationship with money was healed through NLP. There are two statements that I created from my knowledge of NLP that have guided me since the early 90s.

'Money comes out of my trust and my fun.'

'To make a lot of money is really juicy and gives me all the space to be myself.'

I repeated these statements to myself often. I carried them with me in written form for many years. I know the gift of them was that my brain got rewired.

When I was working in the healing centre in Cologne, we were invited to a day's workshop and I had no idea, then, that what we were doing was NLP. I trusted the facilitators, however, so I participated with great energy. The change I experienced on that day has been significant for the past 30 years. The few things I remember were crucial. This confirms for me the power of direct experience because anything I ever truly felt in my body has stayed with me.

We were asked to embody the old conditioning around money. My head was tilted forward, I felt like I was in a race, walking fast, chasing a goal. I felt tense and stressed. I don't remember details of the next few hours, but I do remember – with crystal clarity – what my transformed self, with a healthy relationship to money, looked like.

The new picture in my head was of me sitting on a couch, leaning back, very relaxed. One arm rested on top of the couch. I felt trust, I was resting, being myself. Funnily enough, that's how I often find myself sitting during sessions now. I love my work and it gives me all the space to be myself.

When I lived in Helsinki a few years later my new beliefs around money were tested. Finland experiences six months of very little light from Oct till March. When the sun comes out and it gets warm in July, nobody stays long inside. Everybody makes the effort to go out into the forest or to the lakes. I had been in Helsinki for just three months and was building my business, so I was relying on clients to come for sessions. That special week in July nobody called or came for sessions. I could have gone into survival fear, sat by the phone, desperately waiting for someone to call and book a session.

But, I remembered the guideline. Money comes out of my trust and my fun.

What did I do? What everybody else did. I enjoyed time outside in nature, relaxed and had fun. After about a week, clients started coming back and, in the end, all was good. I made up for the lost income in the cooler months. I am glad I had that experience and spent my time in a nourishing way.

I would now say that I have a healthy relationship with money.

When I first started earning money in Sydney, I felt incredible gratitude every time I received money for sessions. I had worked for so many years but the exchange was food and accommodation. I never saw money and that gratitude has never left me. I know I can live with very little and be happy. Now, I am very grateful for the abundance I have in my life and the financial freedom it affords me.

I also love saving money and am always looking for a great deal. I hate wasting money. I will forever enjoy 'Schnäppchen' (a great deal, in German). I also spend money, generously, for what is essential in my life like a yearly trip to Germany to see my family.

The right use of NLP is an essential ingredient in all my sessions. It allows me to talk to the unconscious in my clients in the most supportive way. NLP can be used in many settings, for career, health or relationship issues, just to name a few of the possibilities. You can let yourself look forward to becoming the best version of yourself with its help.

Beliefs and misunderstandings

I grew up as a Christian. When I was a teenager I left the church but, by then, had had a good deal of exposure in my childhood to its teachings. My mother was Catholic, my father Protestant. (I still don't really get the differences.)

There are concepts I grew up with and, fortunately, don't believe anymore and it'd be interesting to see if they resonate with any of the religious precepts you learned, no matter what religion you come from.

God sits in heaven. He is surrounded by angels.

God is watching over us all the time. He sees everything and everything is written down in a big book of judgment.

When we die, we stand before God and we will be evaluated in terms of how good we were or how much we sinned. If we were good, we will go to heaven. If we sinned too much we will go to hell.

You must try your whole life to get to a good place.

We are born with the inherited sin. (this one is an absurd thought and makes me furious!)

Heaven is eternal peace. (As a child I thought that sounded terribly boring.)

Hell has different stages. There is purgatory, a state in waiting; and eternal damnation, where your punishment is to burn in hell forever in a state of endless suffering.

Throughout my journey, I got more and more in touch with my deepest fears and discovered that one of them was being in a state of endless suffering. For me, this is an Aha moment as this fear came directly from my early training, early religious beliefs.

Beliefs we adopt are not just religious or spiritual. They can be societal, cultural, from parents, family or school. The good news is we can change old limiting beliefs to new life affirming beliefs.

This exercise is a visualisation to change beliefs and can be applied to any and all beliefs.

EXERCISE

BASIC BELIEF CHANGE VISUALISATION

I learned this technique in my training as a Journey Practitioner. I use it regularly, with great success, with my clients. (Thank you to Brandon Bays and NLP.)

1. *You identify an old belief that sabotages or limits you, such as, 'Whenever I feel joyous, something bad will happen'.*
2. *You visualise a safe space of your choice anywhere in nature with a campfire.*
3. *Imagine a big sheet of paper on the ground with the old belief written on it, in big black letters.*

4. *Step onto the paper and feel how the old belief affects you. You might feel a contraction in your body, a tightness, sinking feeling or constriction; stuck or muddy feelings. Then, in order to heal, you'll need to exaggerate the sensations.*

5. *Visualise all that stagnant, dark, contracted energy being washed out of you with a shower of light – choose any colour that works for you. If you are happy to work with guides, wise beings or guardians, you can imagine them doing it for you. This is a metaphysical shower that can clean you on the inside. Your feeling sense or intuition will tell you when it is complete.*

6. *Step off the sheet, gather it with all the rubbish that has left you and throw all of it into the fire.*

7. *Watch the old belief burning and dissolving into ashes.*

8. *As it dissolves, brainstorm what your new, healthy, life-affirming belief might be. Perhaps, 'I enjoy being joyous' or 'It is safe and healthy for me now to feel joyous'.*

9. *Put a new sheet of paper on the ground and see the new belief written on it in a beautiful colour and an appealing font.*

10. *Take a deep breath and step into the energy of the new belief.*

11. *Open yourself to experience living from the new belief. Feel the energy rising from your feet, up your legs, belly, chest, arms, face and brain. Feel your whole body being filled with the energy of the new, healthy, life-affirming belief.*

12. *Once that feels complete, step off and roll up the sheet with the new belief and take it with you. Feel it merging into your heart and mind.*

This belief change works best when you repeat the exercise. You can do this many times for other self-sabotaging beliefs and with enough repetitions you will eventually rewire the brain.

Tools for transformation in action

These transcripts of client sessions (reproduced with permission) demonstrate the power of the tools you'll find in the book.

CLIENT SESSION – JEN

In Jen's session she describes an issue of 'emotional constipation'. She is in her late 40s, married, a civil engineer. Her naturopath, helping her work on her physical body, recommended me and Jen's been coming to sessions for two months.

Today she says she's feeling too full and stuck, something is sitting in her that she can't digest.

> **Me** *Emotional constipation can feel like physical constipation, but it can happen in more parts of the body than just the digestive system. We can feel emotionally constipated in the chest, for example. Let's find out what is going on.*

I guide her into the attitude of the curious scientist. We explore, gather facts and then, at the end of the inquiry, draw some conclusions. She's already learnt to do that and understands that the biggest mistake would be trying to get rid of uncomfortable sensations.

What we uncover is a dark grey, cold, thin metal layer shaped like a rugby ball, covering most of her lower belly below the navel. It sits more to the front of her body than the back. It is smooth to the touch and feels new.

> **Me** *This is called an energetic structure that usually has a protective function. Let's connect with the heart first and then we'll explore the 'issue' in the belly with the support of your open heart.*
>
> **Jen** *I feel a happy warmth in my chest.*
>
> **Me** *Great, now let's find out what could be positive about this structure?*
>
> **Jen** *It makes me feel stable and gives me a centre of gravity.*

Through not rejecting, and curiously exploring, there is a point where you have contact with the part in the unconscious that is responsible for a specific structure.

Using the understanding from NLP that every part has a positive intention, we contact the wisdom behind an old structure and are usually able to change the structure's shape. It's like upgrading software for an outdated computer program.

As we keep exploring, Jen starts seeing yellow light, which turns into the feeling of joy and happiness as if she were walking in a field of sunflowers on a sunny day.

When clients start seeing a colour or light, I have learnt to ask, 'How does that specific colour make you feel?'

Through trainings in colour healing or Aura Soma, I understand that every colour has a different energetic and emotional effect on us. Red, orange and yellow are warming colours with a stimulating or energising effect. Blue and green soothe and calm. When colours come up in sessions, they often have a healing function and are exactly what the client needs. Towards the end of the session we begin putting the pieces together.

Whenever Jen was happy as a child, it was not welcome as her mother was depressed. She was told over and over, 'Kids are meant to be seen and not heard'. She learnt to hide the joy so as not to disturb her mother. The metal layer, then, served to numb and contain the emotion of joy and inner happiness in her childhood, so she could stay contained and stable and centred in her family of origin.

Throughout the session she is able to allow the feeling of joy spreading through her body. At the end she feels joyful, relaxed, grounded and centred. The old protective structure has changed shape – to an expanded heart bigger than her trunk. It contains and allows joy.

She can reevaluate how to express joy in her present life. She understands it's ok to feel her joy and happiness; the old messages are outdated. The old structure disconnected her from the joy. The new structure includes all her joy and it allows all her joy.

THE POWER OF YIN FOR INNER TRANSFORMATION

YOU'VE MOST LIKELY HEARD the terms, yin and yang. Yin is the essence of female energy; yang of male energy. I was introduced to the yin-yang terminology in my metaphysics training yet it is most known through its ancient Chinese symbol, a circle equally divided into black and white teardrop shapes, placed so the curl of one, holds the bulb of the other. White represents the male and black the female energies. All of us, women or men, have both in us. They can be seen as the polarities of doing and resting and both need to be in balance. When we're balanced, we feel good.

Yin and yang have been compared to the moon and sun. Yang the sun, is the active, doing, forward, outward and upward movement. It is hot, bright and shiny light; it has strong colours.

Yin is the moon, the darkness, the night sky. It is cool, restful and restorative. Yin's energetic movement is inward, backward and down. Yin energy allows us to slow down, go in and relax. It's the feeling of letting go, lying on our back and sinking into the ground; it's the feeling of a deep restorative sleep.

In many spiritual teachings, you'll see terms, like allowing or surrender. They are both yin words and mean the same.

CLIENT SESSION – EMILY

At the beginning of her session, Emily describes the experience of an inner darkness. In recent sessions, she's learnt to identify and name the emotions she's feeling. I started teaching her the art of feeling (see *Chapter 5.1*) and as the work goes deeper, it includes becoming present to very subtle sensations and feeling states that are not emotions. While obvious emotions – pain, fear, anger and joy – are distinct, strong, formed emotions, there are also deeper feeling states like calmness or peacefulness, freedom or spaciousness which are, usually, positive. When we learn to feel more, we become more sensitive to these finer states. They are part of true nature.

> **Me** *These colours you are seeing, this dark grey towards black and the moon colours, if you start considering what inner quality this evokes in you, what could that be?*
>
> **Emily** *Balance.*

I explain that this a feeling state, not an emotion and encourage her to explore it more. She mentions an impulse in her physical body to tilt her head to the right. I ask her to do that.

When we work with impulses from the body, I never assume what it signifies. A tilt to the right could be many things. I ask, 'Does your head want to rest?' To find out we explore. I prop her head up with a big pillow so she can lean towards the right and I suggest letting the head rest.

She's relaxing and says it feels so good to have support for her head that she starts crying. Tears of relief. The allowing of, and listening to, impulses is a yin process. We're not forcing, pushing, efforting. Rather, we are following breadcrumbs.

I'm reminded, so often, how wise an instrument the body is. And, sometimes, it takes a little time to decode its messages.

Emily had a specific feeling arise as she drove to the session. As she talks about it, an emotion rises and we explore that further. It is that emotion that leads to an impulse in her head to turn to the right. We find out what that is, which leads to a deeper emotion.

That's how the yin guides the inner exploration. It invites a surrendering into your direct experience moment-by-moment and letting it happen. We learn by doing. Direct experience is the best teacher.

We use our curiosity, learn to trust our intuition and follow our interest wherever it takes us by listening to and articulating our direct experience in any given moment of inner exploration. That's how I learned to trust the wisdom of my inner world, my body, and my being more and more.

Emily eventually feels calm – a benefit and side effect of allowing the yin approach.

She shares that she's found it difficult to tell people what she feels, even express positive things, like appreciation. I invite her to open to the possibility now to learn to do that more. Appreciation opens the heart and can make us feel vulnerable.

Everything that happens in a session is relevant. The more we learn to trust that, the more the process unfolds. So, I've learned to never resist anything that is presented. Transformation is not a doing; it is the **art of allowing**.

We need to be wide open because there is no plan or template. There's no, 'Now you do this and then you do that'. Instead we ask, 'What wants to happen next?'

For me that is an exciting state of consciousness because through that the inner world opens. And we become aware of nuances, of finer meanings. You start talking to yourself, 'Let's just go in and see what is going to happen.'

Personal growth is an organic process. Your trust in yourself – in your individual way of working, and your capacity to apply the right tools – grows over time till the trust is stable.

We include everything. If you don't push back or resist anything that happens, the work unfolds beautifully. That's the gift of the yin, the moon energy, allowing, unfolding, curious. The art of transformation is the art of putting yourself back together, from the disparate, ungrounded, confused being you are, puzzle piece by puzzle piece.

There is a deeper wisdom that's identifying beforehand what wants to be worked with. Some clients have a dream and bring that; some wake up with something in the morning or come with something that happened the day before or just before the session. There is something that guides the work and the more you trust that, the more useful it can be if you just let it happen.

The yin allows chain reactions of healing in the body from a simple relaxation of the breath to a calming of the nervous system. It's an advanced technique – the capacity to deeply, truly relax.

On resistance

In my first training, one of my teachings was about resistance. 'There is no resistant client. If you feel you have a client who's resistant, you're doing something wrong.' I love that teaching. Nothing needs to be resisted. Everything is part of the exploration and deserves attention, nothing in us is wrong or bad. It is vital, and thrilling, to make friends with all our protective mechanisms.

I have learnt – from years of doing this work myself – to understand and trust the process. If I had an investment and wanted the session to go a certain way I'd create a barrier, some resistance and, of course, that's counterproductive and, ultimately, frustrating.

I truly know now that everything we ever learn is well meant. Any protection we develop is the best solution in that situation. How often do you find yourself judging a protection inside yourself like a tightness in the chest that feels limiting and you want to get rid of it? Eventually the judgment of any form of protection will transform into understanding. Later in the book, I talk about protection in more detail.

What does being an HSP mean for inner work?

When I first heard the term HSP, about 18 years ago, from a psychology friend in Germany, it didn't fully register. It took a few more years of unnecessary suffering and misunderstandings till it landed. The term had been used to describe me and it meant that I was a 'Highly Sensitive Person'.

I used an online test on (https://hsperson.com) to self-diagnose. When I ticked 26 of the 27 question boxes, it was clear I had all the traits.

Elaine Aron is the psychologist who first used the term. I feel deeply grateful for her work and highly recommend you find out more about it. There are many resources available.

Once I understood I was an HSP I clearly recognised others who are and saw, soon, that a lot of my clients are highly sensitive. It's why we work well together.

My understanding of HSPs and the information I often use in my sessions, is that:

- It is genetic, which means it has a purpose for humanity and its survival.
- It's not a learnt behaviour. HSPs make up about 20 percent of the world's population.
- Being an HSP is not something to overcome and cannot be changed by thinking it away or changing attitude.
- When humans lived in caves, the HSP in the tribe or community picked up on all kinds of noises, such as a dangerous animal approaching. (HSPs can hear the slightest sounds). They alerted the non-HSPs, the warriors or clan chiefs who were able to protect the tribe.
- In the 20 percent of the world's population that are HSPs there is a spectrum from very sensitive to slightly sensitive.
- One sense can be more sensitive than the others. I see, feel and hear a lot. I can hear the shower dripping across the hallway with the door closed. My husband often doesn't believe what I am hearing. But when he checks, guess what? The shower is dripping. One of my girlfriends is an HSP and she is much more sensitive to smells than I am.
- HSPs tend to be the advisors, philosophers, wise folk, psychologists, creative people.
- HSPs have a more refined capacity to perceive their environment than non-HSPs. When an HSP enters a room their brain is wired to allow them to see, feel, hear, smell more than others.
- Most HSPs suffer in certain situations where there are a lot of stimuli – loud environments, bright lights, chemical smells, too many people in one room with a lot going on.
- HSPs easily get 'over-aroused' as their sensitivity allows so much

in that their nervous system gets too stimulated.

- The most effective advice for HSPs is to give your senses a break when you are overstimulated. Take the time to be quiet, meditate, be in nature, or rest in darkness or with a blindfold. Trust what works for you and give yourself the kindness to respect your sensitivity.

With all this extra sensitivity, it's likely that many HSPs would have grown up hearing judging messages like: 'Don't be so sensitive', 'Pull yourself together' or, the more dismissive, 'What are you on about?'

I recently heard of HSPs being described as **orchids** while other people were daisies. Daisies are more robust and can survive in rougher conditions, they grow in the fields exposed to the elements. Orchids need very specific conditions to thrive.

An HSP will suffer more than others from the wrong conditions but once the right conditions are restored, they recover quickly and can thrive again.

Learning to take care of your 'orchid-ness' takes a while and often there are some rough learnings but once understood, being an HSP is a blessing.

HSPs resonate strongly with trauma healing skills and gentleness of the heart.

Knowing whether you are an HSP is important for all living, but it's most relevant in preparation for doing inner work. I understood late in life that I was an HSP; now I wish I'd known it earlier. It would have made my life easier. I would have worked on stronger boundaries, respected my nervous system more and would have pushed myself less.

Inner maps

I like the idea of different maps for the inner world – it's a way to not only understand the inner territory but also to make navigation easier. No need to be going round in circles; it's like an inner GPS. If we think of a map as a way to show the structure of a place, then the following structures are ways I use and have helped clients to use, to find their way around their inner world.

For me, all maps are different languages used to decode the inner world. Once I had learnt a few of them I started getting confused. For example, the Diamond Approach teaches essences as part of true nature in colours. Red essence for example is strength, yellow essence is joy.

In the chakra system every chakra is associated with a colour. Red is the colour for the first chakra, yellow the colour for the third chakra. Eventually I thought of them being like different languages with the need to keep separate. It made sense, when I thought further, that I don't mix English, German and Italian in one sentence. I learnt to stay within one language or one map.

Maps of circles

This is one of the simplest maps I use and give to new clients. The two outer layers – mask and shadow – represent the **conditioned self**. Conditioning is a mechanism of division where we are divided into what we believe is good about us or bad. If I do this, you might say, I am good. If I do that, I am bad. We work hard to be 'good' people according to what we have been taught.

The two inner layers – essential or true self and universal truth – represent **true nature**, the state of being which is who we really are. It is the treasure chest in the core of our beings that we can learn to find and open.

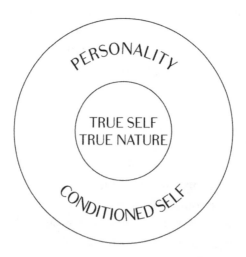

- **Mask** or personality layer, part of the **conditioned self** represents everything we do to be loved and accepted. This is the layer from which we usually relate to the outer world.
- **Shadow** layer is where we find those parts of ourselves – emotions, thoughts – that we believe are not loveable or acceptable. We learnt to reject, deny or repress them. They contain a lot of energy, so once that layer is freed up it makes it easier to drop into true nature.
- **Essential self** layer is the one I used to call 'gifts and treasures' in my women's groups. This is part of true nature, it's our personal expression of it, also often called **true self**. In this layer we become authentic human beings. When we open to this place in ourselves, we start shining, glowing, being radiant.
- **True nature** itself is the deepest place we can drop into. It connects us to universal qualities like love, peace, freedom, strength, stillness.

I created this map in the early 90s as part of developing the women's group that I facilitated for 15 years thereafter. The group was structured around these layers. I found it was then, and now, a helpful way for people to go in.

Another great visual I use to help with understanding how inner work works, is the **image of the ocean.**

The mask is the surface, we have our heads above water and don't know what's below. When we start diving deeper, going in, the next layer representing shadows is possible encounters with sharks, stinging fish, dangerous currents. It's what scares us in our inner world and so we need courage to keep going. We also need to know how to dive so we don't get into real danger.

Then we dive deeper and see more of the beauty of the ocean: the beauty of the unusual sea life, coloured fish, coral, anything pleasing to see.

If we keep diving we end up at the bottom of the ocean, where it is eternally still, untouched by the surface. There could be a tsunami on the surface, and we wouldn't know it. We're in the depth of the stillness of the ocean. This deep place can also be thought of as inner wisdom, connecting us to an eternal wisdom that is way beyond the mind. In the women's work I called it 'The wise woman'.

Introduction to the seven chakras

I learned this system in my Metaphysics training in India and it is the map I use when I read energy in clients.

The seven chakras: Element, place in the body, colour, theme
In my training, I used the location and qualities of the chakras as a way to understand what processes and issues were affecting me and, eventually, my clients.

Chakra	Element	Place in the body	Colour	Theme
1st or Base	Earth	feet, legs, pelvic floor up to the pubic bone	red	grounding, roots, sexuality
2nd	Water	between pubic bone and navel	orange	feelings, emotions

3rd	Fire	from navel to sternum	yellow to golden	power issues: from false power to real power and empowerment
4th	Air	heart, chest front and back, arms, hands	green	love, acceptance, spaciousness
5th	Ether	throat	blue	inner and outer communication, expression, creativity
6th		forehead, occiput, centre of the head	purple	awareness, inner seeing, visions, intentions
7th		just above or on top of the head	white	connection to something bigger

The enneagram: An intro

We all develop specific behaviours to survive and function in the world. The enneagram is a personality typing system; a great map with which to understand different personality types.

Astrology tries to explain how and why we operate the way we do; so does the enneagram, which I use in the work I do. It can be helpful to understand your deeply learnt reactions so that you can work with them and eventually allow more freedom. I often invite clients to study the Enneagram.

The enneagram is divided into nine main types. Each type can be unconscious or integrated and, if integrated it means the person's able to overcome the limitation of their type.

1 is the perfectionist. Right and wrong is very important for them.

2 is the helper. They feel other people's needs more than their own.

3 is the achiever. They want to look good and polish their image. They struggle with deep hidden unworthiness.

4 is the tragic romantic. They can appear eccentric, the artist archetype. They are closer to their emotions than other types.

5 is the hermit. They are very sensitive and protect themselves through withdrawal and building strong walls around them.

6 is the loyalist. They fear authority and survive through finding a sense of belonging through loyalty.

7 is the enthusiast. They are the life of the party and they can look they have it all, but deep down they are as scared as types 5 and 6.

8 is the boss. They can be overpowering, and you notice them in a room. They struggle with feeling their vulnerability.

9 is the peace maker. They do everything to create harmony. It is hard for them to feel anger, it's also hard for them to say, 'No'.

For more in-depth information, there's a wealth of books, an online questionnaire to identify your type, courses and many marvellous accredited teachers.

Chinese medicine and meridians

The beautiful ancient system of Traditional Chinese medicine (TCM) is used to map out the body's energy. It is a solid healing system that has been around for more than 2000 years and its longevity is evidence of how effective it is. Traditional Chinese medicine identifies and uses the body's meridians, or energy pathways. Also, the modalities of acupuncture, shiatsu and a more recent modality, 'Acu-energetics' use meridians for diagnosis and treatment.

Meridians spread throughout our whole body from fingertips to toes, front and back. The mapping of the meridians, so intricate and beautifully interconnected, is fascinating. Each of the meridians relate to body systems and emotions. The lung meridian, for example, relates to sadness. Repressed unfelt grief can lead to problems in the chest area like bronchitis or regular colds.

Acupuncture stimulates points along the meridians to help the healthy distribution of energy. A point can be too full or too empty and, with acupuncture, these points are connected, too full flows into empty spots and balance is restored. I have been a grateful recipient of acupuncture treatments for many years. They work very well to restore energetic balance and I trust it as a healing modality. It's a personal tool.

It's also most useful to think about the meridians in my work with clients. When a client has had an insight or a breakthrough, it's visible or noticeable in many ways that their energy is different. It has gone from stuck to flowing again and I can imagine pathways throughout the whole body being repaired. Meridians distribute energy; just as blood vessels distribute the life preserving blood. Meridians work through the energy bodies or the light body.

Perhaps, with these introductions to maps you've been inspired to study further. I recommend it as each has been most useful in the work that I do.

TIPS FOR MY 21-YEAR-OLD SELF

- The mind can become your friend. You can train it to turn towards your inner world with a kind and welcoming attitude.

- Become the curious scientist on the inner and inquire till you come to your own conclusions.

- Allow yourself to doubt till you've found what is true for you.

- Understand the superego and learn to defend yourself against judgment.

- You can rewire the mind and upgrade it like a computer. You can find many great techniques to do that.

- When you start meditating, don't fight the mind. Learn to bring your attention into the heart or body away from the mind. Shift from thinking to sensing/feeling.

- If you are highly sensitive, treat yourself like an orchid, respect what you need.

- When you start healing lots of old emotions and memories will surface from the unconscious to the conscious mind. In those times of difficult transition remember to 'hang in there'. Ask for help, talk to friends, find a good therapist, read and study to understand how the inner world and healing works. In times of darkness and struggle remember, 'When the night is the darkest, the dawn is the closest'.

- At the core of your being is a wonderful place, your inner treasure chest. It is the end of all suffering and it holds all the answers you need. Venture on your journey, find and open it. You will not regret it.

PART 3

THE WISDOM
OF THE BODY

COMING INTO THE BODY

WHEN I FIRST HEARD the statement, 'the body is wise' it didn't make sense. For me the body was an object that I expected to work, to function. When it worked, was healthy and capable of doing what it was meant to be doing, I was happy. When I got sick, however, I thought my body was betraying me.

The body is wise; it is a teacher

Now that I've experienced some health issues, I know my body is a fine instrument that's giving me feedback all the time. This includes responding to the food I eat. When I eat, it might be straight after a meal or the next day, I get direct feedback if the food was good for me or not. If I've eaten the wrong things for my body, I experience brain fog or tiredness. I've altered my diet and today I don't include gluten, dairy, or a lot of sugar. I always notice the difference if I've had any of those in a day.

My body shows me if I had enough, restful sleep. It shows me what I am feeling. When I hold onto an emotion, I might get tension or tightness in any part of the body.

What makes me happy now, is that I trust my body and, from direct experience, know it never has a bad agenda, it would never betray or manipulate me. My body is innocent, a mirror and a teacher.

I understand now that every physical symptom is an invitation to discover a deeper truth. Anxiety can point towards an emotion like sadness for example. Once the emotion is felt it can lead to rediscovering an essential aspect – like purity or innocence in the heart. This is just one of thousands of possibilities.

Strong symptoms can act like a fire alarm. My chronic illness, for example, was trying to get me to slow down and develop a healthier, more sustainable lifestyle; to stop over-giving and over-extending. My efforts had come from enthusiasm, love for life and wanting the world to be a better place but were not in harmony with my physical reality.

The feedback can come in various forms. It might be discerned by actually talking to the body and letting it provide feedback. It could be heightening our sense of our limbs, or whole body and recognising a range of sensations in the physical.

In this chapter, I will present an overview of different techniques to develop a healthy relationship with the physical body. By doing that, sometimes even chronic illnesses or in some extreme cases a terminal illness like cancer, can heal. Results from being more in tune with the body are an increased level of energy, a sense of relaxation and wellbeing.

You might have heard the saying, 'We are spiritual beings in a physical body'. To learn to express our true nature, who we really are, includes all dimensions, mental, physical and emotional.

Living in this physical body can be compared to driving a car and we all need to take good care of our car for it to drive well. When I arrived in Sydney after living in India for about ten years within a period of 20 years, I was like a well trained driver on the soul level, yet living in a run-down old car and driving on the wrong petrol. I had not yet understood the importance of the right nutrition or supplementation for the physical body.

At 42, I was tired and my digestive system was struggling. It started a long journey of healing the physical body. Lots of experimentation with finding the right way to eat for my specific body and the right supplementation. I learnt so much that I could probably work as a naturopath now, if I didn't love my job so much.

In my sessions I always include what's happening in the body as a crucial tool for inner navigation and transformation.

Talking to the body

When I lived in the ashram we learnt meditations for working with the body that gave me a whole new relationship to my body. One, 'Talking to your mind and body' was very useful and new for me.

One of the more powerful practices from the meditation is to affirm the body every day. When I began that, I started perceiving the body as a friend and I still do. I say, 'Hello body, thank you for everything you do for me every day. Is there anything I can do better for you in the future?'

Some time ago, I got multi-focals (distant and near vision glasses) for the first time. Unfortunately, with the multi-focals on, my vision was blurry when I looked down – a common issue when first trying them, I'm told. So, I missed a step on a staircase and fell. I sprained my ankle. Then I also apologised to my body. 'I am sorry I didn't take better care of you,' I said. As the ankle got stronger every day, and healed very well, I thanked it for the improvement. I do believe in using positive talk to improve the healing capacity of the body.

Sensing the body: Arms and legs

I am a strong believer in working with and through the body in inner transformation. I know that once something is experienced in the body, it's easier to remember. Reading about transformation is useful for information, of course, but when I read I tend to forget a lot of what I've read. However, something I have experienced stays with me for good.

When I talk about direct experience I'm relating it to the art of inner transformation, the subject of this book. There are many topics and books that give relevant information about other subjects that cannot be experienced in the body, like the history of a war for example or a non-fiction book about science.

Let's say, for example, you have a sense of contraction in your chest yet by the end of a session or meditation the tension has dissolved and transformed into a lovely relaxing warmth. That is easy to remember as you are directly experiencing it. To enhance our connection with the physical body I recommend a basic sensing meditation to feel your arms and legs.

TIME TO STOP: BASIC SENSING MEDITATION

*Start on one side of the body and sense the feelings in one
foot, then travel up the leg to where it meets the trunk.
Then, do the same on the other side. Then, feel one hand,
and slowly sense the arm towards the shoulder. Once
you've sensed that, do the same with the other arm.*

Any sensation is valuable: warm or cold, tight or relaxed, numb or alive, tingling sensations. The practice deepens your sensitivity to the body and, in time, we learn to perceive finer and subtler sensations.

Tracking sensations in the body

When I work in sessions, I am always aware that being able to track sensations in the body is an intrinsic component of understanding what is happening internally, emotionally. I ask, 'What is happening in your body right now?' or 'Where do you feel the emotion in your body?' Eventually, when we have the capacity to sense our arms and legs, we can expand that tracking to the trunk and learn to describe sensations in the heart, belly … anywhere, really.

Thinking about where things are happening right now invites us to talk about every sensation we're experiencing. These sensations are movement of energy and, over time we get more adept at describing energetic sensations.

Grounding techniques

Part of learning to connect with our physical bodies is to feel grounded. To understand what feeling grounded is like think of the opposite: being 'off this planet', head spinning, running around like a chook without a head, speedy, spacing out, drifting, floating above yourself to just name a few.

I am sure you know your personal version of feeling ungrounded. Feeling grounded is essential in inner transformation, to be here, present to yourself, this body, this moment. It is quite common in our fast-paced world to be disconnected from our bodies. That was definitely true for me before I started my inner journey.

The simplest way to ground yourself is to feel your legs and feet. One technique is to become present to how your legs move while walking.

A technique that works well, to help you feel grounded is to imagine you only exist up to your navel – your upper body is invisible. Once you can imagine that only the lower part exists, your attention shifts from the head down to the base.

Physical exercise is good, to help us feel grounded. Jumping up and down can help.

Increasing energy levels in the body

In Chinese Traditional Medicine we can identify a map of meridians – energy pathways – through which energy flows in our physical bodies. This flow of energy works for the physical body like fuel does in a car. The clearer and purer the fuel, the more efficiently the car will run. When we work with transformation, we need our physical body to be as alive and energetic as possible. If the body feels tired or sluggish it can be difficult to go deeper.

Movement

Can we intensify energy in the body? Can we feel more alive? It's certainly possible and a simple way to do that is through any form of movement like a walk, running, shaking, dancing, yoga, Tai Chi. Find your own movement practice and be as present as possible during the movement.

When we bring more aliveness into the body, we also feel more. Having more access to our feelings is one of the important steps we can take for any transformation. See *Part 5 Our emotional territory*.

The art of relaxation

Once we become more aware of the body, most people discover how tense their physical bodies are. Which leads to wanting to relax. Yet learning to relax is an art. It is an ongoing deepening skill. Most of us are conditioned to always be a little tense. When we try to relax we're not always successful.

Growing up, I had become good at being tense, not being relaxed had become normal. Does it work when someone tells you to relax, if you're feeling tense? In the early years of my inner journey, my answer to that instruction was, 'Don't you think I would if I could or knew how to?'

When I heard from Osho that 'relaxation is your birth right' I was really surprised. I hadn't heard that before. Think about relaxing as a way to talk to your whole body. Imagine you had a phone in your conscious mind and you made a call to all parts of the body inviting them to relax. Not every part will listen in the beginning.

As you practise to relax, feel into any sensation that's part of the relaxation – a warmth in the chest or a heaviness in your arms, a softening in the belly, a release of tension. Any of those sensations indicate relaxation and by focussing on them, your sensitivity and awareness grows. Focus on the areas that are able to relax, not on the areas that are still tight or tense.

The biggest obstacle

One of the biggest obstacles to relaxation is being in a state of hyper-vigilance. This hyperarousal in the nervous system is a natural and, in many cases, healthy impulse. It's the way our body tells us to be aware of possible danger when we experience our environment as unsafe. Being relaxed, in situations of imminent danger, is not safe. Our primal responses of fight, flight or freeze, were honed from needing to be vigilant about threats of death by wild animals. We were building necessary and life-saving skills. Yet, it is not healthy to stay vigilant at all times. Chronic hypervigilance can lead to exhaustion and eventually lots of physical issues like sleeplessness or digestive problems to just name a few.

How do we turn off the unnecessary vigilance? There will be lots of tools in *Chapter 6.2 Healing trauma: Restoring safety*.

One simple tool I want to introduce at this point is soothing self-talk. Find a message that brings you a feeling that you are safe; that relaxing is a good thing to do. Saying, 'It is safe to relax right now as I'm in a safe environment' might sound silly, even childish. But that's its effectiveness. You're soothing yourself as a parent would soothe a child.

GOLDEN TOOL
EASING TENSION

This technique can swiftly alter your state from tense to relaxed.

Sit or lie down and start tensing all the muscles you
can feel. Hold that and then exaggerate the tension
till it is as tight as possible. Hold the tension for as
long as possible and, when you need to, release it,
naturally. Repeat the sequence a few times.

What's being experienced is the polarity. The opposite of tense is relaxed. The more you increase the tension, the more you'll recognise the feeling of no tension and you can train your body to know how to achieve the relaxed state.

A healthy relationship with tiredness

Feeling tired is often a signal from the body that we need to rest. It can also be a very powerful signal that something emotional needs to be attended to. It can be a strategy not to feel something, like some personality types repress their anger by being tired.

I once gave a session to a number 9 in the Enneagram, the peacemaker. He got in touch with strong anger and a minute later he fell asleep in the session and started snoring. When he came back we both had a laugh as he knew it was a strategy to avoid feeling anger.

In the unhealthy relationship with tiredness we can try to overcome it. We might judge and reject the tiredness; misunderstand it and treat it like an enemy. Through resisting it in different ways we are not opening ourselves to making friends with it.

The healthy relationship with tiredness involves accepting the tiredness as a signal from the body. The body is trying to tell you something important and it would be useful to work with the body as elements of a team towards health and well-being.

This next exercise can be done with any physical symptom. Tiredness is just one example.

EXERCISE

DIALOGUE WITH TIREDNESS

You have two cushions on the floor. One cushion represents the conscious self, the second represents tiredness. You switch positions and take turns sitting on each cushion, allowing each part to speak while you listen to each other – just as you would in a dialogue with a friend that you respect. You take notes in the end about any insights that arise.

Breath awareness

Becoming aware of our breath and how we breathe is a crucial element of getting in contact with ourselves and our bodies. It is part of learning to trust our direct experience and grounding it in the moment.

It is also another way to intensify energy in the body. Breath is life energy and when we breathe more, we feel more alive.

Attention on your breath

This is the first step. Turn your attention towards your breath. It's as simple as that. It is a choice. Instead of being lost in your thoughts or having your attention on anything outward, choose to direct your attention towards your breath.

Once that's mastered, you can learn to experiment with different breathing techniques. They are available in many different traditions like yoga or tantra. I will only give an overview in this chapter and introduce a few basic ones to inspire further exploration.

'Finding the right breath' is one of my favourite techniques and this excerpt from a transcript of a guided meditation session indicates some of what it contains. In this meditation you are giving your body permission to breathe the way it wants to breathe right now.

TIME TO STOP: FINDING THE RIGHT BREATH

As you breathe, feel the movement of the breath in your physical body. How do you want to breathe right now? What is the right breath for you? Maybe the breath will stay as it is, or it might feel good to breathe a little deeper. Let yourself experiment, the right breath will feel right, it will feel good at some level.

RELEASING TENSION ON THE OUT BREATH

Breathing more deeply, more slowly and more consciously can increase energy levels. One simple technique to release tension and increase energy uses the breath in a conscious way.

Make the sound 'Aahh' on your outbreath, and as you do, imagine pushing out old, stale, sleepy, tired, lethargic or numb energy. Focus on the out breath and allow it to be strong.

Next, take a normal breath in and do the long out breath again. After doing that for a while, stop and feel your body and notice if the energy levels have increased.

The relationship between thoughts, emotions and breath

Once you become more aware of yourself, your breathing and the sensations in your body, you will discover that mind, body and emotion are all interlinked. What we think – a happy thought or a sad thought – can lead to an emotion and, with every emotion comes a specific breathing pattern.

EXERCISE

CONNECTION BETWEEN
EMOTIONS AND BREATH

*The next time you feel relaxed, stop and
become aware of your breath.*

The next time you are angry, stop and become aware of your breath.

Try it with different states and then compare. That's how I learnt it.

Breath can be soft and gentle, or hard, pushy and contracted.

We can also use the breath to work for us. If we change a breathing pattern, we can induce a certain state. I use that a lot in sessions, for example, when working with a trauma where emotions and anxiety levels are heightened. In those situations, I invite my clients to relax their breathing as much as possible, thus sending a message of safety to the nervous system and it will, in turn, feel easier to work with the difficult memory.

Breath meditations: An overview

I would now summarise breath meditations into three main categories. The main one is watching the breath. The other two are stimulating or calming techniques.

Watching the breath

You can choose any part of the body and feel the movement of the breath in that part. Feeling it in your chest, for example, will bring awareness to the heart.

Feeling your breath in your belly will bring awareness to your being centre as described in the next chapter.

Eventually we can learn to breathe into any part of our bodies or organs. We can also learn to breathe into the energy of an emotion to bring more awareness to it.

Three stimulating techniques

These techniques can increase energy levels in the body or activate emotions or material in the unconscious.

Rebirthing

Rebirthing is a well known and powerful technique which I've practised and offered for many years. It's vital to have any rebirthing session under the guidance of a trained facilitator. I have many memories from receiving rebirthing sessions, where strong emotions would arise, seemingly from nowhere – pain, anger, or vivid memories would come up.

The breathwork technique used in rebirthing is called conscious energy breathing (CEB). With your instructor's supervision, you'll practise 'circular breathing' – quick, shallow breaths through your nose without any breaks between the inhale and exhale. You'll do this for one to two hours, taking breaks if you need to.

Dynamic meditation

When I lived in the ashram in India, we would do this meditation every morning. By 6 am, the hall would be filled with people ready to meditate. On the sound of a gong Stage 1 of the 5-stage process would begin and you'd hear hundreds of people breathing strongly.

Here I'm focussing on Stage 1, which is called chaotic breathing. It's a continuous breathing exercise where, for 10 minutes, you breathe in and out of your nose as fast as possible and in no particular rhythm. This was always a shortcut into my unconscious. The activity bypasses the conscious mind and its strategies to not feel or protect ourselves from going deeper into our feelings. It is very stimulating and activating.

I'll describe the second stage – cathartic release of emotions in *Chapter 5.3 Transforming anger.*

Stage 3 uses jumping up and down to realign ourselves and it leads into Stage 4 where we stop and stand still. The final, Stage 5 is filled with dancing and celebrating.

This meditation works wonders. There are versions of it online and it's something I highly recommend. Over the 20 years in the commune I did thousands of Dynamic meditations and, from just this one hour's practice, I felt dramatic changes to my inner state. Many mornings I'd wake up and not want to do it but would do it anyway. Sometimes I'd feel sick, still do the meditation and feel well at the end. It is a highly transformative meditation.

Breath of Fire

The breathing technique known as 'Breath of Fire' in yoga involves passive, normal inhalations and powerful, rapid exhalations. The exhale, which requires you to contract your abdominal muscles, is the main focus of this technique. Also, the inhale and exhale should be the same length, without any pauses in between. This is different from slow breathing exercises, which often involve longer exhales.

With this technique, the pattern of your breathing is more important than the speed. So, start slow if you're new to the technique. You can speed it up later on.

Breath of Fire is done in a seated position. It can last anywhere from 30 seconds to 10 minutes, depending on your experience level and preference.

This style of forced exhalation may help reduce stress, boost brain function, improve respiratory health and digestion.

....

FOUR CALMING TECHNIQUES

These techniques allow the nervous system to settle and are great antidotes to stress.

I recommend trying different techniques to help yourself be calm. Try them so you can feel what works best for you. Don't force yourself into any technique. If it doesn't resonate, let it go.

TECHNIQUE 1

One hand on the chest, one hand on the belly. Gentle in breath through the nose, gentle out breath through the mouth or nose. Feel the movement of your breath in your belly.

TECHNIQUE 2

Three-stage breath: On the in breath, feel the belly first, then the middle of the trunk where the diaphragm is, then the chest.

On the out breath reverse: chest, stomach, lower belly. This way
of breathing is used a lot in yin yoga – a very slow version of
yoga where you rest in each position for three to five minutes.
I have been a fan of this style for the last seven years.

TECHNIQUE 3

Breathe in deeply, hold and breathe in more. Then breathe out.
This can be very relaxing and helps to discharge pent-up energy.

TECHNIQUE 4

Breathe in normally and on the out breath push
the belly out. This relaxes the diaphragm.

If any of the above techniques suit you, practise that specific one for a few weeks. It will make it easier to remember it when you need it.

Hara: *Gathering, containing and sustaining energy*

Our Hara – a term that derives from ancient Eastern cultures – describes our true centre of being. It is one of the most fascinating places in our inner world, as important or even more important than the heart. I mention the hara in this chapter as it is also relevant in feeling grounded and centred in the physical body. I will come back to it in *(Chapter 7)* on inner guidance.

It is described in every Eastern tradition that I am aware of and have studied. The Japanese call it Hara. In Chinese tradition it is the Dan Tien. In the Ridhwan School it is called Kath, centre of presence, or being centre.

Hara was the term I used when I was in the Mystery School in Pune. In the past eight years I have been a student of the Diamond Approach Australia. Here it is called the being centre but I use the terms interchangeably.

'We have to work on the shift from the head to the heart,' said Osho. 'The movement into the hara happens naturally.'

When I was 21, after my first experiential therapy group, I had my first experience of the hara. I was completely centred and sat in meditation, resting, waiting, without knowing or being concerned about what came next. I waited for impulses and followed them or simply sat. That state lasted for about three days.

I hadn't known that something like that place even existed in me. I felt I could just be, just be without a goal. It was a very profound and fulfilling sensation. Now, because it showed me what was possible, I'd call that experience a 'spontaneous' awakening or opening, a glimpse of what is possible. It made me 'hungry' for more of the same, also called a longing or divine discontent.

When it changed after three days, I started the long and arduous journey to cultivate the capacity to stay connected with the hara.

And now, I am able to help clients learn to connect to the being centre. It's physical location in the body is roughly five centimetres below the navel. When you first try to locate a feeling in that area, there's not likely to be much. With attention, it does eventually become more obvious and a feel-able presence. The ancient Buddhist tradition of vipassana teaches people how to connect with this centre.

Basic vipassana

Vipassana has become more and more known in the last decade as part of the growing interest in meditation and mindfulness. There are different well known vipassana centres in the greater Sydney area and all over the world. Many of my clients have been there for 10-day retreats. I believe its popularity is based on it being an ancient technique that is simple, powerful and efficient.

One of the simple instructions is: 'Feel the movement of the breath below the navel.'

Bring your hands to the spot roughly five centimetres below your belly button. You can cup your hands, fold one over the other, intertwine them – whatever works. One thumb can rest on the belly button. Then you feel the movement of the breath under your hands. The rise of the belly on the in breath, the fall of the belly on the out breath.

The more the diaphragm relaxes, the stronger you'll feel the movement in the belly.

When the mind wanders – and it will! – notice and bring the attention back to the breath. This is a practice of cultivating attention.

Think about it as calling all the farmhands back into the main house after a long day of working in the fields or with the animals. At the end of a busy day everybody comes into the kitchen, eats a nourishing meal and sits around the warm fire.

The more we are connected to this centre the more it can feel we are gathering our energy, containing and sustaining it, which gives us a centred and grounded feeling.

Going in

We use the tools available to access our inner world. This ancient technique is so central and important to going in and can be a ready access point. For some people, it is easier to start the diving in by opening the heart, the topic of our next chapter. Though it's not a strict division, there is a tendency for women to have more ease by using the heart as the access point. Men tend to find it easier to start with the belly centre.

Source of energy

It's useful to think of an analogy to truly understand what the hara is. Originally, I was trained in metaphysics and the chakra map. In this map there are seven chakras – each relates to a different part of the body.

The hara was explained to me as 'the main water supply' into the house. Imagine that you're in a seven-storey building and every chakra is one floor, starting from the base chakra as floor one. Every floor needs to be supplied with water. That's where the hara comes into its own. The hara is the main water supply for the whole house. It comes in from an outer source and fills us up in the centre. Another good image for the hara is to think of it as a well. In order for the well to be full so that there is water when we need it, we need to fill the well, gather water. The gathering quality is crucial. No water in the well, nothing to supply.

Learning to feel centred in our belly can feel dramatic, like a ride on a wild horse but finding the hara and staying centred is part of the process of taming the mind by bringing the real boss – our consciousness – back in the picture. Thoughts and thinking can be very chaotic, consciousness is always harmonious.

TIPS FOR MY 21-YEAR-OLD SELF

- Value your physical health when you have it.

- Relate to your body as being wise, relate to it like a friend.

- Listen to any physical symptoms as a message from the body.

- Take good care of your physical body.

- Nurture and cultivate good habits:
  - Eat the right food for your body
  - Make sure you get enough sleep
  - Find a form of movement or exercise that you enjoy.

- Become aware of your breath: slow it down and deepen it, you can never go wrong with that.

- Practise a basic meditation: Hand on either the heart or the belly, feeling the breath in that part of the body.

PART 4

OPENING TO THE HEART

MEETING YOUR HEART

I love love
In all its forms and expressions
It is the deepest expression of the heart
I love love for life itself, love for people, not just family and friends
Love for animals, love for plants, love for beauty.
Variations, flavours of love, self-love, gentle love,
passionate love, compassionate love, caring love
fierce love, peaceful love, forgiving love.

I love love

As I've journeyed to understand and care for my inner being, there've been two constants that I value most. One is truth; the other is love.

My heart has become the place from where I relate to myself and the world around me. It is my centre and I love the feeling of love welling up in my heart. I've also discovered and, value deeply, the fact that the source of love is deep inside my own heart.

I made a commitment about 16 years ago to live from love; to do that each and every day. I was 47 and had spent 20 years in a commune and my first five years in Sydney, in shared accommodation. Then, I lived in a two-bedroom apartment on my own and, for the first time in my life, had my own lease. At the end of each day, I'd look back and I see where I'd lived from love during the day. Also, where I hadn't.

The more I practised it, the more the capacity to come from love grew – in my work and with my clients; with my husband, family and friends; my women's group and Diamond Approach study group. I even love cleaning and making our home beautiful. I have noticed, though, that it's not entirely possible to be present in love with anything computer related. Still, I love expanding my capacity to come from love in every aspect of my life. It is an ongoing practice.

I hope you'll enjoy this next story, just as a child might enjoy a bedtime story read to them. It's the story of my process, of making the transition from being lost and scared, to discovering the inner landscape that is all-embracing and comforting.

My journey to the centre of the heart

I am lost. How did I get here? I don't recognise anything. I can see trees, but where am I? Nothing looks right. I know this is a forest, but which way am I meant to go?

I start walking into the forest as the outer landscape, these barren fields don't look attractive at all. At least there's some green in the forest.

There is no obvious path so I make my way through the trees, walking on leaves. I move deeper into the forest but still have no idea which direction I'm meant to take. Then, my heart begins to relax a bit; something about this feels right. I keep walking with a little more determination drawn to, what I assume is, the centre of the forest. It's not too bad here. Actually, quite nice. Birds sing and the sun is shining through the trees.

Suddenly, I reach a massive metal wall, too high to climb over, solidly closed, no door in it. I start walking around the wall but any way forward is blocked. Damn! I start banging the wall till it hurts my hand. The wall is rusty and cold and I don't have any tools to cut an opening. I start feeling very upset, disappointed and helpless. Why this? Why now? Why here? I feel miserable and sorry for myself. Doom and gloom set in.

I try to will this away, to overcome the obstacle. I'm using all my mental and physical force. But the wall doesn't care, it doesn't move or change at all. Eventually, I'm so exhausted I sit down.

A voice gently whispers through the trees. 'Acceptance is the key. Acceptance is the key. Acceptance is the key.' Am I meant to accept the wall and do nothing? Collapse, resign and give up moving forward?

Walking back is not tempting at all, I don't even know what to walk back to.

I sit down and think about acceptance. If I were to accept this wall, how would I do that? I'm curious, walk along it, touch its surface. I'm interested in why this wall is here. Does it have a story to tell? As I touch the wall, I get waves of feelings. Sadness arises, a memory from a past relationship that failed and I felt rejected. Tears roll down my face.

The temperature under my hand gets warmer. Do I have contact? Are we communicating? It gets warmer still. It doesn't even feel metallic anymore but soft, even rubbery. What is the wall protecting? What's on the other side? Is the wall protecting me from getting hurt?

Eventually the wall changes, a door appears and opens, and I am in the next layer, a very soft and vulnerable one. A whole different landscape presents itself, and it's full of soft and pastel colours.

As I keep going deeper, I land in the secret garden of my heart. A deep sense of love floods me and my cheeks are again wet with tears. I remember something that feels so real and intimate. I'm enveloped by a deep embrace and it's caressing my sore heart, taking me in, like a most loving mother holding her baby, protective and caring. I have never felt more loved, seen or understood.

Why did I ever leave this place?

What is the heart?

The heart I talk about is the spiritual heart, also called the heart-chakra – an energy centre located, just as the physical heart is, in the middle of the chest.

I learnt about the chakra system through my training in esoteric sciences. Chakra is a Sanskrit term denoting an energy centre in the human body, that's associated with the spinning energy that helps regulate the body's processes, from organ function to the immune system and emotions. There are seven chakras in our body and an understanding of the seven chakras is more mainstream now, introduced a great deal through yoga and mindfulness practices.

Energy is the deeper life force that flows in everything. Life energy has different names in different traditions. It is Chi in China, Prana in India, Ki in Japan. Without this life force we would be dead.

In esoteric study we use a map to understand chakras, which comprises concentric circles, each circle representing a layer within the chakra.

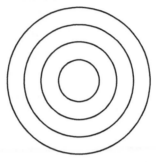

As part of my spiritual journey, it was vital to understand the many layers we need to uncover as we find our essence, our true nature. Layers are peeled back till we come to our core, our centre. The more we gather the tools to find that centre, the more we gain the calm knowledge that the core is always beautiful.

The deeper we go, the closer we come to opening the treasure chest. Yet, on the way we will pass through difficult layers. We can access pain that may have begun in childhood, and at different stages, all the way to our present life. Any time we experience pain but repress it because we can't cope, it is stored. The painful memories go into the unconscious storehouse we've previously mentioned.

When you finally open into old, stored pain or begin to digest old material it is likely that your stored feelings pour out and tears flow. It's invariably followed by a feeling of relief. It feels good.

The centre of the heart

Our essential being, our true nature, is always positive. As you learn to connect to the centre of your heart, you begin to experience aspects of true nature. For me, during those many times of connectedness, I'd check whether I might find any of those emotions that usually create suffering. Was there any fear there? Pain? Unworthiness? Shame? Guilt? I couldn't find any of these.

This is my direct experience, so for now, consider it a hypothesis. Then, it is vital you confirm this for yourself. As with any spiritual inquiry, direct experience is the best teacher.

Once you are in the centre of the heart you will find it a deeply enjoyable place to be. The truth of that makes my job as an inner tour guide very rewarding. The experience can be accompanied – depending on which of your senses you use to access the centre – by a feeling, a knowing, a message, a guidance, a fragrance, a picture, even a taste.

I'll describe different ways to connect to your core, to true nature. Once you begin to use this roadmap, you'll more easily navigate the territory of the heart and, indeed, your whole inner world.

This simple heart meditation can give you a first glimpse of what I'm talking about. Do this meditation sitting or lying down, for five to 20 minutes. Make sure you are undisturbed. I offer more meditations which you can access in a separate booklet that accompanies this book. It can be downloaded, for free, from https://inneralchemy.de/heart-meditations.

....

SIMPLE HEART MEDITATION

Bring one or both of your hands to the middle of your chest, allowing them to touch your own heart space. Sense the touch of your hand on your chest right now.

Now, imagine your in breath starting to touch the chest area from the inside.

Allow yourself to become aware of the immediate physical sensations. Maybe it's the tender touch of your hand, or you might feel the temperature of your hand or its pressure on your chest. Just notice the physical sensations. Is the chest tense or relaxed? Hot or cold?

Start to familiarise yourself with what is there. Maybe you see something when you connect. Colours or an image, a shape? Maybe there is an emotion? Maybe it's numb. Maybe you hear something? A word, a sentence, a song?

At the end of the meditation let yourself slowly come back into the room. Then, when you are ready, open your eyes again.

....

Be gentle with yourself

One of the keys to connecting to the heart is gentleness. Your heart will reveal itself in its own time and its own way. The softer or gentler we are in our approach to the heart, the more it responds, opens. It doesn't like to be pushed and will contract and hide from you if it's feeling forced to respond in any way. Let your inner scientist, the curious inquirer, be present in a soft, gentle and receptive way and then your heart has a chance to open. You're looking for a direct experience and that can't be pushed or forced. It needs to be allowed.

The purpose of all heart meditations is to connect the heart to all our senses – feeling, seeing, listening, tasting and smelling. You'll find heart meditations in the free online booklet at https://inneralchemy. de/heart-meditations.

Get a sense of your senses

Do you know which is your primary sense? Is there one that is more immediate for you than others when you connect with yourself? Most people name seeing, feeling or listening as their primary senses. Smell and taste are, generally, not as immediately accessed. Once you identify your primary sense you can develop others more.

It is important to understand your primary sense so as not to put unnecessary pressure on yourself when you start experiencing your heart. Seeing something is as valuable as feeling something or hearing a message. It is hard to connect deeper. Rejecting your natural way of perceiving the inner world can make it even harder.

My primary sense, for example, is seeing, or responding to visuals. But I have learnt to develop the feeling sense and the auditory or listening sense over the years. Just recently, I made a vision board with images that looked appealing, triggered feelings and spoke to me. A simple way to learn to connect the visual with the feeling sense is to ask yourself when you see an image, colour or shape, 'How does that make me feel?'

Occasionally now, my senses of taste and feeling combine; I might associate a feeling with a metallic or very unpleasant taste, or it might be appealing, like the fresh taste of drinking water. I rarely get fragrances on the inner realm of my senses, though I once had a spontaneous fragrance of rose when I was in deep meditation, which clearly didn't come from anything outside. When we learn to open our hearts, we become more receptive, sensitive to and patient with ourselves. We learn to trust our experience, moment by moment, we learn the art of true acceptance.

Your heart may talk to you when you experiment with heart meditations. Let yourself say, 'Yes' to whatever you feel in your body, whatever emotion might be present, whatever you see or hear.

The heart teaches us the art of being present. When you are present, you are in your heart.

Now let's explore more, deepen our understanding of the heart.

My journey discovering the heart

I will never forget the first time.

> *I open the door and see the ocean of pink and green pillows on black mattresses. I love the smell of rose water in the air. But there is something else, a vibe, a field. My heart starts singing with a sense of recognition. I feel like I've stepped into a magical world; one I've been longing for but didn't know was even possible. I feel embraced by the energy in the room and, immediately, feel safe.*
> *My mind asks, 'Why did I not know this before? Why only now?'*
> *I know I am home.*

These are my impressions from my first heart group. A three-day process – Opening to the Heart – to explore and open the heart-chakra and learn to connect all the senses with the heart. The atmosphere in the room was pregnant with acceptance, expansion, beauty and gentleness. I had done groups before but some of those experiences were too harsh or didn't work for me.

With this, however, I fell in love with the heart, there and then. I didn't know what I was missing till I entered that space. I ended up running this group and kept a group like this going, for 15 years.

Home is where the heart is

In my first experience of that group I began an exceptional journey of discovering my true heart, the spiritual or heart-chakra. Thirty years later, the exploration continues.

I call myself a devotee of the heart. It keeps teaching me, showing me its treasures, its depth and wisdom. And it gets never boring or repetitive. Once I found the heart, I felt like I'd come home.

My German upbringing instilled the idea that the head was always bigger, vaster, more important than the heart. The brain knew it all whereas the heart was, essentially, for kids. It was designed for love, that was certain, but also for play time, and was certainly not the best support for living your life. Love was merely an addition to the elements of our psyches.

Once I started exploring the depth and beauty of the heart, its transformational power, I understood that the heart space keeps expanding. At first, the heart was a little flower and at some point, it grew to be a bush. Next, a tree and then, many trees. Now it is a forest that still keeps expanding.

There is no limit to how big our hearts can get. We can always love more, feel more compassion and empathy, understand more and more aspects of our human experience. The heart makes space for all the different emotions we can have and all the paradoxes of being human.

I live with the ongoing question, 'Can I accept this too?'

Once a certain level of acceptance has been reached it naturally expands to the next level. This continues in our lives until each emotional challenge, repressed part or shadow is faced and overcome. Then we understand ourselves and feel more integrated. We become whole.

Signs of an open heart

When the heart is healthy and open, we can both give and receive love.

This allows us to let someone love us. When the heart is closed love can't come in.

When the heart is open you can receive appreciation, positive feed-back, and much more. It is nutrition for the heart, like good food for the physical body. When the heart opens, we have access to intuition, the wisdom of the heart starts guiding us. We can learn to listen to the voice of our hearts again. It is often much quieter than the mind, peaceful, easy. Sometimes it's only a whisper in the beginning.

When you start living from the heart you will experience a shift in consciousness.

Once we learn to open our hearts, 'the laws of the garden' – a term I was introduced to in my metaphysics training – apply: When one wins everybody wins. The heart thinks in terms of win/win. It works towards a solution that is beneficial for everybody involved.

The true heart is about connection, love, acceptance, a deep sense of benevolence, which means 'well-meaning and kindly' or to wish well. Benevolence is intended for everybody, not just one's self and it includes other living beings, the land and the environment involved.

Symptoms of a closed heart

When our heart is closed, we can feel cold, distant, isolated, hard, arrogant, disconnected, insensitive.

When the heart is closed, we follow the 'laws of the jungle': Only one person can win. We think in terms of competition, climbing the ladder, being the best, the first, the only one. It is about territory, hierarchy, superiority and inferiority.

Synchronicity

A side effect of deeper connection to ourselves and others is the idea of synchronicity.

This is a great way to explain synchronicity. You have a string instrument on one side of the room and play a note on it. A similar string instrument at the other side of the room will start resonating and make a sound too.

When I first started experiencing synchronicity during a conversation with a friend – when both of us were deeply connected to our hearts – the feelings, insights and connections which arose were so special. Synchronicity allows us to tap into a deeper intelligence – the wisdom of the heart.

Why do we close our hearts?

The most common reason for closing our hearts is that we have experiences of past rejection, hurt or pain. Everybody will have such experiences, either large or small. Either in early years or later.

Pain of rejection

Whether there was not enough love growing up, pain with the first love, loss of a loved one through death, or divorce of one's parents. There are so many reasons we feel hurt.

The easiest protection against feeling more pain is to close our heart. One other reason is not to feel fear.

Understanding protection and working with it

When we close our hearts, we develop layers of protection. It can feel like the heart turns to stone or a metal shield can cover it. We can have our walls up.

When I work with energetic protection, we compare it to outer physical structures. I always ask clients, what material could this be? It can be any material like stone, plastic or glass.

Description of a protection from a client:

> *It feels like my heart has turned into a plank of wood. I had to become rigid so I couldn't break when 'people walked on me'. It feels like my grandmother was sitting on my chest and I was trying not to break. My diaphragm feels tight, my ribs feel glued together. When I fall asleep, I hold my breath, pretending I am dead. It is not safe to breathe deeply.* —ELISE

Usually there is a protection around fear. A client might have a sinking feeling in the heart or contraction. When we learn to approach fear and open into it, it will be vital to explore the protection layer around it. The best antidote to fear is love. And understanding.

In *Chapter 5.1 The art of feeling* there will be a good deal of detail about how to develop a healthy relationship with our emotions.

Elements of protection

When you come across protection there are three elements to be aware of:

1. Every protection has a positive intention. It is a part in the unconscious that got created at some point because it was absolutely needed. I am convinced that we truly do the best we can in any given circumstance with the resources we have at that moment in time.
2. Ask what is being protected inside yourself.
3. Ask what you are protecting yourself from on the outside.

The stronger the protection or reaction the older is the memory it is protecting us from. What hits us strongly 'in the now' usually comes from the past.

In many cases the protection is outdated as it is generally developed in childhood. It would be like wearing a raincoat because there had been rain but wearing it when you're lying on the beach on a sunny day. Not quite appropriate, is it?

'When you come across a protection in a client,' said one of the metaphysics teachers in my Energy Reading Training, 'always look for what is being protected'.

Consider this example: A person's heart is closed, tight and contracted. They can't feel their heart, which means they can't feel love, warmth or acceptance – those pleasant warming feelings that we probably all like very much when we can feel them. What they are likely protecting is their vulnerability. They have been hurt in the past, rejected at some point by someone important. It hurts! If we experience that hurt repeatedly, we close the heart and stop feeling.

What we are protecting from is often a person or a situation from the past. A cold rejecting father. A demanding mother. An overly attentive mother who invades a child's space. An intimidating teacher. Bullying classmates. The list of what can hurt the heart is long.

Often a situation in the present can remind us of someone in the past and trigger the same shutdown. This mechanism is also called projection or transference in psychology. We are projecting someone from our past onto a person we are in contact with now.

Healthy protection

When we explore the issue of protection, it is important to include the understanding of healthy protection or the right level of protection in any given situation or environment. Old outdated stagnant protection – if worked with rightly – will eventually transform into appropriate flowing alive protection, that is not limiting but enriching.

When I was 34 I moved to Finland because of a relationship.

Helsinki was a very interesting city. It was a city where drinking, to excess, was quite common. I would regularly see people tumbling, drunk.

For me that felt very unsafe. In my inner work I was learning more and more to keep my heart open and be vulnerable. But I didn't really want to do that on the streets of Helsinki. I read about a technique for visualising a bubble of white light around oneself for protection.

At the time I hadn't done my training in metaphysics, I didn't understand energy fields and the concept of a light body was unfamiliar. As I didn't know what else to do, I started practising. The results were faint in the beginning, but it did make me feel better.

One could say it was a placebo effect. Just thinking that I was safer made me feel safer. Or it worked? One day I was standing in a full tram and a very inebriated man was standing not far from me. Suddenly he dashed towards me. I got scared as he stopped right in front of me trying to hug me. But then he said, 'I love you!'

I'd never met him before but, from that moment I started trusting my bubble of light protection more as nothing dangerous happened. Maybe it was a sign to help me trust, but that didn't matter. I made the decision to never go out in any environment that felt unsafe or where people were mostly unaware of what they were doing, without dressing up in my invisible protective cloak.

For the past 30 years I've used this technique successfully. I've shared it with many clients.

I've studied further – light healing and metaphysics – and understand that we have the capacity to use the different lights we see in visualisations for different healing and feeling effects.

GOLDEN TOOL
BUBBLE OF LIGHT

Visualise a bubble of white light around your entire body. The bubble could be round or oval and it could also be colours other than white. Notice how it makes you feel. As you visualise the bubble make it as big as you need.

When I used this technique in sessions, clients might choose more than one colour. It might start with a layer of yellow and change into a dark blue; it can be figurative, like a painting or abstract, like a pattern. But it is whatever feels right to the individual.

In speaking to clients, it seems the most common size is about an arm's length around one's body. What is being described, in essence, is our human energy field.

My own bubble of protection evolved over time and I added an outer layer with a semi-permeable membrane to the visualisation. I learnt, when I studied physiology, that every cell in our physical body has a semi-permeable membrane. This simply means that certain molecules or particles can get through and others not.

In a healthy cell anything that is good for our health passes through. Generally anything that helps the inside of the cell to make energy, like amino acids, etc. can get through. A healthy cell doesn't let harmful substances in. Fungi, bacteria and viruses which would make us sick are blocked.

There are key receptor cells, that open or close according to what is in front of them. They're a bit like a bouncer in a club selecting who can come in and who stays out.

How does that translate to a human energy field?

If you imagine the outer layer of your bubble of protection is a semi-permeable membrane fuelled by an intelligence that selects what is good for you and what isn't.

Human fungus, virus and bacteria are rejection, judgment, unfair criticism, blaming, shouting, unsupportive, sabotaging behaviour, misunderstandings, someone in a bad mood dumping their rage on others.

Positive energy is love, support, healthy feedback, appreciation, acceptance, being seen, understood, consciousness, peacefulness. You get the picture.

Once understood you imagine that everything that is not good for you, stays out. The membrane closes and becomes impenetrable.

In the long-term this is a great way to learn about healthy boundaries.

The different layers of the heart

The heart-chakra's many different layers are like concentric circles from the periphery to the centre. When you start exploring your heart you will get in touch with any given layer. And then you learn to go deeper. Going deeper into the inner layers, happens through a sense of melting, going through a door, moving a curtain or just telling yourself to do it. Whatever works for you is completely acceptable.

Sometimes when you go deeper, what you experienced before deepens. It might be a sadness, joy or silence. It can, also, be the opposite. You might be sad and when you go deeper you feel joy. You might have seen something red and orange and suddenly it gets black or grey. What's important is that you trust yourself as you go deeper. With each new layer, you start fresh with what you are experiencing in that moment.

How to recognise that you are coming into the centre of the heart? You'd be feeling very relaxed or comfortable, peaceful or spacious. Your inner world might be silent or, if you can hear anything, it will be very harmonious. It might look very beautiful. You might see colours or a beautiful image of something.

You are creating a pathway from the head to the heart, which can feel like cutting a swathe through an overgrown jungle. In the beginning the way is not clear. You are reconnecting, rediscovering, remembering the beauty, preciousness and truth in the core of your heart. We all have this preciousness. We all have the beauty. And yet, sometimes there is also a jungle to penetrate before we find it. Protective layers, shells, can cover the core.

It's like a treasure hunt. The core of the heart is the treasure chest with lots of beautiful surprises. And you are the treasure hunter getting to know the territory and find your way back to the core.

In time you will learn to trust to find your own way, to move from your head to your heart, to not get lost in the jungle.

When you travel to the core of the heart, true transformation can happen. Sadness can change into love, numbness into presence, anger into strength.

The importance of the heart in inner work

My understanding today is that going in without opening our hearts first is a complete waste of time. Our heads judge. To really get to know ourselves and navigate the inner world we need the acceptance of the heart, its capacity to make space and not judge, to bring kindness to difficult issues and courage to face typical challenges. We'll expand on this in the next chapter.

Challenges that respond to an open heart

The heart has the capacity to embrace paradoxes, opposites. The heart doesn't divide – unlike the mind. The heart will not make you choose one feeling over another. However, there are typical challenges on our inner journey. To face all of them we need our heart to be open.

When we open our hearts, we may experience our **repressed emotions**. Typically, sadness, anger and fear start surfacing. When the heart opens, we start meeting our **shadow aspects**, those parts that we learnt to reject.

In my upbringing, for example, strength was greatly valued and weakness wasn't. So, I had to learn to embrace and accept weakness over many years. And, in recent years, that's included the challenges and perceived 'weakness' of a chronic illness.

In *Chapter 5.1 The art of feeling* we'll look at our shadow aspects in greater detail.

An open heart helps us to transform **protection** layers and meet inner places of **resistance** with love and kindness. It helps us to be comfortable with feeling **lost, uncertain, in transition, or not knowing**.

The transformative power of the heart

In 1997, I had a remarkable experience and through it, I learnt that the heart has an exceptional power to transform suffering into bliss.

In that year, I was at the beginning of a new love affair. I'd met a man earlier that year while I was living in India and he was visiting from France. We only had a very short, yet wonderful, time together as he had to go back to France to work. We stayed in touch and six months later he decided to come back to India for three weeks to give our relationship a chance. We decided to spend time in Goa, India, on the beach.

I was overjoyed, very excited to see him again. I also had no idea what inner challenge I was about to face.

The Frenchman was four years younger than me and very good looking. His last relationship was with a woman younger than him – a very attractive model and I was not only older than him, but didn't have a great sense of self-esteem around my looks.

So here I was in Goa, in this perfect romantic environment with the man of my dreams. Beautiful Indian climate, warm balmy nights, the sound of cicadas, glorious night skies under blankets of stars. Swimming, sunbathing, eating fresh healthy food in the day.

Heaven, right?

No. I was in the hell of unworthiness!

The devastation hit me like a wave and knocked me out. It took over and blocked me, made me feel separate, entangled in my head, disconnected and definitely not present to the gorgeous man in front of me. It was agonising. I was drowning in feelings of unworthiness, tortured by the monster in my own head which didn't give me a break. 'He is too beautiful, I am too old for him.' I spent a lot of time visualising his ex, comparing myself to her, and on and on it went … mercilessly.

After three days of this we had to admit that our connection was obviously not working. Yes, this was a 'test run' … but I had failed.

I went back alone to our accommodation, feeling devastated. I had everything I wanted in front of me, but my head blocked it all.

And then I lay down and began to meditate.

Stage 1 (length about 1 hour):
As I didn't know what else to do, I stopped resisting the pain and opened into the feeling of unworthiness. It felt like I was dying. The idea, the sense of unworthiness was everywhere.

Stage 2: (about another hour)
Somewhere a faint memory of a powerful Buddhist meditation called **Atisha's Heart meditation** – named after the Buddhist teacher, Atisha – came back. *'Breathe in suffering, breathe out blessings.'* Some deeper wisdom started guiding me. On the in breath I started breathing in the sluggish swampy energy of unworthiness and on the out breath I held the intention to feel love.

It took about 20 or 30 minutes to feel the first benefits of doing this, but at some point, there was a definite change. I started to feel lighter, less stuck. This encouraged me to keep going.

The feeling of love kept growing and at the end of those life-transforming two hours I was love. Love was in me and around me.

The ocean of unworthiness had transformed into an ocean of love and my heart was the magic transformer. It had gobbled up the energy of unworthiness and spat out gorgeous, all-consuming love.

At the end of that experience my French lover came home, and he couldn't believe the change, he could feel my transformation.

Finally, I was present as love, open and available. After that we had a great time in Goa and it was the beginning of a very nourishing, healing, intimate relationship.

QUALITIES OF THE HEART

ALL THE EXAMPLES OF inner transformation would not exist without the power of the heart. The heart's qualities are crucial to understand. They are essential for its extraordinary capacity to transform suffering into a healthy state.

Love

The main aspect of the heart is love. Love is the heart's language. The same way our nose enables us to breathe, an open heart enables us to love.

Self-love

Love includes self-love, which is crucial in our journey towards becoming whole. If we come across challenges like shadows or repressed emotions without love or self-love, it would be impossible to integrate those aspects.

Unconditional love

At the core of the heart is one of its most fascinating aspects: unconditional love. I believe that we are all longing to be loved unconditionally. It was one of my great discoveries that this quality is one of the many treasures to be found in the heart.

Connection

One of the many qualities of the heart is connection. The heart allows you to feel more connected with yourself, with other people, animals, nature and everything around you. When heart and mind align, a different way of thinking arises.

TIME TO STOP: MEDITATION FOR CONNECTION

Think of everyone in this world experiencing exactly what you are experiencing right now.

At any given moment other people, thousands or even millions might be going through the same thing. This way of thinking has started happening spontaneously more and more in the last decade.

I remember thinking, during menopause, of all the other women having a hot flush, when I was having one.

In moments of loneliness or hardship I become aware of everybody else in any other country, of any age, social status or religion who might experience what I am experiencing. I immediately feel more connected when I think that way and experience more acceptance.

Compassion

Compassion is one of the main qualities of the healthy heart. It translates to 'feeling with' and, as such has a rich sense of connection from us to others.

Compassion for ourselves is as important as feeling with others. A lot of transformation happens through compassion. For example, fear can transform into love, peace or relaxation.

If a loving parent is present with a scared child, the child will eventually relax and feel safe again. Love and compassion allow that transformation.

Gratitude and appreciation

Gratitude has a role along with the power of appreciation. There is a growing awareness in the world around the power of gratitude. Gratitude and appreciation open the heart.

One of the ways I have seen this repeatedly is in my work with couples. They usually book a session when they are in some sort of trouble, stuck with each other or fighting, misunderstanding each other.

GOLDEN TOOL
APPRECIATION EXERCISE FOR COUPLES

Partner 1: *'[Insert Name of partner], I appreciate or feel grateful for ...' (a quality in the other like listening to me, washing the dishes, earning money, cooking a beautiful meal, how you take care of our children)*

Partner 2: *'Thank you' and in answer: '[Insert Name of partner], I appreciate or feel grateful for ...'*

I usually let couples do three rounds of this exercise. Every single time I have experienced this with clients, it's gratifying to see how a simple appreciation exercise puts a smile on their faces.

What is true forgiveness?

I have had an interesting journey with forgiveness and my association with it started in my mind. I heard, I learnt that forgiveness was helpful in one's healing.

Looking back I now understood it as a valuable beginning to reprogramming the mind and introducing a new concept. Though I don't remember that thinking about forgiveness created much of a change. I do believe, however, that it started building the foundations for real forgiveness.

I kept experimenting over the years with forgiveness.

Then, one day, in a seven-day meditation group, a spontaneous feeling of forgiveness arose in me. Someone from my past, who had hurt me a great deal, popped into my mind. Suddenly I had a vision of us moving towards each other and we were hugging. Within minutes, a deep sense of forgiveness began flooding my heart. It welled up from deep inside, an unknown place at the time.

I wasn't thinking about forgiveness, it arose from a source way beyond the mind, which I now call my inner wisdom.

That was the first time I started understanding that forgiveness is a real quality. I would now call it an essential quality of the heart. It is part of the treasure chest in our hearts that we can learn to open. It had a liberating and truly transformative power, thus allowing a **real let go** of the wounding of the past.

Years later I trained in a modality called Journey work – created by Brandon Bays. This work is most rich and there is a wealth of resources online and in print, if you'd like to explore this work further. The Journey work uses the idea of cellular healing to clear old emotions stored in the body. It's work is to clear the kind of emotions that can cause pain or disease.

I came to see that I had a **misunderstanding** around forgiveness. The idea to 'forgive and forget' made me repress emotions like resentment, anger, hurt or disappointment, just to name a few. I didn't know that they needed to be expressed not repressed.

One exercise from this work is to imagine a **campfire** where you are in a dialogue with someone from your past. You allow old, repressed emotions to come back into consciousness. The emotion leads to a memory. Then you express these emotions with the people involved in the memory.

The final outcome of many well designed steps in this process is forgiveness. That's how you check if you have accomplished what needed to be done.

You would begin by asking, 'Am I ready to forgive?' If the answer is no, you keep going. The key is emptying out old raw emotions by finally naming, feeling and releasing them.

Imagine you always felt rejected as a child at home by a parent and you could never address it. In this campfire setting, you talk to the parent and they listen. They understand your side. You understand their limitation. Once all raw emotions are emptied out through expressing them fully and feeling them in the body, there is a point where the emotion feels released. You keep checking until there is no resentment, pain, hurt or charge. Nothing is left. When that is done thoroughly, forgiveness starts flooding in.

At that point, when you ask, 'Am I ready to forgive?' you will get an honest 'Yes'. It will not be manipulated or forced and you'll recognise the difference.

Forgiveness and true nature

You can't 'do' forgiveness. All you can do is clear the way for forgiveness to arise naturally. It is the end point in any healing, and it has a transformative power. It liberates you, expands your consciousness. But you need to 'get down and dirty' which means facing all the unpleasant and hurtful feelings. You need to not be afraid to do the work.

If you can eventually be in front of somebody (in spirit or in present time) and feel completely clear, without reaction, and feel 'All is forgiven' then the work around forgiveness around this person is done. That is the final test, the 'forgiveness test'.

....

SELF-FORGIVENESS MEDITATION

It is hard enough to learn to truly forgive someone, but it is even harder for most people to forgive themselves. To help with that I created this self-forgiveness meditation.

Imagine somebody that you feel you have forgiven already.

Allow the energy of true forgiveness to arise in your heart. You can visualise it as a colour. Golden light works well for me, but you can change it to any other colour that works for you.

Now, imagine golden forgiveness showering down from above and flowing through you and around you.

Sit in the energy of self-forgiveness. Remember a difficult time and feel the feelings from that time again like unworthiness and surround those feelings with the energy of self-forgiveness.

....

Softness

Softness is one of the most beautiful qualities I ever discovered in my heart. The softness emanating from the heart can feel like feathers caressing your skin. Or a soft mist gently descending. When essential softness penetrates your skin, the world feels ok. It feels like everything is ok. There is a deep sense of acceptance. The softness can feel like an angel at your side, protecting you.

When I first experienced my own softness, in a meditation, it felt too good to be true. Having grown up in Germany 12 years after the end of World War II, I was surrounded by war survivors. All my grandparents had suffered and, now I understand that all of them had PTSD.

Everybody around me in my family, was affected. They had all been on high alert and in survival mode throughout the War. There was no space for softness.

I became a survivor in their midst. I became strong and tough in their image.

There are many more qualities that the heart embodies. Let this list be an inspiration and then make your own list. Add your own experiences and find your own names for the treasures in your heart.

Acceptance is the master key

I have listened many times to this powerful quote from Osho – one of his core messages about acceptance – and it's never lost its relevance or importance for me. If I had to choose one quality of the heart as the most important one for healing and inner transformation, I would pick acceptance. It is the master key.

The only problem with sadness, desperateness, anger, hopelessness, anxiety, anguish, misery, is that you want to get rid of them. That's the only barrier.

You will have to live with them. They are the very situation in which life has to integrate and grow. Accept them, they are blessings in disguise. If you want to escape from them, then the problem arises – because if you want to get rid of something, you never look at it directly. And then the thing starts hiding from you because you are condemnatory; then the thing goes on moving deeper into the unconscious. It moves into the basement of your being and hides there. And of course, the deeper it goes, the more trouble it creates – because then it starts functioning from unknown corners of your being and you are completely helpless.

So, the first thing is: never repress. Accept it and let it come in front of you. In fact, just to say 'do not repress' is not enough. I would like to say, 'Befriend it.'

A person who can be patiently sad will suddenly find a happiness arising in his heart from some unknown source. That unknown source is godliness.

Difficult moments will be there, but one day you will see that those difficult moments gave you strength because you encountered them. Those difficult moments are hard when you are passing through them, but without them you would never have been integrated, centred, grounded. —OSHO

As we open our hearts more and more to ourselves and others, we start integrating different parts of our personality. Once we have learnt to embrace a new part or emotion, it will automatically be easier to accept that same capacity in others.

We all have specific traits that we cultivate as we grow up. They are traits that we believe are loveable and acceptable – this is the definition of conditioning. And this conditioning is a mechanism of division. We nominate one aspect of ourselves as good, and the opposite as bad. Like in my example: strong is good, weak is bad.

For many, anger is unacceptable. If we judge our own anger and feel it is negative and unhelpful, we will judge it in others. Yet, once you are ok with feeling angry, then you let others have their own expression of it.

What are your learnt judgments? In my conditioning being busy, productive, efficient was good, being lazy, unproductive, inefficient was bad. We all have our favourites. The mind is trained to judge and divide.

The heart embraces, integrates, brings all parts home and accepts opposites. In time, more and more parts of yourself, will knock on your door, calling out for acceptance. It is an organic process that keeps working till we accept ourselves completely.

The meditation 'Becoming Whole' in the meditation chapter – available for free online – allows a direct experience of bringing rejected parts home.

Peaks and valleys: Accepting change

This is one of the many beautiful quotes from Osho that has guided my inner explorations.

> *One has to learn not only to rejoice in the day but rejoice in the night too – it has its own beauty. The peaks have their glory; the valleys have their richness. Whatever comes, enjoy it as part of natural growth. Just remember one thing: accept everything that life gives to you.*
>
> *If you are alive, climates will change, seasons will change; and you have to learn through winters, through summers, through rains. You have to pass through all these seasons with a dance in your heart, knowing perfectly well that existence is never against you. So, whatever it gives, it may be bitter, but it is a medicine.* —OSHO

This is a theme I feel passionate about and I guess it is one we all have a story about.

I grew up with the illusion that progress is linear. Life, I'm lucky to say, has taught me to understand that everything happens in rhythms and cycles. I was educated to think about things being linear. That, for the purposes of the book, I will call an aspect of the 'male way of thinking'. It's rational, logical, linear. This is not a statement about men and their qualities. We all have both sides in us and two brain hemispheres with different functions.

The 'female way of thinking' is intuitive, feels, has hunches, 'knows', reads between the lines, sees things in pictures, follows the gut, has ups and downs, knows life is a process. The sense of life's changes can feel like 'birthing' something.

For women, the menstrual cycle affects moods and energy. For older women, a bigger cycle signals the end of our menstrual cycle – menopause. Then, there is the biggest cycle – that of birth and death – and that affects everyone, regardless of gender.

My old model for success in life went like this. Learn, get good at something, achieve, learn more, get better, achieve more. Yet, it turns out, that isn't the whole picture. Is it?

There was a whole lot this linear model didn't explain. If this was the roadmap to happiness, why did I feel so lonely and empty as a teenager? If, as happened, I was best in school and did everything right, why did I feel so much was missing?

Clinging to a high and rejecting the low

One of the biggest traps on the path towards freedom (and I've made this mistake hundreds of times over the years) is the idea that we should hang on to the happy place we find; that the goal of all our inquiry and interpersonal work is happiness.

The way it manifests is as a determination to 'stay happy'. Happiness is the achievement for all the work. Yet this linear way of considering life doesn't, truly, make a lot of sense. Life really doesn't flow just like that.

Living a conscious and fulfilled life means being real, and honest and asking ourselves: 'What is my truth right now?' Sometimes, the answer may be a so-called negative. It might be that we need to cry or vent our frustration. This is part of being alive. Mental states change, emotions change, physical states change. Life changes and if you can allow that, be aware of its shades and movements, this is a growth in consciousness.

I wasted a lot of time attaching myself to peaks and believing 'That's it!' I've found my answer – peace and happiness.

This massive misunderstanding created a lot of unnecessary suffering for me. I held onto a specific state for longer than it actually lasted, and the result was stress and exhaustion. It's also hard work to reject negative experiences. What is not helpful, when we're trying to be sensitive to life and awake to its possibilities, is to manipulate our experience according to our own ideas or fantasies, instead of letting life unfold the way it naturally does.

One particularly strong experience of this happened on a retreat about five years ago. Every learning and experience happened very quickly. All was accelerated and my experiences kept changing – bliss to shock, pain or disconnection to bliss again. I was the least resistant I'd ever been; like a kid on a roller coaster with the wind blowing around my ears; I met whichever state was present. And, it changed all the time. When I didn't resist a difficult state, it soon moved to a lovely experience. I experienced a sense of grace and freedom while being with highs and lows, the natural movements of life.

Accepting sadness

Sadness was one of my great teachers in accepting that life has peaks and it has valleys. When I started my inner work at the age of 21, I often found myself crying at the end of a group, without knowing why. It was confusing. According to the linear model, I should have been feeling happy!

So, one day I asked my meditation teacher a question about my sadness. His wise and simple answer: 'Acceptance is the key'. It wasn't the answer I expected.

At that age I had no idea what that really meant but it started my exploration. I thought he would solve my problem and make my sadness go away.

Now, things are different. I am a total fan of acceptance and I practise, teach and live it as much as possible.

I understand today that I had so much repressed pain stored away in my unconscious. It started surfacing in the safe and supportive environment of therapeutic groups. Since my first encounter with sadness, I have learnt a lot. Ongoing exploration has taught me the difference between resisting and accepting sadness. *Chapter 5.2 Transforming pain* will have more detail about this understanding.

The feel of sadness

It's a rainy day inside. The climate has changed. What happened? Last week the sun was shining, I saw blue skies and felt a gentle wind on my skin.

Sometimes the weatherman doesn't warn you. Nobody announces the change of wind or air currents. There is no obvious trigger. Something old surfaces from the recesses of the unconscious.

A cloudy sky, everything looks dark grey. No colour anywhere. You can smell the moistness of the air. Heavy rain clouds are on the edge of bursting. What will allow the skies to open?

It is difficult to breathe. There's nervous tension in the stomach, an ever alert inner guardian watching out for danger. Fear of breathing too deep. A deeper breath could break the damn. The old hesitation: can I handle the intensity of the emotion?

After initial resistance some acceptance creeps in. Every hour a little more. The breath deepens slowly. My consciousness is still testing: can I handle this?

There were days when none of this was even considered. Before the sadness reached the surface so many mechanisms were already in place to numb it, dull it, deaden it. Shallow breathing, hypervigilance, distraction through doing. Faster, faster, faster! No time or space to feel. Feeling was dangerous. Memories of similar atmospheres earlier in my life line up.

This is a softer version, quite bearable. All it needs is acceptance. Opening my heart to the sad part and the magic happens: it softens and warms up. It turns from enemy to friend.

The longer I relax into it, the friendlier it becomes. A softness, a deep sense of letting go. More space for the feeling. Not imprisoned anymore.

Remembering times when all I could do was 'be in the cave and lick your wounds'. In the early days of learning to feel old pain and hurt it would feel like every second was too long. It took everything I had to just stay present with the overwhelming intensity of the pain.

It's a valley and it is always dark. Acceptance changes the temperature from cold to warmish. The fragrance of the air gets sweeter. The feeling on the skin is less abrasive. Though, some guests are hard to welcome, I can learn to say this.

Welcome home, sadness! Be my guest!

TIPS FOR MY 21-YEAR-OLD SELF

- Get to know your own heart.

- Start with a simple meditation for five to 10 minutes. Bring your attention and/or one or two hands to the chest area and feel your breath moving the chest up and down. Start noticing what is there. Apply the idea of being the curious scientist, gather information (*Chapter 2.2*).

- Meditations that fit into your life easily are the best.

- When you start opening your heart you will have some very beautiful experiences. But very likely you will also start remembering past rejections because the heart is all inclusive.

- Remembering past hurts, rejections, will bring up a fear of getting hurt and is the biggest barrier to staying on track.

- Do not give up when that happens. You *can* learn how to transform old pain (*Chapter 5.2*).

- Visualise the heart-chakra as a map – a map that has many layers of concentric circles from the periphery to the core. It will help you feel calm when you are in a difficult layer, because if it feels difficult, it is not the last layer.

- Once the heart starts opening, it will keep revealing more and more amazing qualities.

- Acceptance is the master key.

- There is no end to the beauty you can discover in the core of your heart.

- One of the most important things you'll find is that the source of love is right inside your own heart.

- Your heart is a wise guide and can become your best friend.

When we learn to open our hearts more, we start feeling more. The expansion of the heart, the heart-chakra creates more space in our inner being and a deeper connection to ourselves. This includes more capacity to feel emotions and, in the next chapter we will delve into the idea, the art, the benefits for wholeness of truly understanding what it means to feel.

Meditations you can do

Here is a link https://inneralchemy.de/heart-meditations to a free meditation booklet. It contains most of the meditations that I used in a three-day experiential workshop: Opening to the Heart. I recommend practising some of them before you get into the next chapter.

PART 5

OUR EMOTIONAL TERRITORY

THE ART OF FEELING

ALL EMOTIONS – THOSE WE TERM good as well as those we think of as bad – are part of our human experience. We can learn to feel them all without labelling them. It's vital to feel them all if we are to live a conscious life. They are what they are.

'Good' and 'bad' feelings

As we grow up, we generally learn to discriminate between good and bad feelings. Examples of the 'good' feelings are happiness, joy, peace of mind, love, confidence. Most people label pain, anger, hatred, fear, hopelessness, disappointment, revenge, disgust as 'bad' feelings.

Yet, an emotionally healthy human being knows that while the feelings such as happiness and joy exist, so does suffering. When we interact with people, there will inevitably be times when they trigger us, wound us and these hurts happen in childhood as well as throughout our lives.

Working with that understanding that all emotions are acceptable allows us to develop a healthy emotional body.

In this chapter, I'll give you tools to understand and accept your emotions and transform what might be negatives into positive states.

Letting go of emotions

In my earlier days, in the hope that I would be able to let go of negative emotions, I resisted them. It turns out, I was living under a big misapprehension. I thought letting go meant pushing against them or repressing. I thought if I did that, I didn't have to feel them.

When I started meditating, I learnt about witnessing and letting go and saw that to understand each of those ideas, was an important step in my journey. At that time, I misunderstood letting go and thought it was the spiritual method of repression. I thought I was witnessing, but by repressing emotions using what I thought was a spiritual technique, I went wrong again. I came to see that witnessing means fully **allowing** all emotions. It was the beginning of understanding the art of feeling.

Turning point

When I learnt that letting go of emotions meant first letting go into them, it was a real turning point. In the core of loneliness, for example, it is possible to find many positives – sweet self-love or beautiful healthy aloneness. When we feel our sadness fully it can turn into relief, relaxation, even joy and laughter. Our anger, healthily felt, can become strength and aliveness; our fear, fully felt, can turn into courage.

So, the journey is to learn to really invite the feeling into consciousness, allow it, feel it in the body, get to know the energy of it and understand how it wants to move through us.

Once that is learnt the letting go happens naturally; those waves of emotions break and with the release, calm is restored.

What is the art of feeling?

The art of feeling happens progressively. Once I understood that a negative emotion is the raw material for a positive state, I was sold on the idea of diving deeply into my feelings. When I had my first breakthroughs, it felt like magic or, at times, merely good luck. But, once I began to get results, I understood how important and useful it would be to learn how to change a feeling each time I felt stuck in it.

My process was to start with one emotion and an understanding of how it works and from that, develop a skill. Then I'd practise with another – one that might be more difficult. Once I got good at the identification and deep investigation of a feeling, the difficult, more repressed emotions started surfacing.

All emotions will transform if we approach them in the right way. The emotions that are more deeply buried, or repressed, might be ones we judge as the most negative – disappointment, terror, heart-wrenching grief, rage (even murderous rage), hatred.

I had a client who struggled with frustration his whole life. Growing up, he got very good at repressing it, as his family and friends reacted badly to any expression of it. So, he learnt to pack it up in his stomach, not say anything and keep it stuck.

Through his current relationship the stuck frustration was brought into awareness. We worked with it and he was more ready than ever before to stay present with it. Our work together allowed him a kind of loosening up of the territory, a softening of the ground.

In one particular session, he allowed the feeling and energy of frustration to expand and spread up through his chest and arms. We invited it into his mind and brain and he started moving but with jerky, awkward movements as it released through the body. Eventually it moved to his legs and he kept allowing the body to release. At some point he looked like a child throwing a tantrum. But as he was doing this with full awareness and in control of what was happening there wasn't a moment that he felt overwhelmed.

And at some point, not very long into the process, he said he was starting to feel better. Such a result is always the case, no matter the emotion being released.

When he processed the feeling for long enough it transformed into a feeling of relaxation, aliveness and, even, a compassion for his partner. He felt more trusting and grounded.

E-motion is 'Energy in motion'

Emotions are flowing energies that live in the body. When energy can't flow healthily or be released or transformed it will get stored somewhere in the body or the mind. Even when we try to disconnect from emotions – numb them out, deny them, pretend they are not there – the original energy of the emotion is still there. These stuck energies can create havoc. The chaos can present as physical pains, tension, tiredness, indigestion and relationship problems. It could even extend to mental illnesses such as anxiety, depression, even suicidal thoughts.

The danger of turning emotions against ourselves

Sometimes, when we are not able to fully feel a difficult emotion like anger, frustration, hatred or disappointment, we deal with it by turning it against ourselves. Repressed hatred turned inward becomes self-hatred. This can be very subtle and not easy to identify. But it's important to understand. I have done this very thing; repressed my hatred for something. I see this learnt behaviour, this pattern, in my clients. It's an example of what can happen when an emotion is stuck.

For example, frustration with yourself can show up in the mind as harsh self-judgment. 'I am so angry or frustrated with myself!' 'I hate myself!' 'How stupid am I?'

Stuck pain can show up as depression. 'It's all my fault' 'If only I didn't …' 'It's hopeless,' 'There is no point …'

Originally these are coping strategies that we've most likely learned in childhood. When a child can't express frustration with a parent, they learn to turn it against themselves. Repeated a few times and it becomes a habit that's not questioned anymore.

When you become aware of any negative emotion you are directing at yourself, imagine turning it away from you. It doesn't matter whether you know where it comes from, turn it towards something on the outside – like punching a pillow when you are angry – so it stops circulating in you and creating harm.

These negative symptoms of turning emotions against yourself will disappear once you develop a healthy relationship with all emotions.

Transforming emotions: From e-stuckness to e-motion

What I had learnt growing up – how to not feel or not let that energy flow and move – I now call e-stuckness. Once understood it is so simple, and I only really got it as I developed on my spiritual journey.

How I wish that all the emotional tools and processes I use with, and teach, clients for how to evolve a healthy emotional body, were taught in school, from as early as Year 1. I believe this is as vital a part of our education as learning to read or doing maths.

Taking the steps to healthy e-motion

Often, when I ask clients what they're feeling they're not able to name the emotions. I ask them to close their eyes, stay curious and answer the question, 'What am I feeling right now?' It is important to not force or push an answer. Sometimes it takes patience to wait till a name arises that resonates with the feeling. Labelling our feelings isn't easy but with practice, we can develop our vocabulary for stronger emotional states like anger, pain or fear, and finer feeling states like gentleness, softness, expansion, freedom, relaxation. Once we have the capacity to name emotions, we recognise them faster, and so we lessen the gap between our conscious mind and the emotional body.

Feeling and naming our emotions is part of being healthy inside and out. If we find it hard to feel an emotion directly, it can arise as symptoms in the physical body. Instead of feeling sad, for example, we might have a sore throat. This was a pattern with me, but as soon as I understood the link, I started looking for the sadness whenever I had a sore throat. When I was, eventually, directly in touch with my sadness, the physical symptom disappeared.

Once named, we learn to allow the feeling to move the way it naturally wants to express itself. This is called emotional release or transformation and you'll find more detailed examples of this in the next chapters.

TIME TO STOP: NAME AN EMOTION

*Stop and ask yourself: How would I name
what I am feeling right now?*

Be patient, wait. Breathe softly till you come up with a name.

The right recipe

If we're keen to change from one state to another it's vital to have the right method. Making a delicious cake means using the raw ingredients, combined in the right quantities and sequence and baking at the right temperature. There is a recipe for emotional freedom and I offer, here, the different elements in the art of feeling that are crucial to attain that goal of freedom.

Recipe for emotional transformation

These steps remain the same for the healthy release of any repressed emotion – positive and negative.

Step 1 – **Welcome** the emotion, be interested, accepting, friendly.

Step 2 – **Identify** the energy of the emotion in the body and breathe into it. Ask:
- where do I experience the feeling in my body? Chest, stomach, belly or anywhere else?
- how does the energy of the emotion show up in my body? Is it hot or cold? Numb? Stagnant or chaotic? Does it have a movement?

Step 3 – **Release** it in the appropriate way.

Step 4 – Keep going till you start **feeling better.**

You will be familiar with some forms of release, for example, crying when we are hurt or grieving, screaming when we are angry, shaking or trembling when we are scared, smiling when we're happy.

Ride the waves, or get to the dessert

Waves and dessert? I love to use this term – learnt from a teacher of mine who was a surfer – when I teach clients the art of feeling. I've never surfed, but I value the idea of riding something out, conquering it. I value the idea of enjoying the ride.

When emotions start moving, they come in waves. Just as water does in the ocean: building, peaking and rolling out on the beach. Some waves are small – a little wave of sadness might cause a welling up of tears. A monumentally large wave can bring a heart-wrenching release of pain with lots of sobbing and sounds that cut to the core of your heart.

Whatever size they are, we need to learn to allow the waves, experience them fully and not interfere with them. Eventually any repressed emotion will transform into a good feeling. If a positive feeling like joy was repressed, it will deepen when it is allowed to flow in its natural way.

If you were to interfere and stop the ride too early, you wouldn't get to benefit and experience the best part, or what I sometimes jokingly call 'getting dessert after eating spinach'.

Freeing up stored emotions is crucial for our wellbeing on every level. With this, we can move from e-stuckness to e-motion. For example, the relaxation and relief most people feel when they were able to cry.

What of extreme emotions? A challenging statement for me was that the way to peace is through allowing our hatred consciously. Can hatred be transformed? I have explored this for many years and now, I know its truth. To find peace, we don't need to act emotions out destructively. We do, though, need to be conscious of those emotions that we might associate with dark and unacceptable feelings. Our shadows, our dark side. With knowing and consciously identifying them, we become whole again.

Our courage and the capacity to face difficult emotions is like a muscle we can train. It gets stronger once we start practising. It develops so we can lift heavier and heavier weights.

I will go into more detail about this in the chapters on transforming pain, anger and fear.

Three basic emotions

There are many emotions in our human repertoire. Yet sadness, anger and fear are the three basic emotions from which many others flow. Each of these can vary in intensity, in expression, in flavour. Sadness, for example, can be an expression of love or gratitude, like feeling deeply touched and tearing up when you are reunited with a loved one after a long time. It can be the pain from loss and grief. It can be soft and gentle or heart-wrenching and unbearable.

CHAPTER 5.2

TRANSFORMING PAIN

WE HAVE LOOKED AT the transformative power of the heart and, a key to transform pain is having an open heart.

In *Chapter 2.2 The right attitude for inner exploration*, and *Chapter 3.1 Coming into the body* you'll find the basis for the exploration of this next step – transforming pain. When I learnt to feel sadness more astutely, a crucial ingredient was the capacity to slow down my thoughts. Sadness is the water element and water is a powerful symbol for letting go – showers, rain, waterfalls, rivers flow. Water invites us to relax. If we are too fast, racing in our thoughts, rushing through the day, it is very difficult to feel sadness. So, taking enough time to breathe into the lower belly, will allow us to slow down.

The feeling centre or second chakra is located in the lower belly. Many of us in second-chakra groups during my metaphysics training, got headaches on Day 1. This was a direct result of shifting gears internally; moving from the head into the belly. The common response was interesting and we came to understand that the headaches were probably because we were resisting feeling into the second chakra. Now, I breathe down into my belly automatically and with that, I get the vital sense of feeling connected to my body and my feelings.

Resistance or acceptance?

Suffering is not in the fact but in the interpretation of the fact. —OSHO

What does Osho's statement mean with regards to sadness arising, for example? Try the following practices (call them recipes) and see how each makes you feel and which you'd prefer. The two practices demonstrate the difference between resistance and acceptance.

Scenario 1 – Recipe for suffering

- Say **no** to the feeling, listen to your mind warning you about what might happen if you did feel sad. 'It's endless, once you let go you will never come out, don't be weak, keep it together, nobody will like you, what will others think of you' … **Judge** sadness as bad, a sign of weakness, unnecessary, inconvenient, a waste of time.
- **Hold** your **breath**, keep it shallow, breathe as little as possible.
- **Tighten** the **body**, **contract** your muscles and organs.
- **Stop** the sadness from arising, push it down and **resist** it.
- Get creative in **numbing** yourself: eat too much, drink alcohol or take drugs, **distract** yourself with work, TV or games

Scenario 2 – Recipe for inner peace

- Say **yes** to the feeling, adopt a welcoming attitude in your mind, make **friends** with sadness.
- **Relax** and soften your **breath**, imagine you are breathing into or with the feeling.
- **Relax** the physical **body** as much as possible, feel your muscles and organs relaxing.
- Imagine the feeling of sadness is a guest and your body is **making space** for it. Let it grow into a bigger and bigger wave that will peak and ebb naturally.
- Stay **present** with the feeling, give it all of your attention.

Not running from pain anymore

Imagine yourself in the middle of a terrible heartbreak. A relationship that you put all your hopes on is finished, the dream of getting married smashed. You thought you had found 'the one' and they decided to leave you. To make it worse, they tell you it is over via voice message.

You feel rejected, unlovable and unworthy. You'd usually do anything to not feel the pain, make it better, make it go away, drown it. You distract, get busy … to name a few strategies.

This time you decide to stay with the pain. You cry, you sob, you let the waves of sorrow move through you. You don't know where the strength comes from, but you keep crying till it stops naturally.

At some point the space starts changing. You don't know where the change is coming from, it is not a decision you made in your mind.

It keeps changing and you find yourself in another dimension. Where you felt like drowning in high waves before, you begin to feel like a bird lifting and flying in the blue sky. Everything gets calm, you feel freedom, space, a deep sense of peace and harmony.

CLIENT SESSION – EMILY ON GRIEF

My client is experiencing grief from the breakdown of her marriage some months ago. She still feels overwhelmed and scared of the intensity of it.

> **Me** *The mind can learn to befriend grief and welcome it. For most minds, grief is a terrifying overwhelming 'no go zone' in the beginning. It is normal to fear it and most of us haven't been educated in the right relationship with grief and we tend to shut it down in many ways.*

The new recipe or paradigm is to let the mind be interested in grief. How does it show up in the body? What sensations can you become aware of? This healthier way of thinking is possible when we retrain the mind. In the process of reeducation, the old mind is welcome to object and argue.

Start the **diagnostic stage**. Can you describe the sensations in the body. How big is the feeling? Where in the body is it?

> **Emily** *I feel tension in my eyes, jaws and in my belly.*

> **Me** *This is the tension from containing and keeping it in. How big does the grief feel?*

> **Emily** *Endless*

Me *If your mind could find out a little more about it, how would it start describing the shape of it?*

Emily *Like a large orange.*

She had never experienced a loss in her life before her marriage ended. Naming the sensations makes her feel less overwhelmed. The size she is describing is small compared to some clients who experience their grief like large deep lakes.

Me *You are 'digesting' your grief. When something is too much for us or new, we store it in the unconscious till we are ready to deal with it. As soon as we are ready to deal with it, it comes back into the conscious mind. Once it is digested, it is gone. It's the same as eating food. Bite by bite. Eventually the plate is empty.*

To help with digesting her grief I give Emily a homework assignment. She will burn a special candle she still has from her wedding for a brief time each night as a daily ritual to let go and feel the grief till our next session.

Me *What we are doing today is the beginning of 'befriending grief'. We start out interested, curious and we acknowledge it. The long-term strategy is to befriend it till all resistance is gone. You will learn to let go into the emotion, allowing its energy to move, flow and release, most likely in the form of tears. Eventually you will learn to trust that you can cope with the waves of grief when they arise. You work with the feeling, breathe into it, allow it. You 'Ride the waves'. It builds, it peaks, it breaks, like the waves in the ocean. My learning after decades of exploring, is this: When the waves come, we are ready otherwise they wouldn't arise. Different waves can have different intensities. In time, we learn to ride them all. Sometimes it can feel like you are at your edge, you can't handle any more. When waves come in an environment where it is not appropriate – in the supermarket, for example, you can talk to the pain. 'We will do this later once we are at home.' If you make a promise like that make sure you follow up on it. This is how your emotional body learns to trust you.*

She agrees to do the crying meditation every night as she burns the wedding candle.

Me *After every wave of sadness there is generally a good feeling, like a relief or lightness, even joy, warmth or self-love, more compassion for yourself and others. This is an in-built reward system of true nature.*

Towards the end of the session, because she was able to experience some good waves of grief, all the tension had left her body.

Teaching

This is a recipe. An application of the art of feeling in relationship to pain. This is how we transform old, stored grief. Once understood, you use the recipe and the pain stops being a problem.

Emily digested a good portion of her grief that day through accepting it and crying.

Towards the end of the session, when she spoke about how her mind was feeling, she said it felt fine. Her mind's relationship to grief had changed within one hour.

She rated the size of the wave she experienced as a five out of a possible 10.

At this time, she's good with that. Eventually she'll be at six or seven. Then, even 10 waves will be ok, which also means that the fear of pain won't be a problem anymore.

Towards the end of the session we focused on what was feeling better, Step 4 of the recipe for emotional transformation. I invited her to describe anything that was positive for her at that moment.

She saw a pink colour which made her feel warm. Her body was more relaxed, she felt calmer, peaceful and harmonious – a direct result of transforming the stuck grief. Once it is flowing again it turns into an alive positive energy, an aspect of true nature.

Once we experience it, we can know it. I believe that fear of pain is behind most of our suffering. Once the mind understands and knows it, it can start cooperating. Emily can now imagine not being afraid of grief anymore; knowing that it's part of life and we can learn to feel it healthily and, also, transform it into a state of wellbeing.

Resistance to what is, is the only suffering

This is such an important understanding. Grief itself is not the problem or the suffering. The resistance itself is the suffering.

Pain is part of life and when it is there, we need to learn to feel it, to allow and transform it. If it is not felt, it can turn into numbness, depression or a resignation. We may give up on love.

Men and women are no different in this regard. We all have the same capacity to feel pain. Men, traditionally however, have more conditioning to repress and not feel their emotions.

'Noble suffering'

There is a difference between real pain that can't be avoided and pain that is created through destructive or unhealthy thoughts – unnecessary pain. The superego creates pain through judgment, negative self-talk and outdated messages.

Grief, loss, hurt can cause real pain, also called 'noble suffering' or unavoidable pain in the Buddhist tradition and The Diamond Approach.

Learning to discriminate between real and unnecessary pain is important for emotional health. If you feel sadness because someone is sick or died, then it's healthy to cry. When you lose a loved one it's healthy to grieve. The pain needs to be released otherwise you store it, shut down physically or mentally. You will still need to process it later.

In this Buddhist teaching story it becomes clear that some painful emotions are softened when we understand that everyone has experienced grief at some point in their lives.

A disciple came to the Buddha with unbearable grief through the loss of her child. He gave her the task to go into the village and knock on people's doors to see if she could find a house that had not suffered the death of a family member.

She was not able to find one family or household that had never experienced loss. That helped her with her grief.

'False' emotions

Emotions have many shades and one of those is the issue of false emotions. Your real emotion is sadness but instead, you get angry. Or you're feeling angry but resist feeling it and try to cry as an expression instead. However, that won't give you the same relief that you can have when you feel the real emotion and find the appropriate release.

Generally women tend to channel their anger into pain or tears. Men tend to get angry, instead of feeling pain or hurt. It comes from our cultural conditioning that has begun in our childhood. Men are more often allowed to express their anger, and women are allowed to cry.

Layers of emotions

Emotions can be layered. They can sit one on top of the other. The surface emotion might be a shut down or numbness, the layer below could be pain and, under that, anger. Perhaps under those is fear or any variation of emotion like disappointment, disgust ... The healthiest way to work with the layering of emotions is by feeling one emotion at a time. It's useful to allow one, then you explore the next. This way you drop deeper and deeper into your emotional body till you reach the last layer. Then, you will eventually drop into true nature, a sense of calm, peace, joy or freedom.

Between true nature and the surface of our personality can be any number of emotions. I have seen clients drop through one strong emotion into true nature. I have seen some go through four or five, even 10 layers.

When we don't feel each layer separately, the build up can turn into a feeling of chaos or overwhelm as explained in *Chapter 5.9 Shock and overwhelm*. This becomes especially potent and uncomfortable when anger, pain and fear are mixed into one.

It's useful to think about the three basic emotions as the three primary colours red, yellow and blue. They are beautiful and distinct on their own. Yet when you mix them the result is a muddy, sometimes dark, unappealing brown. None of the primary colours are recognisable anymore.

Hierarchy of emotions

When I began my inner journey, I was fairly numb and unable to identify whatever it was I was feeling. The first emotion I learnt to feel was pain and, gradually, became more aware of my anger.

Years into my journey I eventually became aware of fear and it has led me to offer this structure in the book. I think pain and anger are interchangeable and, one or the other might be closer to the surface in different people. Yet fear is, generally, more hidden in most people.

Feedback from clients

As preparation for writing this book I spoke with a range of clients. Their feedback here is fitting for this chapter. Note: When I refer to a lake of sadness in sessions, it refers to when clients experience a lot of old pain.

Not being able to feel pain

I knew from the session before that I was experiencing overwhelming grief and that by following the tools slowly everything might settle, and it was, slowly but surely. But there was one thing that didn't seem to budge and that was that I was finding it hard to release emotion, particularly, I was struggling to cry.

*I would have a long period of not being able to cry, then I felt that I desperately wanted to and then in brief moments it would be as though all flood gates were open, which felt incredibly intense. After discussing this, Karima suggested a **crying meditation**.*

For 30 minutes every day, I sit and just allow myself to feel, creating a space of acceptance so that eventually I can know and feel with my whole body that I have permission to actually experience and feel what arises without letting it bottle until the flood gates break.

Lake of sadness

You shared the vision of a lake of sadness and how with each stored emotion the lake gets fuller. When time comes it is important to process a little bit of the sadness from the lake at a time, rather than a large flood. You also shared that one day you will look for the lake and it will be gone.

This made a lot of sense for me and the thought of sadness needing to flow ... like water really relates to how I feel the emotion. This also helped me understand how I became so full of sadness and wasn't able to process any of it until starting the work.

How my subconscious mind worked to try and make me process this largely stored sadness blows me away – just incredible.

Flat line or not?

My AHA moment was when my goal of being a flat line all those years ago was not the best ideal/goal to have. It's normal that life has its ups and downs!

You can't have a mountain without a valley, they both need to exist and slowly I've learnt that all emotions are welcomed and not to shun any – still practising though, as it's sometimes hard to welcome those difficult emotions.

CHAPTER 5.3

TRANSFORMING
ANGER

I AM TEACHING A new client how to release anger, consciously.

I start by explaining that the three basic emotions of anger, sadness and fear are each a type of energy – anger is fire, sadness is water, fear is air. Each has a flow, a movement and specific characteristics. The natural energy of anger has fiery, hot or warm, upward flowing movements. Inner fire is often perceived by clients in red, orange, yellow tones, just like outer fire.

'Anger is the in-built emotional response to real or perceived unfairness', is a favourite definition of anger as taught in The Diamond Approach. Every human being is born with the capacity to experience anger. It gives us the energy to do something about unfairness and take the right action. So, when we are treated unfairly, or witness unfairness happening to anybody else, we are meant to get angry.

Preparation

For many people learning to feel anger can be overwhelming in the beginning. As part of the preparation for a client to transform anger, I invite them to imagine a tap that they can learn to turn on or off; to regulate how much anger to allow at any moment of the session. The tap analogy helps them understand that we can control how much we deal with, by measuring and adjusting what we're able to cope with.

Step 1 – Welcome the emotion

As in all explorations, the first step is for the mind to be your companion. It needs to be open and welcoming. For my client, the idea of accepting and welcoming anger is new. Her old conditioning – to repress it, judge it as bad and feel guilty for feeling it – is a very common reaction.

Step 2 – Identify the energy of the emotion in the body

She identifies where the anger is stored; describes a contraction or tightness in the stomach. I explain that the contraction is not the energy of anger itself. It's the part in us that has learnt to repress anger and stops us expressing it. I ask her to imagine it like a fence around the natural energy of anger. The body erects that fence through compressing, contracting or tightening a part of the body.

Step 3 – Release it in the appropriate way

Once we identify the energy of the emotion in the body – for example, like a volcano in the belly – we need to find the body's 'instinctual release'. Anger is part of our instinctual self, the ancient part of the brain. Our limbic system and the amygdala are associated with feeling fear and anger which arises with a perceived threat. When threatened, the instinctual part in us will do whatever is needed to protect ourselves, just like an animal. The angry expression might be felt in the jaws or the throat, might come out through growling or angry sounds or through swearing. It can be in the arms and hands, and be acted out by punching, tearing apart, scratching. In can be expressed by kicking or stomping. As you practise how to identify where it's located, your body will teach you how it wants to release stored anger. See **ABC of cathartic release** below.

Step 4 – Keep going till you start feeling better

With the right way to express your anger you'll feel a release or an expansion. The best way to express any feeling, is to savour every moment. If you want to punch a pillow; do it with full awareness, feel the muscles in your arms.

You may feel shitty doing this, your stomach may cramp and you may want to vomit. If you keep going, that uncomfortable overcharged feeling will diminish and eventually turn into a comfortable feeling. Stay present and know that the expression will allow you to stop rejecting the uncomfortable emotion. You will come to accept that it has been there and can be released.

You will begin to feel alive, and you release till you feel there is a natural change. Then you shift to feeling calm or joyful. It is an honest, real transformation. Don't stop before you have discharged the anger, otherwise the fear of the feeling will remain and stop you having more anger release. The more the anger is released the more peaceful you will feel.

ABC of cathartic release

This is a refinement of step 3 and specific to the release of anger or any other fiery emotion like frustration, irritation or rage. It is often called cathartic release.

Find the movement of the anger you're dealing with, find the sound and breathe with it. It is ok to visualise any form of angry expression in a safe therapeutic environment. You won't harm anybody with that. These are the three components:

- **Movement**: Find the right movement by listening to the body. Give it full permission.
- **Sound**: Allow sounds, words, a statement or a growling sound.
- **Breath**: Breathe *with* the movement, not against it. For example, if you punch, breathe out on the punch and don't hold your breath.

Ground rules for safe anger release

- **Don't hurt yourself**: Don't punch a wall and break your wrist. Don't punch yourself.
- **Don't hurt others**: It might feel very tempting to punch somebody when you are angry. But rather than a person, use a pillow or take a rod to a thick pile of paper.
- **Don't destroy favourite objects**: Don't throw your computer at the wall in the heat of the moment or act on the urge to see the vase shattering on the floor. You will regret it. A great way of mimicking destroying something is taking an old towel you don't need any more and trying to tear it apart.

Healthy and unhealthy anger

Healthy anger is the natural response to unfairness. Unhealthy anger is dumping, name calling, physical violence, violent crime of any kind that hurts others or which is directed towards a loved one, or yourself.

Dangerous anger release

Most people resist feeling their anger, thinking it's a negative aspect and needs to be repressed. If we do that, it gets stored and the charge builds until we can't contain it anymore. The stronger the charge the earlier the memory, generally.

When anger releases as a bad mood, bad temper, shouting, arguments, judgments it's acceptable as long as there's no harm done. When it turns into criminal expressions, like hurting others, going on a rampage, etc, the anger is out of control.

Most people had experiences of witnessing unhealthy anger as they grew up. It could have been either explosive or passive-aggressive – the repressed version of unhealthy anger.

Working with anger

A couple comes to see me, both are stressed and cranky. It feels right to teach them about anger as they are expressing their anger unhealthily with each other. I give them the basic teachings on anger and introduce the ABC of cathartic release. I ask them to identify where they are feeling the energy of anger in their bodies and explain that anger can be transformed into strength and right action.

CLIENT SESSION – ROB AND CAROL

Me Anger is an instinctual energy, part of our survival instinct. Emotional release can look raw and wild. It is not polite, or pretty. Most tribal traditions have rituals to express it like wild fiery dancing around the campfire, for example.

How it shows up in the body

Me If your body could express it, what would it like to do?

Watching kids throwing a tantrum is a great example of full body emotional release. You're beginning with this so trust any first impulse. The body knows.

Once you find the right expression there'll be a sense of relief. It could come as a deeper natural breath, or a smile or laughter. It is hard work to not express feelings, contain them or shut them down. It is more natural to release it. Then the body can return to a state of equilibrium. Anger is fire energy, warm or hot and it moves upward. Water flows down, fire burns upwards. Learn to harness the energy of anger, master and transform it and it will start working for you.

They both identify the need to scream.

Me *How would it feel if you allowed yourself to scream? Anger is part of your emotional repertoire; part of every healthy human's emotional body. People who don't express it healthily can carry anger around all the time. An unhealthy relationship with anger can also get passed from generation to generation. In looking at this you are changing your relationship with anger, from misunderstanding and judgment, towards acceptance.*

They feel encouraged and both like the idea of finding ways to scream healthily.

Me *First you need to learn to identify when you're feeling angry. And then it needs to be released in the right way, till it transforms. The in-between step is to take yourself away from the trigger – not shouting at your partner, is the hardest one in the beginning. Once learnt it becomes normal. It is just another skill. You can get creative where and how to release it. It is important to respect your neighbours and scream into a pillow so you don't alarm them!*

The three of us brainstorm different ways for them to release anger: in the gym, boxing, running, dancing, practising kundalini yoga.

I suggest doing five minutes of safe anger release whenever

needed, to learn to accept the anger, and as a long-term solution for greater emotional health. I also suggest they discuss their anger more with each other and include it in their relationship as a valid aspect – so they don't judge it anymore.

Benefits of transforming anger
I mention that once we learn to release it safely, anger can lead straight to a good space like strength or aliveness. Yet some-times it can uncover another deeper emotion like sadness, for example.

At the end of the session we discuss why it's valuable to learn this. They come up with clearer thinking, the ability to take healthier action steps in response to life, more creativity and aliveness.

Who will you be?
I finish with a **future integration:** 'Who will you be when your relationship with anger has healed?' We project one month ahead, three months, six months and a year into the future. More on this in *Chapter 7.2*

> **Carol** *I would be nicer.*

> **Rob** *People would want to be around me more.*

They both agree that their relationship would improve.

> **Me** *What we are learning is a conscious release of anger where you master the energy and you choose how and when to release it. Learning this doesn't mean you become an angry beast who expresses themselves in the world in an angry way. You regu-late the release, transform the anger into strength, aliveness, self-assertiveness and healthy boundaries. You become more functional, a better, more responsible human being.*

Teaching children
As they have a five-year-old son I let them know how to share this learning with him.

When a parent has learnt how to release anger consciously,

they can share it with their children. It might mean playing 'monster' together, making faces, growling. Getting playful. The child gets the message that feeling angry is accepted. It also teaches them to have healthy boundaries and they need less therapy as an adult to repair this.

You teach the child the same rules as you have for adults.

Imagine if every child learnt this in school? How good would it be to have a class on emotions, healthy release and the transformation of it?

ANGER RELEASE MEDITATION

5–10 mins of anger release. Your body will teach you as you experiment.

5–10 mins of quiet restful time after to integrate.

Anger covering needs

This next client example introduces the relationship between anger and needs. We all have basic physical needs for water, shelter, food and clothing. We have psychological needs like the need for safety and belonging. There is much written about the hierarchy of human needs. But it's important to discern whether emotions like pain and anger might be covering up deeper needs. See the client session that follows.

CLIENT SESSION – SARA

Sara, a client in her late 40s, married with two teenage children, starts the session describing her strong resistance to feeling emotional pain. In our last session, we'd come across a lot of old pain and she feels angry with that, with her pain, which expresses itself outwardly as frustration with her teenage children.

Me *The thing is, any reaction in us, is valid, deserves attention and to be inquired into. This is how we understand ourselves more and more. Especially reactions that don't make sense to us or our rational mind yet, can be precious, they help us to discover more about ourselves. When we work with our emotions and when there is a big lake of tears, there will also be anger and fear.*

I explain the hierarchy of emotions, that we are generally more aware of one emotion rather than another. We might feel our anger but not the pain or the fear. Or vice versa. Once we learn to feel one well, the next layer will show up.

Most importantly, once we identify an emotion, the next step is to learn how to healthily release it.

Me *To become more aware of the resistance I want you to exaggerate it. Hold your breath, be against the pain in your mind, tense your muscles, tighten your body. Make the resistance more conscious, stay with it as long as possible and then release.*

We discover that under her anger is the need, an essential need, to feel respected. This need is real and will never go away, even if we try for a long time to not feel it.

I invite her to say, 'I need to feel respected' to reacquaint herself again with this need. Thinking and saying it like a new phrase is an important step in befriending repressed needs. I use the technique to repeat healthy statements a lot in sessions.

Me *Not feeling respected doesn't feel good to anybody. It is a universal need and for our needs to not be respected can lead to anger, a healthy anger as it's the right response to unfairness.*

Sara feels relieved as she understands herself better at the end of the session. Her daughter keeps using her laptop and leaves it for her with a run-down battery and she feels rightly disrespected. She looks forward to finding a new way of letting her daughter know that this needs to change.

Once we know our needs and respect them again, we can learn to communicate more consciously from a place of vulnerability and connectedness to our needs which opens up a whole new realm of communication.

It might help her daughter to understand that mum is not just the all-giving, all-knowing, all-providing, should-cope-with-everything-entity. That mum is a human being with feelings and needs, not just an endless supply station.

I believe when we are really stirred up or triggered there is possibly an essential need deep down in the mix that hasn't been met.

It's crucial that we all understand there is always a way forward out of discomfort or pain. We are all trying to do the best we can to become the best version of ourselves. It is imperative to be compassionate in the process and defend from the inner judge.

My experiences with cathartic release

At the beginning of my journey, as I began to get in touch with my anger, it took a lot to dig it up, get to know and, eventually, befriend it. I was afraid of my anger, had completely shut it down and learnt to judge it.

A moment with a client comes to mind. It was in a session in Sydney in the early days of my business as a holistic therapist and I was helping her feel her anger.

I held a big pillow against the wall and, sure that the insulation was sufficient between her fist and the wall, I encouraged her to punch it. She was struggling with feeling and showing anger surrounding an issue with her mother. At some point she stopped, opened her eyes, looked at me. 'This is as normal for you as having a cup of tea, isn't it?' she said. 'Yes, it is, keep punching!'. We both burst out laughing. Then, she continued. What a journey to get to that point.

Steps on the journey

In Pune, our day began at 6 am with Dynamic Meditation. In those meditations I learned the skill of emotional release. The practice put me in touch with all emotions. The one, very difficult one, was anger. I'd fake anger, sometimes. Then, I got glimpses of the real energy of anger moving through me. It had been deeply buried and needed time to come out of hiding.

I will never forget my first very long anger release. I was in a group of 50 people, and we were all bashing pillows. It was many hours until everybody was done.

When I started the cathartic release, I was resistant and thought I might last for a few minutes, but certainly not hours. When all the resistance dissolved, I happily released whatever was there till all the anger was gone.

Anger's power to transform

My first direct experience of the *transformation* of anger into joy, aliveness and laughter happened in my counselling training in 1987. My trainer supported me in really allowing my anger and exposing it to the group. After some time of releasing – most embarrassing to start with – it changed. How could this horrible, 'bad' emotion that I had tried so hard to not feel, become joy?

Since then, I have participated in hundreds of hours of cathartic release either through shorter meditations or therapeutic group structures. Eventually I started facilitating cathartic release sessions like the one I'd experienced, in my women's groups. It is a very uplifting experience to witness stagnant energy become alive again.

My biggest teaching around discharging till the storeroom is empty was after a relationship breakup in 1994. It was in the ashram and my boyfriend had left me for another woman. By that time I had learnt to feel my emotions and was practising the releasing.

Most of us ate together in the ashram, under open Indian skies in a massive canteen. Every lunch time I sat where I could see my ex-boyfriend and his new girlfriend. After lunch, I'd go to my room and use the rest of my lunchbreak to allow any emotion that had been triggered – pain, hurt or anger – without judgment. I got good at it. It became a new habit or lunchtime routine. While doing it I was aware that there was a lot of old anger releasing that had nothing to do with him.

After about a month, I sat down, and watched them, ready to feel whatever would be triggered, but that day, I couldn't feel anything. 'Maybe I am disconnected today?' I went to my room trying to feel any strong emotion, but still nothing. I pulled a tarot card and it said, 'Personal victory'. I was done!

It took a few more days to start believing that the charge was truly gone. Yet it was and never came back. Eventually we became friends again and I was ok and relaxed when I was around him.

That was a direct teaching on releasing charges. Same trigger, no more charge.

Where am I now?

Now, I accept anger and have a healthy relationship with it. When I see anything in the news that seems unfair to me, for example, I ask myself, 'Is there anything I can do about it?' If not, I notice the anger and let it move into aliveness.

I don't judge it anymore. It is part of me and my natural emotional expression. It is a crucial puzzle piece in this journey of becoming whole. I understand that every emotion has its place in our human experience. What creates the suffering is the judgment on anger, and the repression of it.

TRANSFORMING FEAR

I can remember one session though that stands out mainly because I was so distressed at the time. I called you for an emergency session, I was so terrified I could hardly breathe after my ex said he would get the kids. You told me to feel this fear through my body and start shaking. It was only a 30-min session but after shaking for some time I did move through it and on the other side I felt I could cope not only for the next five mins but for the days ahead. I felt happy when we finished, yet nothing had outwardly changed. Only I had.
—LAURA

Most people grow up rejecting or, ironically, being afraid of, fear. I grew up with that conditioning. Fear was judged as weak. In my mid-30s I read *Face to Face with Fear* by Krishnanada and Amana and it made a dramatic difference to my thinking.

Before that, I had never thought fear was ok. The understanding that everybody is afraid started the process of finally allowing it. It was liberating to develop a healthier relationship with fear.

Healthy and unhealthy fear

Fear is part of a healthy emotional body. There is a healthy place for it. It warns us of something dangerous or potentially harmful. It tells us when something is wrong. If allowed, it strengthens our intuition when we do listen and learn to trust it.

Unhealthy fear, like paranoia, making up stuff that isn't happening, can be a distortion in the mind. Attaching meaning to something that isn't real. In time, and through more awareness, we learn to discriminate between what is real and what isn't.

Eventually there will be a healthy relationship with fear, where the **fear of fear disappears**.

As explained before, different emotions can be compared with natural elements; pain with the water element, anger with fire and fear with air. If fear is recognised it might show up as a trembling, shaking or quivering somewhere in the body. You can feel it in your jaws just as you might ache or shiver when you are cold. You can feel it under the skin or anywhere in the body, in your arms or legs. If fully allowed, fear can consume the whole body.

Deep fear, terror or dread is an extreme form of the feeling. I will talk more about that in *Chapter 6.2 Healing trauma: Restoring safety*.

Approaching fear

First, we need to identify fear to know what we are dealing with. Once we recognise and name it, we can learn to approach it in the right way. This is a refinement of Step 1 in the recipe for emotional transformation – Welcome the emotion.

Love is the antidote to fear

The right way to approach fear when you recognise it in yourself, is with loving kindness, compassion and gentleness – all qualities of an open heart. When we do that the fear starts settling – just as it might when a mother soothes a frightened child. If the child is supported long enough and in the right way, talked to, cuddled, the fear will dissolve, the child will relax and feel better again.

Imagine a baby bird has fallen out of his nest. What would you do? Would you pick it up gently and put it back in the nest? When I think of the scene, I pick the bird up and I can sense the relationship of my hands with the baby bird. This gentle kind holding is the same as the holding we need to practise – in our own minds and hearts – when we meet fear inside.

After learning to approach a feeling softly it has quickly become 'the puppy dog approach'. When a feeling arises, I take a moment to acknowledge it and then hold it softly like a puppy. It taught me to trust that I can handle the waves of emotion and that approaching feelings doesn't have to be hard, holding them softly helps me remember that. —KARLA

There is also a right way of using the breath that helps ease our relationship with fear. We can let our breath be friendly, soft and welcoming with the emotion, to surround it gently. Breathe into the emotion in a supportive way.

The opposite of that is, what I'd call a rejecting breath. This happens when we don't want to feel fear and try to avoid it. We hold our breath and it becomes short and shallow.

I recently started describing this to clients as the **science of self-love:**
1. Developing the right attitude to any emotion.
2. Getting in touch with how the energy of the emotion shows up in our bodies.
3. Learning how to release it in the appropriate way.

This is a variation of the basic **recipe for emotional transformation** above. It is a skill learned after practice. Just as we'd do for all emotions. We don't *do* transformation; we can only learn how to allow it. Once fear becomes a flowing energy again, it starts releasing through the physical body and transforms into a positive state like peace, joy or relaxation.

Fear of fear

It can be hard to connect to fear. In my life, very much as part of general German conditioning, I was taught to be strong and not show fear.

I had learnt to hide fear in my bones, in my bone marrow, the same way we put money and valuables into a vault and lock them away safely.

During my metaphysics training, at some point in our explorations of chakras and energetic fields, I experienced an energy evaporating out of my bones, like smoke. It was very confusing. But fortunately my metaphysics teacher understood what was happening, explained that this was old stored fear releasing and supported me through it.

My fear was inside my bones and I had become so disconnected, I was not aware that I was scared. I believed, as a teenager, that I had no fear. That idea is, now, unbelievable to me.

MEETING FEAR AND DREAD – EXCERPT FROM A SESSION

My client has a strong physical sensation in her chest. I invite her to describe it but to make sure she does it from a friendly distance. She describes it as cold, dark and dense and names it as dread – very deep fear.

I encourage her to stay present with this very difficult emotion. I let her repeat out loud: 'This is dread and fear'. 'I feel dread and fear'. 'I feel a lot of dread and fear' helps her in naming and befriending the feeling. As she starts allowing it more, she begins to tremble.

At some point she feels very heavy and her throat wants to close yet she manages to stay present with the sensations in her body and allows different waves of trembling. It starts in her jaws and then moves into her arms. She is shaking and releasing in waves, which she understands from previous sessions. I help her to stay with it as much as possible and encourage her to keep going till she feels the first little change, the beginning of a sense of relief, relaxation and lightness. She has begun to feel better.

Eventually we change the statement to, 'I am able to stay present with a lot of fear and dread', which is her truth at that point. In her past that wasn't the case. It was too much and overwhelming.

Her fear of the fear is dissolving, which makes it easier to feel the real fear. She befriends this difficult emotion and at the end of the session she describes a sense of liberation.

Fear is transformed

The relationship with fear changes through working with it. At first, the feeling controls us. We feel that we can't cope, and do what we can to disconnect from it, dissociate. Through doing the work to bring it into our conscious mind, our consciousness gets stronger and the capacity to stay present with difficult emotions grows. We don't have to run from the fear anymore.

Your physical body will thank you for learning this as one of the ways fear can show up is through nausea. Once fully felt as an emotion the body doesn't have to get nauseous anymore. We don't have to avoid this emotion anymore.

This is the mastery of emotions.

CHAPTER 5.5

FROM REVENGE TO JOY, AND EVERYTHING IN BETWEEN

This being human is a guest house. Every morning a new arrival.

A joy, a depression, a meanness, some momentary awareness comes as an unexpected visitor. Welcome and entertain them all! Even if they are a crowd of sorrows, who violently sweep your house empty of its furniture, still, treat each guest honourably.

He may be clearing you out for some new delight. The dark thought, the shame, the malice, meet them at the door laughing and invite them in.

Be grateful for whatever comes because each has been sent as a guide from beyond. —JELALUDDIN RUMI, THE GUEST HOUSE

In this chapter, you'll find a kaleidoscope of different difficult emotional experiences and how to deal with them. I have used transcripts from several client sessions and though they don't cover all possible difficult emotions, they will, hopefully, be an inspiration for how to deal with challenging emotions.

Understanding and transforming revenge

Revenge is a shadow related to repressed pain. We need courage to explore it and expose it to ourselves before it can transform. Revenge is one of the emotions that permeates a lot of activity in the world. It is, often, why wars start; why families fall apart... there are far too many examples of how destructive acting out of revenge can be.

Yet, when we are hurting and don't want to feel the hurt, we don't necessarily process it. So, it doesn't go away and then it turns into vengeful thinking.

The thinking behind revenge, when it's on a personal level is, 'I am hurting, I want you to hurt as much, if not more. I'm going to do whatever it takes to make you pay!'

Thinking of expressing this gives us a feeling of power, in an otherwise powerless situation.

CLIENT SESSION – ON REVENGE

My client, female, mid-30s, single feels rejected by someone she has started dating. She feels unheard, as if she's not listened to. This present experience with a new love interest triggers a wounding from her childhood. Her sisters and her father didn't listen to her.

I invite her to connect with the pain from childhood to feel the helplessness. It is difficult for her. She starts feeling overwhelmed as we go back to the memories that originally triggered the hurt.

I use a guided meditation – the visualisation of her safe space (see *Chapter 6.1 Healing the inner child*) – to resource and ground her. Once she is relaxed enough, I ask her to visualise the part that feels revenge, separate from her and to simply watch it. And to not judge it.

Acceptance of what is

Acceptance of what is, is always the first step in inner transformation. In this case it means consciously accepting the mechanism of revenge.

I ask, 'What happens when you do that?' She starts feeling a bit teary, good teary, coming to terms with revenge being part of her. This is part of her relief at not having to fight with that shadow anymore.

Healing comes with learning to understand more and more parts of ourselves. Acceptance allows us to reconnect with lost parts or rejected emotions. In this case, the vengeful part needs to be understood. The pain behind the revenge needs to be felt, the inner child needs to be healed and that allows new conscious choices to come into our present life.

If revenge is not understood, it gets acted out unconsciously. If it is understood, it is not a shadow anymore that could create sabotaging behaviour. Anything that is not part of true nature will transform in the process of inner transformation. Anything that is already part of true nature will deepen or get stronger.

DIRECT EXPERIENCE OF TRANSFORMING DISAPPOINTMENT – DREW

Drew, a single businessman in his mid-40s, shares that he is experiencing repeated disappointment in his search for the right romantic partner. This issue has been going on for years.

As we start exploring, he describes a sensation in his heart. It feels like a block from the throat down to the navel. The image that unfolds is of a tree stump, old and grey, with lots of hard knots, rotting as if it had been in a swamp.

I ask him to look at it like a piece of art in a museum and to invite the curious scientist. The name of the sculpture could be: A lifetime of disappointment.

Drew and I have worked together for some time and he understands well how transformation works. He is able to enter the position of the curious scientist. He describes holes, where branches got snapped off.

Me *What do the holes represent for you?*

Drew *Dead opportunities, stale opportunities that died off.*

This energetic structure has revealed itself with such accuracy and detail. By staying present with it, it starts shifting, releasing, opening, changing.

Me *Stay with your experience and keep describing it.*

I invite him to see what this old rotten stump once was. What reveals itself is an image of the trees original state: a pine tree in the mountains in the snow, tall and beautiful, part of a beautiful lush dark green forest. A majestic tree in a majestic forest. Somewhere along the way it (the tree – him) started dying of disappointment.

Me *What happens in your heart when you remember its origin?*

Drew *It brings up feelings of freedom, freshness and a sense of belonging.*

I invite him to feel these feelings more.

Me *The great news is, that in the inner world the stump can return to its original shape.*

One possible pathway to this rebirth, is by releasing the emotion consciously, to make what was stuck flow again. To be able to do that we need to develop a healthy relationship with the stump, to start communicating with it and not rejecting it. Then step-by-step, it will transform.

As feeling disappointment is difficult for him, I use another emotion as a resource. He has done a lot of work on anger and developed a healthy relationship with it. He can identify it, feel it, and release it till it is transformed into strength and aliveness.

He understands already that any emotion has a specific feel, flow, colour and movement in the body. And that once the specific emotion is befriended and he doesn't resist it anymore, it stops being an issue. In this case, he is able to change the rigid structure, and the dead tree stump dissolves.

He starts exploring what his inner experience of disappointment is like.

Drew *It smashes you, like falling into an empty hole bracing for the impact, you don't want to believe it is happening. Then it starts hitting you, the shock waves hit the heart over and*

*over again. It is disorientating, very confusing, like a bomb
going off, it comes in from all sides, it hits hard. There is an
initial impact that keeps exploding, more like an earthquake,
a rumbling. The mind starts freaking out, doesn't know how
to get away.*

Another way he describes it is like a car rolling down a hill,
rumbling and tumbling, totally overwhelming. No still point
anywhere.

Every time he tries to meet a girlfriend and it doesn't feel
loving, it rocks him to the core of his being; no part feels
untouched. The impact of that experience leaves him exhausted
and can last for weeks.

From the intensity of his inner experience today, I can see
he's describing a very real deep sense of existential survival fear.

At this stage I propose that the experience might go back
to early childhood because of its all-consuming devastating
intensity.

We start exploring some memories. He remembers his
mother crying.

As he describes the memory, I share a vision I get of him as
a baby sobbing and sobbing, till it is so exhausted that nothing
is left. It looks like we are dealing with a birth trauma as he puts
more pieces of his history together, pieces his father told him
and he decides that he will talk to his mother about what she
remembers of his birth.

He feels very proud of himself. I applaud him for his capacity
to describe such a difficult experience so accurately.

Me *How is the stump right now? Something will have started
changing either in size, colour, density or moistness.*

Drew *The bark has come back, and the tree isn't as grey
anymore. The swamp scene is fading, and the healthy mountain scene is coming closer.*

I am excited from a healing perspective as the tree, which represents a part of him, is coming back to life. The 'original tree' is
still in there.

He can even see a little sapling and starts describing the happiness and aliveness of this sapling excitedly looking forward to growing and living, having purpose.

His heart feels good at this stage. His inner scientist is fascinated with what he uncovered today. He understands the wisdom behind the amazing creation of the stump in relation to the issue. The wood is still there, the knots contain the heart-wrenching disappointment. The stump represents the rigidity, frozenness and deadness that allowed him to survive. Without that strength, he could have collapsed or given up.

The earlier the experience, the stronger the impact

With such an early impact, in his case possible birth trauma, it makes sense that he is terrified of disappointment later in his life. If someone had an easy childhood with very little disappointment and later in life, maybe in their early 20s had their first big disappointment, they might just brush it off.

His heart was still raw at the end of the session, but his belly was quiet.

Dealing with disgust

Most of us grow up learning to feel ashamed or guilty each time we feel disgust, hatred, hopelessness and disappointment. These feelings are part of the group of emotions that are generally low on the scale of things that are socially acceptable.

They are, commonly, also judged by others who are affected by or witness our expression of these emotions. So, we learn to believe that *we* are bad, or it is bad when we feel specific emotions.

It is stressful to repress or suppress emotions for a lifetime. It's hard work. There will, even, be physical symptoms as a result of trying to not feel a particular emotion. Repression affects the breathing, it leads to contraction in the muscles, the organs and tissues.

Yet, all that tension can be released.

Imagine the stress eventually dissolving. Once you begin the process of investigating and being conscious with these (and all) emotions, you'll notice changes in how you respond to events and people around you.

Then, with consistent inquiry, you go up on the inner acceptance scale. One day you check, and you can sincerely say, 'I am 100% ok with this specific emotion. I fully accept it. I can identify it and name it. I recognise how it shows up in me – where it starts, how it moves. I know how to release it if needed or contain and transform it.

This is the art of feeling and it's a mastery.

CLIENT SESSION – SANDY

Sandy shares her struggles with feeling disgust. She has never consciously explored disgust before – I'm looking forward to guiding and helping her.

I introduce the idea of an 'acceptance scale' of emotions: 10 is full acceptance, one is very low. When I ask her which emotion is easy for her to accept, she chooses love. She rates her acceptance of it a 10. She rates sadness a five and disgust as a minus one.

I invite Sandy to imagine what a 10 on the acceptance scale of disgust could feel like. 'Liberating,' she answers. She's articulated a universal truth. When we learn to accept the feelings in us that are the most judged, or the least accepted, we can experience the biggest liberation. As a healer, I know there is gold to be found in places that have been rejected.

My own breakthrough with disgust was in a primal group in the early 90s. Primal therapy is a trauma-based psychotherapy created by Arthur Janov. It is used to reexperience childhood pain – felt rather than conceptual memories – in an attempt to resolve the pain through complete processing and integration.

I watched a participant being able to, with a good deal of support, express her disgust. I could see a glow around her while she expressed it. And, as she accepted her feelings, I suddenly also believed that disgust wasn't awful anymore.

I didn't understand the deeper metaphysics at the time, but it was obvious that the acceptance of a very judged emotion had its own beauty. Disgust has a place in our human experience.

We are given the capacity to experience emotions for a reason; it is not some weird mistake.

I guide Sandy through the following exercise:

Me *Close your eyes. Consciously choose to accept disgust a little more than you may have ever considered. If you experiment right now with accepting this feeling of disgust a little more what would happen?*

She describes a lighter feeling.

Me *Feel the disgust in yourself right now. What would your body really like to do when you feel disgusted?*

She makes a disgusted sound as if she's throwing up.

Me *Give it as much permission as you can right now. It wants to be expressed. Feel the muscles that are involved. Support the flow up and out through the sound and the movement.*

She allows more disgusted sounds and she starts feeling better, less tense and stressed. At the end of her release we design a 'disgust meditation' for her to do.

She chooses five minutes of release per day. As always, I suggest balancing the release with the same or double amount of quiet time afterwards to allow the integration.

Me *Memories might come up, understanding of the reasons for the disgust. In time the acceptance of it will land more and more in your cells. It will go way beyond a mental understanding. Disgust will teach you what it is, why you are disgusted, what to do about certain situations that trigger disgust. When you get triggered in your family, notice, and then bring it into your next meditation. The more you accept disgust, the more fun you can have with it. It gets easier. It can even feel energising. You will feel more self-love and more at peace eventually because you are not fighting with a part of yourself anymore.*

I talk to her about discharging old, stored energies and explain that when the storeroom gets too full, we get overcharged.

When it gets released, we are in balance.

> **Me** *Disgust releases in a specific way. It usually moves up from somewhere deep inside towards the face and mouth and then wants to be released. Like vomiting or spitting, making a disgusted face, using disgusted sounds. Disgust likes to involve the tongue. You can discover a lot of face muscles that you usually don't use when you make a disgusted face.*

Disgust is a powerful emotion. It makes us rebel, push back, spit out, not do something. We learn to control these powerful emotions to be good people, to be adapted. We don't want to look like crazy animals.

The purpose and gift of a therapeutic environment is to really allow the emotion, and its raw expression. Imagine what you would like to do, to say if you could fully express it?

Once it is released enough you choose how to express it on the outside. You use your functional self to discriminate where and how it can be expressed or not. In the beginning it can feel endless, but that is not true. It just means there is a lot of it stored.

Transforming loneliness into beauty

In my childhood and teenage years, I felt lonely. It was my secret. Nobody would have known as I had lots of friends and peers that respected me. The loneliness was on the inner, missing real contact. The kind of contact I only really discovered in my grown-up years, especially when I discovered meditation.

Loneliness and aloneness: One coin, two sides

When I first heard Osho say that loneliness and aloneness are two sides of the same coin, it didn't make sense to me. I hated the feeling of loneliness. I felt a lot of it growing up and if there was one emotion I never wanted to feel again, it was that. But as I trusted Osho, I started experimenting, and thought more deeply about how it could be true.

My experience in Finland

In the early 90s, I moved to Finland with my Finnish boyfriend. He'd lived in Cologne for about 10 years and wanted to move back home so I joined him, but I left all my friends, and a great community, behind.

When we first arrived, I was on my own a lot. He was very busy establishing himself in Helsinki again and I was alone, in a new country, with a language I didn't speak. Fortunately, a lot of people spoke English. I started allowing the loneliness when it arose, stayed with it, cried or felt the emptiness of it. It took some weeks but often, after those times that I really stayed with the feelings, I would find myself in lovely states like self-love, peacefulness, deep relaxation, contentment with myself, a sense of okay-ness just being me.

I eventually lost my fear of loneliness. I became too aware of the treasures at the core of it. Loneliness became my friend. I was alone, but it felt good.

Healthy aloneness

The deep difference between loneliness and aloneness is that in a state of aloneness you are content. You don't need or miss anything. It is a fullness, a deep connection with one's self, a sense of wholeness. Healthy aloneness is an aspect of true nature.

Loneliness can be a by-product of our need to belong, to follow others, to orient ourselves towards the outside, outer rules, outer guidance. In healthy aloneness we are no longer a sheep in a crowd, following blindly what we are being told. We stand tall, listening to who we truly are and living our truth.

The more you are connected to yourself, the more being alone will feel fine. My favourite synonym for aloneness is 'All-one-ness'. All is one, we are whole.

On rejection

When we don't reject ourselves anymore outer rejection doesn't hurt as much.

Imagine you feel joy. You feel it directly in your body as if you're being filled with sunshine and you know it's real. Let's see joy as a field of sunflowers and then, imagine a friend with sunglasses who cannot see the yellow.

Perhaps, there's someone walking past, disconnected, in their heads, lost in their own thinking, not noticing this beautiful field of flowers. Does it make your experience unreal? No!

You only feel rejected if you reject yourself. If you don't reject yourself, you don't hurt even if you are being rejected. I had a breakthrough moment when I was dating. The clearer I was around my needs and my attractions, the more I expressed what I wanted, the less rejected I felt.

One of Osho's many teachings for us was to become Zorba the Buddha, to join two iconic characters and bring east and west together. That meant allowing equal space for the inner and the outer. The spiritual and the material. Going in and going out.

When I was in the ashram, we'd all gather for meditation for an average of two hours every night and then have a meal in our canteen. Those who still had energy would head over to the bar, no different from any pub in the world. Except there was never any destructive drunken behaviour.

Drinks were served under an open sky with high bar stools to rest your drink on and people chatting, laughing and hanging out. Music was playing in the background. Our world was a mosaic of monastery and marketplace.

I was in a period of dating and understood, more and more, whom I was attracted to and why. At that time, with my study of metaphysics and chakras I was beginning to identify where the attraction was in my body and in my energy centres.

One evening, going against my upbringing that it was only men who did the asking on dates, I approached a man whom I found very attractive. The attraction was to his looks and I expected a good sexual chemistry. I had enough courage at that time to ask him for a date.

He said he already had another date. But when I went away, I did not feel rejected. Now, in my 'old book' I would have felt rejected. But I didn't. How was that possible?

The secret was that I did not reject myself at all. I knew exactly what I wanted and asked for it. There was no inner rejection afterwards, no negative self-talk or inner judgment.

On joy and positive emotions

We don't usually struggle with states like joy, excitement or happiness. You're not likely to hear people say, 'I feel bad that I feel happy'. We generally want to feel good, so we don't resist these positive states.

It's when we cling to them or prefer them above all others, and hold on to them, sometimes with masses of effort, that problems arise.

I used to believe that the whole journey of enlightenment was designed to help me feel good and stay in that state. I have done many rounds, over many years, of clinging to positive states and rejecting negative states.

But slowly, ever so slowly, the understanding sank in that suffering comes from clinging to or rejecting emotions; they're all part of the same cycle. Being neither for nor against what is; just being present with what is, is the right attitude for transformation and spiritual growth.

Cultural messages make a difference

It is important to see that we absorb beliefs and cultural messages against feeling unbridled joy. Many people are afraid that they can only feel joy to a certain degree, but then it becomes too much. There's a fear that it will change, but also that it has to change. This comes from experiences in childhood, when we were having fun, then something went wrong, and we got punished for it.

Like missing a meal because you had too much fun running around outside, tearing your clothes, making yourself dirty. We learn that a bit of fun is ok, but too much is not.

Because of that it also takes practice to stay longer in good feelings like joy, not just in difficult emotions like old pain or anger. Once we reclaim our natural joy, for many people there is a point where a voice in our head kicks in and says, 'That's enough now, something dangerous will happen, if you keep feeling joy'.

Antilibidinal ego

It is a structure of regulation put in place in our conditioned self in childhood, that regulates how much happiness/joy we are allowed to experience. There are cultural messages like: 'Roosters that scream in the morning are dead in the evening'. 'If you stick your head out it will be cut off'. 'Kids are meant to be seen and not heard'.

What this induces is a fear of joy and, behind that, is the deeper fear of rejection and punishment. At some point this mechanism becomes automatic and the joy gets cut off before we even know that we are feeling it.

There are extreme examples of the unhealthy expression of joy and it's worth looking at those.

When someone experiences the sense of joy and freedom for the first time again in adulthood after repressing it for a very long time, they might feel free as a bird. Worst case scenario: this feeling could be so real that they become delusional, stand on a roof top and try to fly like a bird. Not a good idea, right? Or someone else in this state could feel so overwhelmed by this sense of freedom and joy, all boundaries dissolving, that they start celebrating by running naked through a supermarket. Not a good idea either.

Causeless joy

As that name suggests, there are times when true happiness arises on the inside for no specific outer reason. And it is exquisite. It is a flavour of true nature.

All the states of true nature simply exist within us. They don't need any reason or trigger or justification.

Feeling states of true nature

There are so many different ways for true nature to show up in us. It can make me feel effervescent with tingling energy rising and it can create a state of intense happiness.

The states experienced in true nature, are only positive. You will never find anything stressful in this dimension. Fear, guilt, shame and a sense of unworthiness don't exist there. It is the end of suffering, paradise or heaven on earth, it's what I believe we all long for. And it is available to anybody who is ready to do the work.

Once connected to true nature we can experience many positive states like peace, love, joy, happiness, freedom, spaciousness and gratitude.

The conditioned ego-self – a poor imitation of one's true nature – tries to achieve these states with effort or artificially. They are copycats but not able to create the real thing.

Their basis is illusion. And one of the biggest illusions in modern society is that financial success will bring happiness. Of course, financial freedom is useful, comfortable and has many positive outcomes. But I have seen many cases where being rich doesn't guarantee happiness.

One that strikes me now is the story of a friend who, 20 years ago, when I first met him, was a millionaire. He was also severely depressed and struggled with his mental illness for 13 years. Eventually, he killed himself.

Another is a billionaire who had sessions with me around 2003. He spoke, often, about the games rich people play – competing in San Tropez to see who had the biggest yacht, for example. He came to me for therapy because he was unhappy and struggling with intimate relationships.

We've begun to look at true nature (*Chapter 1.2*) and will look at it in more detail in Chapter 8.

UNDERSTANDING AND TRANSFORMING GUILT

ALL HUMANS EXPERIENCE SUFFERING. In my study and work, as well as, very deeply, in my own life, I understand there are three main states of suffering that human beings experience. These are guilt, shame and feelings of unworthiness.

When I experienced these states, I thought my suffering would never stop. Even with all the work I had done, all the understanding and tools I'd gathered, I still wasn't able to eliminate the trio of suffering. Then, I discovered one thing.

True nature has no guilt, shame or unworthiness

I finally understood that these three – shame, guilt, lack of self-worth – do not exist in true nature. That is the only place where we can experience relief from them. True nature is the end of any suffering. It is in the art of inner transformation, that we can move from guilt, shame and unworthiness to true nature.

What is guilt?

Have you ever been punched in the gut? Or, if you haven't, can you imagine what it would feel like? That's what guilt can do to us.

What if you could learn to stop being punched, and instead feeling uplifted, supported and encouraged?

Guilt is a learned response. Everybody gets the voice of guilt implanted in their heads from early childhood. Guilt gives us ideas of how to behave, of how to be, or how not to be. The essential message of the guilt voice is, 'When you do *this* you are good, when you do *that* you are bad.'

Guilt is like a trance or hypnosis that holds a promise; guilt makes us believe a statement about our behaviour or our personality, is in our own voice. The statement might be, 'If I follow what the voice tells me I will be a good person; I will do things right and be the best I can be. Then, I'll be loved and accepted by others.' But as you'll see, the more you investigate the root of that statement, the more obvious it becomes that it's a false promise.

Guilt creates contraction

Guilt makes you feel awful, it contracts you. If you're beset by guilt, you are not at your best at all.

Let's explore the mechanism of guilt, element by element. Once you understand how it works, you can practise the actions to break the trance. You'll need repeated practice to release yourself from the hold that guilt imposes. Begin by identifying a typical thought that makes you feel guilty. Then, use these four actions to release the hold that guilt imposes. Repeat, as necessary.

Step 1 – Identify

Step 2 – Externalise

Step 3 – Separate / defend

Step 4 – Replace

Judgment

The superego, the inner judge, uses guilt as one of its strategies. To understand the mechanism of guilt I want to refresh some of the teachings on judgment.

- Every judgment hurts.
- Every judgment contracts us.

When we listen to the voices that make us feel guilty, we are trying to identify the deeper implied judgment. What that means is the thought we originally hear might not sound so bad. To understand the effects of that judgment, we need to feel the impact of thoughts on the body. This is not easy in the beginning of any inner work; we usually have strategies to not feel the impact, to soften the blow. One way we do that is by numbing it out.

But if we really open to the deepest layer of the judgment, it usually has a strong negative physical, emotional and energetic effect. You will see this in the client interviews.

CLIENT SESSION – SERENA ON GUILT

My client, Serena, 28 years old, is married and the mother of a little boy. She is very busy providing for her family but her guilt arises around having more 'me' time in her daily life. In a previous session, we'd reached a place where she came to see that it's healthy to have time out.

It was useful to identify a particular and strong trigger for her guilt; in this case – the wish to read a book and be on her own to enjoy it.

Step 1 – Identify

I ask her to identify the voice in her head that makes her feel guilty, turn to it and listen, attentively. She needs to know her enemy and, as it is in this case, the voice of guilt is not necessarily loud and obvious. It can be quiet, hidden or, even, subliminal.

I call this process, hunting it down or becoming Sherlock Holmes – it's all good detective work.

Me *What is the thought that makes you feel guilty?*

Serena *There is so much that needs to be done. Get up and do something!*

When Serena identifies what is operating, she looks deeper into the idea for the implied or hidden judgment.

> **Me** *'There is so much that needs to be done' doesn't sound too bad, right? What is the hidden judgment in that?*

To help her identify it, I ask her to consider the opposite.

> **Me** *When you get up and do something, how does that make you feel?*

> **Serena** *I feel good when I listen and follow the voice.*

> **Me** *Now let's look at the reverse. Imagine staying on your couch and enjoying reading your book so much that you want to keep reading. If you did that, and you stopped listening to that voice, how would the voice judge you? What kind of person are you, lying on the couch reading your book for long periods of time?*

> **Serena** (after some pondering) *Lazy.*

This is a deeper layer of implied judgment, but not yet the deepest. How will you know when you've reached the deepest? You will feel it, energetically. The core of the judgment will create some form of contraction. You might feel as if something hit, punched or poked you.

> **Me** *I'd like you to close your eyes and feel the impact. Imagine you're lying on the couch. The voice asks you to get up, but you resist. It feels so good to read your book, right now. The voice gets stronger: 'You are lazy!' You still ignore it. [Pause.] How would this part judge you if you kept reading the book and didn't listen?*

She struggles to identify the deeper judgment. This is a common problem, we protect ourselves from the real judgment, because it feels uncomfortable or hurts.

I keep helping her.

> **Me** *What kind of people waste tons of time in their life? What's the negative judgment on that?*

She eventually uncovers the answer.

Serena *Useless.*

That is a deeper layer, it hurts.

Often, people uncover statements like: 'You're worthless! You are really, really bad! You're a horrible person!' In severe cases, we can feel as bad as a criminal destined for a high security prison.

And the inner guilt voice continues: 'Get up and do something so you can prove you're not this useless, really bad person'. It's this mechanism we are taking apart.

I ask Serena to consciously open to the impact of the judgment.

> **Me** *Close your eyes, take a deep breath and become really curious about where you might feel the contraction. Imagine someone that matters to you, or someone whose opinion matters to you, saying to you: 'You are useless'. Where would you feel that? Check head, heart, stomach or belly, include the whole body.*

> **Serena** *Well, it's as if my heart's skipping a beat, like a shock.*

> **Me** *Imagine this person you trust really believes you're useless. How would that feel in the heart?*

> **Serena** *It would really hurt, a lot.*

Serena tells me that to avoid that pain, she'd stop reading her book and do something 'useful'.

This is a defence mechanism. To avoid the pain, we do whatever we believe will counter the judgment. Our defence mechanism needs to be detected and made conscious.

Step 2 – Externalise

I suggest to Serena that the guilt voice is not the voice of truth. It is an implanted artificial voice, like a chip in the brain. When Serena is able to externalise, she will learn to stop believing that voice.

> **Me** *Visualise us taking that part of your brain out and making it into a separate character. It's not you, it shouldn't look like you. It can be male or female, any age. Let's say you were a*

movie director. What would you want this character to look like? Create anything you like. Trust your creativity.

Serena had watched a science fiction movie the night before: 'Oh, it's a yellow evil alien with a big head. All he does is make people feel guilty'.

Me *How far away have you placed him?*

Serena *Right close, next to me.*

Me *That's very close. Are you able to move him further away? Can you move him three or four steps away?*

She struggles with moving the character further away, and she can't yet imagine not hearing the voice but, eventually, succeeds. I keep encouraging her.

Me *From my experience and after a lot of examination, I now call guilt a virus like the flu virus. It makes you sick, weak, feverish and you ache all over.*

Step 3 – Separate

Me *Imagine there was a chance to have separation from this voice, turn its volume down. Who could you be, would you be, without that voice telling you, you're bad?*

Serena *Free.*

Me *You know, that's the most common answer I get; I really encourage you to trust that. And how about trying this for yourself. If the guilt voice could be uninstalled, right now for good; if it truly never came back, who would you be?*

Step 4 – Replace

Me *We need to add another piece here. We need a valid voice that tells you what to do and what not to do, when you stop listening to the guilt voice.*

Serena (who came up with the words, instantly) *My heart.*

Me *I call this the voice of truth. Heart, intuition, gut instinct, conscience, feeling sense, your intelligent mind, your intrinsic morals and values. All of these will replace guilt and guide you.*

Serena *Is that enough to replace the outdated voice?*

Me *Once the trance is broken, you're not rudderless. You don't turn into a terrible person, who has no morals. Dealing with guilt is like riding with support wheels on your first bicycle. They need to come off eventually, so you can ride freely. You will be completely functional, even more functional when you let go of guilt.*

Let's test that. Imagine going back to your couch, reading your book and enjoying it. Isn't there a feeling sense to let you know you are enjoying this? What would your voice of truth say to you?

With a sigh of relief, she says: *Keep reading.*

Me *Till what time?*

Serena *Till I don't feel like it anymore. I will eventually get up and do something else.*

Me *Yes. Not listening to guilt doesn't mean you'll read your book for the rest of your life. Rather, your feeling sense will tell you when it's the right time to stop. You'll find your own right balance between resting and doing.*

I ask Serena to visualise that healthy scenario. It's still hard to imagine and, as with most people, it will take more practice of these steps. But Serena is happy to have a tool and looking forward to learning how to use it.

Step 3 – Separate

This is possibly the hardest one in the beginning. So, I make a few suggestions for how she can practise the idea of separation.

Me *You can put a wall up, out of stone, metal or any other strong material between you and the guilt character. You can*

*put a soundproof box around that character. You can even
add a volume button to manage the guilt voice. Just as you
would with a remote control, turn the volume down.*

She chooses thick, soundproof unbreakable glass for the
container. I suggest a volume control button in the glass as
extra security. I guide her through turning the volume up
and down a few times. I'm helping her learn she can control
that voice, be the boss. This will feel very unfamiliar in the
beginning.

Me *Can you imagine turning the volume down to zero?*

She eventually gets a glimpse of what it could feel like when she
doesn't feel judged. I invite her to create an external character
for her voice of truth now.

She chooses a fairy godmother who is very kind, older and
only wants the best for her. She feels better now. She needed that
extra protection.

I encourage her to start practising these steps regularly. That
will break the trance.

Step 4 – Replace

Me *Eventually, the voice of truth will replace the voice of guilt.
You will not be identified anymore. It needs a lot of retraining
and practice. The brain will change eventually. Why should
you not be allowed to read a little longer? Does it really make
you a bad person to read your book for another 10 mins? Or
30 minutes?*

She agrees that having fun reading her book doesn't make her a
bad person. Then she asks me if I still feel guilt. 'Oh, yes,' I say.
'I still have the voice, but I do not believe it anymore. I can turn
it into a little mosquito that flies around yet can't sting because I
have mosquito repellent on.'

Once these four steps are learnt they become part of our tool
kit for a conscious life. The more we rest in the heart, feel, trust
our gut, the more the guilt voice loses power.

Unfortunately, there is no uninstall button, yet the voice can lose its power over us. It takes patience, but the skill to soften the voice can be learnt.

CLIENT SESSION – JO

To **identify** – which is step one as noted above – is to become aware of the implied or hidden judgment. This step is difficult for Jo. Confronting this consciously is uncomfortable. As we're growing up, we learn to believe that the voice is true and trustworthy.

Jo runs her own business, a health clinic, and she has several employees. She is married, in her mid-30s and has a six-year-old son. She feels the guilt, as a judgment, that she is selfish when she takes time off work, and, for example, has fun skiing with her husband. She is afraid to be seen as not caring.

The judgment feels like tension and contraction in her stomach.

> **Me** *If someone were to believe you're a selfish person, maybe even unemotional and uncaring, and you trusted this person and believed them, how would that affect you?*

She struggles to identify the deeper impact.

Strategies to avoid judgment

I can see Jo acting distracted and kind of squeamish; her discomfort is obvious.

It's not unexpected. We all develop strategies so that we're not affected by external and internal judgments, which are called primary defences.

In Jo's case, she can identify a reaction on her skin, which then uncovers a feeling of frustration. She tells me that if she really believed it, she'd feel depressed.

Here, she's detected the lack of ease or dis-ease. That's a hard thing to do but this step is forensic, in a way. Like having an x-ray to detect why you are coughing.

Step 1 – Identify

Identifying the exact nature of the guilt, or what I call the diagnostic stage, is the most challenging.

When I learnt to hunt down my guilt voice, I discovered sentences in my head straight from the Bible. They opened, 'Thou shalt not…'. I was shocked as I don't remember ever studying the Bible. I grew up Catholic but left the church in my late teens. And I wasn't exposed to a strict religious upbringing. I definitely hadn't been exposed to any Bible statements for more than four decades. So, this conditioning, with its religious, societal, familial influences, goes deep.

When we're growing up, we tend to do everything to be good, so that we're accepted, loved and, definitely, not be attacked.

Step 2 – Externalise

I ask Jo to externalise the voice of guilt as described with Serena.

She chooses a witch – a cartoon character from her son's storybook and as we go through the steps, she is easily able to move that character further away from her.

Step 3 – Separate

Jo chooses a brick wall as her barrier. We turn the volume down and she names freedom as the feeling when guilt is turned off.

I invite her to become more aware of guilt arising and being able to counter the voice, in the future.

Source of judgment

How do we identify where guilt comes from (so we can counter it); what are your triggers?

If you hear someone voice a judgment and it gets to you, then it's likely you have the same or a similar judgment in your own head.

The guilt voice is a mix of messages we've learnt from family, society, teachers, religion and from collective messages. My messages from the Bible demonstrate this well.

Imagine these two scenarios.

Scenario 1

Someone says 'You are green' to you, meaning it as an insult. Now, you are not green, haven't played with green paint, have absolutely nothing green on you or about you. You have no negative associations with green. In this case the judgment wouldn't affect you at all. You are immune.

Scenario 2

But if someone says, 'You are greedy' and you have negative associations about being greedy, it will affect you. Perhaps being greedy was a negative judgment in your family or you have a value system that doesn't appreciate greediness.

A signal that there is a judgment somewhere will come from the body; we'll contract in our bodies or energy. Whenever we make it more conscious, we get better at detecting/identifying and separating/defending.

Eventually we have an overview of our main guilty-making voices.

In Jo's case, her guilt arises from working too much – the perspective of her family – and not working enough – the perspective of her employees. As long as she believes the guilt voice, she can't win.

I suggest homework for her. She can practise identifying, separating from, and protecting herself from, the guilt voice.

In time, and with practice, we won't need to externalise the guilt voice anymore. Step 2 – Externalise and Step 3 – Separate – can happen inside our own heads. First, it's diligent detective work. Then it becomes more automatic. Once learnt, you recognise the voice immediately and don't give it any more attention. You become immune to the guilt voice the same way a virus can't penetrate a healthy immune system. Breaking the trance is the most important step in freeing yourself from guilt.

Parallel to this you keep strengthening the voice of your truth, intuition, gut instinct or knowing. *Part 7 Inner guidance* will provide more information about how to do that.

UNDERSTANDING AND TRANSFORMING SHAME

TRANSFORMING SHAME BEGINS WITH becoming conscious of it. Then, we can heal it. Shame is more subtle than guilt and harder to detect. Shame can be so hidden that most people are not aware of it at all. For most of my clients the ability to work with shame happens once they have done a lot of other work before.

That's why I go into a lot of detail around Step 1 – Identify. It's a complex operation. I provide additional tools that are specific to shame – understanding it as a trance and that it needs a reality check. Once shame is identified, you can apply the same four steps that you used to transform guilt.

There are four elements in identifying or becoming conscious of shame.

- Physical symptoms
- Metaphysical substance
- Shaming voice
- Its function or role in society

Physical symptoms of shame

The effect of shame is that when we feel it, we cringe and wish the floor would open and we'd just disappear. Typical symptoms that are signals that what we're feeling is shame, include feeling shy, insecure or nervous, turning red on different parts of your body (typically cheeks and neck), blushing, not being able to think straight.

Shame, like guilt always contracts the body or your energy somewhere. For example the heart can feel like it's imploding. The stomach can feel like it is twisting in on itself. It can be experienced in any part of the body or all over. Shame also includes a sinking feeling. It feels uncomfortable to varying degrees and, the physical symptoms make things worse because they are more visible. If you already feel ashamed and then blush or can't think straight it only makes you feel more ashamed.

Metaphysical substance

From my training in metaphysics, I understand that the cringing, twisting feeling is the metaphysical substance of shame. Shame can be transparent. It wraps itself around real qualities like strength or aliveness and then distorts them – it's like a metaphysical cling wrap. If your sexuality was shamed, it could be wrapped around your genitals and pelvis. If your innocent kind heart was shamed, it would be wrapped around the chest. Glad wrap symbolises the contracting quality of shame well and the transparency of the material. It is hard to detect. Not like guilt, which can feel like a heavy dark sludgy substance.

Shaming voice

The shaming voice also plays a part in exacerbating the feeling. In the nearly invisible structure of shame we tend to hear voices – not those of the psychotic. It's those voices – an aspect of the superego – that create the shame. Experiencing shame relies on having been shamed in the past.

Shame can be there even if there's nothing to be ashamed about. In the reports from rape victims we hear, over and over that while it's not their fault, the victims still feel shame.

The more we detect the shaming voice, the more immune we can become. The voice can be silent, hidden, subliminal. We need to find it and turn the volume up so that we can hear what we need to counter.

Hunting the voice down is crucial. We need to know our enemy. Find it, face it, listen to it. Then, we can expose its lie.

Shame's function in society

The positive intention or function of shame is to make us good people, to be accepted and loved. We don't want to be bad.

How do we make sure that we are still good people without shame? Our inner healthy guidance system will replace shame. It is like support wheels on a child's bicycle. When we can ride freely and keep our balance, we don't need the support wheels anymore. So, consider whether your heart would allow you to do something destructive. The answer is, no, it wouldn't.

When the functional social self and the inner guidance system are fully established we don't need shame anymore (see *Part 7 Inner guidance*).

Are there truly bad people?

I don't believe that anybody is truly bad at their core. Yet there is truly bad behaviour and certain people – psychopaths, sociopaths, narcissists and all those with minds turned to criminal acts – have done truly bad, unforgivable things. It is ok to judge people who hurt, violate others, as destructive, as bad.

What I ask you to reconsider is feeling bad from shame that is not justified. When you pour shame on yourself, you are in your own courtroom. Shame can make you feel like you are a criminal and you are the accused, as well as the judge and jury. When shame is triggered it contracts the heart and blocks the capacity to feel love.

Shame needs a reality check

One of the ways to help heal shame is a reality check. The reality check could be exposing what you find shameful and having the confirmation that there is genuinely no need for shame.

When we believe what shame tells us we are in a trance; believe we're bad and deserve to be punished. It is psychological torture. We believe the shamed reality and are scared to have it confirmed. It lurks, and also makes us afraid to ask questions; to get to the root cause of the feeling. Yet, as we grow up we come to believe, from parents or religion, for example, that shame is necessary. It's a controlling emotion that keeps us behaving 'well' for fear if we don't, we'll be shamed.

But shame is not a real emotion. It's artificially created. Can you imagine a life without shame? Truth enhances the real and dissolves the false. Shame can dissolve and this demonstrates that shame doesn't exist in true nature. To know this is a relief.

The following two sessions demonstrate how shame was transformed. Both clients, Emma and Nancy, have done a lot of work with me before. I use mainly Steps 1 and Step 4 with them, from the Recipe for emotional transformation.

With new clients, for example, Serena and Jo, I always use the four steps in the beginning. This recipe can heal any form of judgment we suffer. The recipe is about disidentification. With more experienced clients I can often skip Step 2 – Externalise and Separate in the way shown above. With the next two sessions I introduce more advanced ways of disidentification through love and presence.

CLIENT SESSION – EMMA

Emma describes the experience of shame when someone told her that her husband – who is ten years older than her – looked like her father.

Emma *Shame hits the forehead like a fist punching me when the words reach me. It triggers a chain reaction like ripples going through the body.*

Me *Let's look at the space you were in before your friend said this.*

Emma *My heart was wide open. I was sharing how much I love my niece and was showing pictures of my niece to a friend. One of the pictures was of my husband with the niece. That's when my friend asked, 'Is that your Dad?'*

Emma was shocked that her friend would think it was her Dad. That's why her comment went in like a punch.

Open-heartedness and judgment

We explored why the comment hurt so much and traced it back to her childhood. When Emma was growing up, she'd been repeatedly bullied in school. When there are lots of bad memories and something triggers it in the now it can feel like an earthquake inside. This is called an imprint.

A repeated experience imprints itself on our soul. It is like scratching a word into a tree. The longer you scratch the deeper the groove will be.

Her repeated experience was of feeling innocent – like Bambi in the forest and a car coming her way trying to run her over.

Defending with love

I choose to work with a technique called walking through the **corridor of time.** This is replacing Step 2 and 3 – externalising and separating.

I suggest a healing visualisation where she walks down the corridor of time with compassion. I invite her to visualise a corridor going all the way back to childhood, either by visualising herself at different ages getting younger and younger as you walk down the corridor or imagining pictures on the wall of different ages.

Emma chooses the pictures. To get her into the right space I let her feel the love for her niece to allow the feeling of love and compassion to fill her heart.

> **Me** *Now stand in front of the first picture. The most recent memory. Allow the same love and compassion you feel for your niece to flow towards you. Flood and surround your wounded self with compassion and love. This is the remedy to stop shaming voices from tormenting you. Speak to the wounded self in an affirming and supportive way.*

> **Emma** *You have done nothing wrong. You heart was wide open, you wanted to share the love. You did not expect any judgment at all.*

I let her repeat the message till it reaches the wounded self.

Shame as a substance

The next step with Emma is to view shame as a substance or structure.

After some thought, she describes it as a grey, heavy cloak.

Me *The identification with shame can be very deep. We don't know who we are without it.*

Shame as a disease

Shame is like a metaphysical disease, like a virus causing the flu. It feels horrible. But because of that, it may feel we have no control over it.

That's not true. We can help the self who feels shamed come out from under its grip.

At this point in the session I suggest that Emma has a change of cloaks. The old cloak of shame can wrap itself around and contract her. I invite her to take it off and replace it with a new, beautiful cloak of light around the shamed self so it feels protected.

Me *Does the new cloak support the connection with the heart? Would the shamed self eventually consider not needing the cloak of shame anymore?*

Emma has a brilliant insight: I am an even better person without the shame cloak. Thus transcending the shame trance, which says, 'Wear me, so you are good. I make sure you are not bad. I make you better.'

Me *The truth is that in shame we get so disconnected, discombobulated that we can't think straight. It's evident to us that we are not our best selves at all. In fact the opposite is the case. Even highly intelligent people can't think clearly or don't know what to say, if they are in shame. Shame can make us harsh and judgmental with others, protective, defensive, unkind. That happens because shame acts as a harsh inner attack. With that happening, we lash out.*

Imagine eventually you are completely buffered from a shame attack. The thought happens, the memories are there.

But so is the new cloak; it's staying there for good, protecting you and keeping the healthy guidance system intact. You are immune to the virus. Everybody else might still get the flu, but you don't.

Your energetic immune system is strong. Learning to defend yourself from shame is a skill. It will get easier in time. You can start with a specific symptom to track the voice down. Become your own Sherlock Holmes. Find the culprit who makes you feel bad, unworthy, crappy or weird.

The stronger the connection to your own heart, the more you are buffered. True nature is very kind. It would never put a cloak of shame around you.

At the end of my session with Emma, I decide on a heart meditation for her to do. The easiest image for her is play time with her niece. With that symbol, she can practise turning her attention back to her own heart and feeling the love.

CLIENT SESSION – NANCY

A female client in her mid-30s starts the session describing feeling confused about her new relationship. She had finally met a good man after years of failed attempts. Her present partner is caring, understanding and committed. He listens to her and is empathic. They are having fun. A few months into the relationship her shaming voices try to tell her that she should break up with him.

She has done a lot of work with me before and so I build on those foundations. I start with an overview of the most important teachings around shame.

Step 1 – Identify

Me Shame distorts reality, it creates isolation, disconnects you from yourself and others. It's a tricky bastard. It is an artificial emotion and not part of true nature.

We will now detect it together so you can learn to protect yourself better in the future till you don't believe it anymore. The shame voice lies and distorts reality, it is not your truth speaking to you. Yet, if we could rate how much you believe the shaming voice from 1–10, if it is a 10 it means you take it as the truth. That trance needs to be broken.

All of that makes sense to her and she understands, already, that it is part of her upbringing trying to make her a 'good' person.

Me *So, let's identify how the shame voice speaks to you, how it makes you feel and which emotions and body sensations it creates.*

Her shame voice tries to convince her in different ways that she should break up with him. She hears taunts like:

'You are not fit to be in a relationship.'

'You will destroy it eventually, anyway, so better leave now.'

'He will leave you eventually like many others before.'

'It is just not gonna work.'

'This is too good to be true.'

This is typical of the commentary of the superego or conditioned self. Each of us has aspirations and dreams. They might be of meeting the right partner, having the perfect job, finding a beautiful home, having enough money … whatever we have been dreaming of. Yet, when we grow and expand into what we really want, these countering thoughts can be triggered.

An effective way to think about your good fortune is to say: 'It is good, and it is true!'

During the session Nancy works out that she really likes being in the relationship. And therefore, she's confused that there are all those shaming thoughts in her head.

Shame can feel as if you are locked in, in a bubble and, while there's the illusion of being protected it also feels yucky, murky. Like a heavy blanket. The shame bubble is very different from a healthy protection bubble. The protection bubble always feels wonderful, expansive and protective.

Nancy feels more and more relieved as she understands what created her suffering.

Step 4 – Replace

Because of her previous experience with this work she can skip Steps 2 and 3. I ask her to remember some beautiful moments in the relationship. She immediately smiles. We highlight the voice of truth as an antidote to the lie of the shaming voice; that voice of truth is an immune booster helping fight off a virus.

Her truth is, 'I don't want to break up at all'.

If he was a terrible person and mistreated her, the voice of truth would, hopefully, tell her to break up, yet her situation is the opposite.

EXERCISE

AWARENESS OF SHAME

Identify a shaming voice.

Start doubting it, question it.

Do I really want to listen to this? Is this true for me?

On transforming shame

I was standing by the fence, at the gate.

The words 'You have permission to be happy' opened the gate, inviting me out of that old field, that was preventing me from being my fully expressed self, into this new space of genuine, authentic, effortless happiness.

With that came a hesitation and apprehension. Hesitation to step out of the gate and apprehension that if I did, and I trusted that happiness, that it would be ripped away. That it would hurt. The fear that opening my heart and fully trusting in happiness would result in me being shamed.

I was moved to step out of the shame, as though I was stepping out of a cocoon. When I stepped out of it, immediately the urge to squirm and writhe, the nausea and the pain dissipated.

When looking at this crumpled cocoon with love I could see that shame had valiantly tried to protect me with this thin cocoon. Its purpose was to help me determine right from wrong, from the context of society and conditioned beliefs, to enable me to fit in with the 'shoulds'. To blend in. Yet, as a result, to not live fully expressed in a space of effortless joy.

As I continued to look at this cocoon of shame with love, the cocoon melted. It morphed into a puddle on the floor.

My whole being was emanating a powerful, far reaching white light. I could feel energy flowing unrestricted through me. An ability to move courageously out of the old, confined field and into the space of permitted happiness with trust and openness. A sense of being fully aligned, fully expressed, a sense of excitement and anticipation for wonder. —HELEN

UNDERSTANDING AND TRANSFORMING UNWORTHINESS

A SENSE OF UNWORTHINESS is, like it is with guilt and shame, an artificial, learnt emotion.

Before we can transform it, we need to understand its mechanism. Our first step is to identify the voice or thought that makes us feel unworthy.

This transcript of a session with a male Australian client, Dan, in his early fifties will indicate some of the process we went through when he presented to me with the issue of unworthiness. Dan experiences this sense despite running his own successful business as an Osteopath and being happily married.

As he explains his thoughts and feelings, he demonstrates well that feelings of unworthiness aren't tied to the reality of a person's place in the world.

CLIENT SESSION – DAN

Me *What is that thought or voice you hear?*

Dan *I will always fail!*

Me *Can you change the statement to 'You will always fail'?*

During the session, I used the same four steps in transforming this, as we need when looking at guilt and shame:

Step 1 – Identify

Step 2 – Externalise

Step 3 – Separate / defend

Step 4 – Replace

I suggest that to help him with the process of disidentification, he needs to look at Steps 2 and 3. As long as he believes it is the voice of truth, he won't be able to separate from it. The voice is his superego, the inner judge camouflaged as inner guidance. Naturally, he listens and believes it.

> **Me** *What is the quality of the message or voice?*

> **Dan** *It is like a rule. A law.*

> **Me** *How does that make you feel?*

> **Dan** *I shrink, feel small and collapse.*

Superego disguised as truth

Superego messages – disguised as the truth – are the nastiest of the messages we tend to get in our mind. False voices like this one create contraction, whereas the voice of truth creates expansion. You will never find the feeling of unworthiness in the dimension of true nature or your true self. It only exists in the conditioned self. It is a mind-created emotion. That's why I call it artificial. For his externalising, in Step 2, Dan visualises a robotic computer such as the one in Star Wars. In Step 3 he sees it being crushed from above – his defence. He was then able to listen to the real voice of truth again which encourages him to keep going, to not give up when he fails and to acknowledge how well he is already doing – a clear proof of how wrong this old thought pattern is.

Unworthiness is a mechanism

I had one of my strongest teachings around unworthiness when I was doing my metaphysics training. At the time, I felt very alone in my unworthiness, but I learned that unworthiness is a collective mechanism – everybody suffers from it in one form or another. It creates a sense of isolation and makes us believe we are the only ones feeling so terrible.

The 'Unworthiness Equation' I received as a teaching has helped me a lot since.

An 'Ideal' minus 'Reality' equals 'Unworthiness'. As an equation it looks like this: Ideal (Should) – Reality (Is) = Unworthiness. Or in other words:

Should and Is are enemies

That's a rather cryptic statement so, what does it mean?

- There is an ideal, a 'should', that we compare ourselves to
- There is our reality in this moment
- There is a gap between them
- The bigger the gap, the stronger the sense of unworthiness

Let's look at examples of it being applied:

You have curly hair; you would like to have straight hair.

Your friend is most engaging in social gatherings; you don't know what to say.

You are a certain weight; your ideal weight is 10 kgs less.

You earn a certain income; you believe you should earn at least double that amount.

You should be good at sport; you are clumsy.

You should be good at gymnastics; you just can't get a specific skill no matter how hard you try.

Your friend dances gracefully; you move like a wooden doll.

All your friends are getting married; you are the only single person in your friend group.

Ideal versus reality

Each example can create a feeling of unworthiness. The gap between the ideal and the reality can bring on a sense of failure which leads to feelings of unworthiness and the belief: 'I am not good enough.' If only I could ... be like x, achieve my goal, find a partner. There is always a *should* in the mix.

When I ran women's groups for about 15 years, I heard many say, in the sharing, that they felt unworthy and what struck me is that the reasons were generally vastly different. What made one woman feel unworthy, was no issue for another. It is a subjective mechanism, brought on by conditioning and learnt values and ideas.

Because of that, because of its subjective nature, we can take it apart and retrain ourselves to not feel unworthy anymore. One felt she was too tall, someone too short, one too loud, the other too quiet.

A very common thought pattern is that 'the grass is greener on the other side'.

Relaxing into unworthiness

In my training, we did an exercise to learn about the metaphysical energy of unworthiness. The fifty people present made a big circle in the room. Then we imagined the big circle was filled with the energy of unworthiness. I visualised an ocean of vomit. It looked disgusting.

Then, we were guided to take the next step and it was one I definitely didn't expect.

Now, an ocean of vomit isn't one of the most attractive energies. All my old instincts would tell me to move away from it. Yet here was the next step. We were all invited to step into the energy of unworthiness. Really?

I did it. Despite all the resistance I had and expectations of a horrible experience. I've always been a courageous seeker, curious and hungry to learn.

I can't recall exactly what those first few moments were like when I stepped in, but I do remember that after some time we were invited to relax into the unworthiness, to stop fighting it.

Falling into a changed world

I did and it changed. It blew my old mind.

It was like falling through the vomit layer into a deeper layer that felt deeply relaxed, peaceful and ok.

At that time, this level of transformation was still revolutionary for me. Now, thankfully, it is normal; in fact, I take it for granted. I also facilitate it daily for clients in their sessions.

Within the core of that unworthiness was a healthy relaxed comfortable place. This is one of the experiences I never forgot.

Now I know that part of true nature is a state of intrinsic value, where there is no need to prove anything or do anything special. Beingness is enough in itself.

That technique is one of the most powerful I've used and use, to transform unworthiness. You are asked to face it, relax into it and drop through into a healthy place in the core of it.

Stepping out of the trance

Another technique is understanding shame as a trance and stepping out of it.

With this, you visualise a circle drawn around you, then stand in the circle as if you are in the trance of unworthiness. On the count of three, you step out of the trance and experience yourself without unworthiness.

Both techniques work in different ways towards disidentification from our sense of unworthiness.

Artificial versus real

We learn to feel unworthy. It is related to thoughts and learnt concepts. It is not part of true nature. That's why I call it an artificial emotion. Whenever you catch yourself thinking 'I should ...' or 'I should not ...', stop, examine and ask, 'Is that really true?' Start doubting the idea and then connect with what is true for you in that moment.

One of the antidotes to unworthiness and one of my favourite mantras, is to say, 'If I trust myself right now, what is my truth?' I now treat 'shoulds' as enemies. The moment a thought starts with 'should' I lose interest and disengage.

The more we open our hearts to ourselves, learn to feel our bodies, become fluid with our emotions, the more we are protected from artificial emotions. The more we are present to our truth through direct experience, the more we are buffered from the old thought patterns of unworthiness.

SHOCK AND OVERWHELM

IT FEELS IMPORTANT, AT this stage to mention, the concept of shock in a therapeutic sense and how to deal with it. The feeling of shock can easily be a by-product of feeling shame, guilt or any state of overwhelm. I use the word shock to describe the result of too much going on. In order to cope when we are feeling too many emotions at the same time or one that is too intense, we shut down or shut off. We become numb to stay functional.

It is like the main switch in the power board blowing.

In that sense, saying 'I am not feeling anything' is just another layer of feeling. As with all layers of feeling, the key is to relax with feeling nothing, be gentle till you get in touch with a real feeling.

The only remedy for shock is love or self-love

This is one of the most essential teachings I ever had around shock. When I learnt to identify the state of shock, I would remember that specific teaching and it would allow me to come out of shock. Love melts shock, it allows us to soften, to think clearly again and identify what we are actually feeling. Only then can we address the underlying reasons.

Energetically we can look at shock as a pressure mechanism. When in shock, we experience tremendous pressure in our thinking: 'I should cope, I should do this, I should do more of/ less of', it goes on and on. The inner critic, judge or superego will be very active and busy. If you examine your physical body in shock, you will discover a lot of tightness, muscle tension and overall contraction or the other polarity – numbness.

The concept of shock is also important in understanding how we relate with each other. I have witnessed many times in couple sessions that partners polarise. It can especially show in their mental processing. Some people can't think anymore, the mind gets blank. They stare blankly at their partner, they can't compute or process what is being said. Others start racing in their thoughts, can't stop talking and bombard their frozen partner with words or demands. That specific dynamic can lead to a couple spiralling down more and more. The opposite response to shock escalates the suffering they are experiencing.

I have seen many times, when I explain this concept, how a light bulb goes off in both partners triggering a sense of relief. They stop the negative cycle or spiralling down even further and switch into compassion for each other. Then they can hear each other again. They can see that the behaviour that was triggering them more and more was just the desperate attempt in the other to cope. No strategy is better than another. But when they are polar opposites, it can get very bad.

I always love simple recipes. The one for shock is simple: **switch back to love**. Open your heart to yourself and your partner again.

I remember during the first few years of running heart groups, I would often find myself in shock in the evening of day 1 or 2, my mind was busy and loud creating pressure asking what to do next, what I could have done better, how to respond to a challenging situation, planning the next day. Once I understood the concept of shock, I would stop engaging with the pressure cooker, slow down, feel whatever was touched in me and come back to loving myself.

A beautiful simple key to come out of this specific suffering.

GOLDEN TOOL
OVERWHELM AND CHUNKING THINGS DOWN

I guess we all know what overwhelm feels like. It is a universal experience that overwhelm feels uncomfortable. In overwhelm we are not able to think clearly or make good decisions.

The overwhelm I am talking about here is not the overwhelm we can experience when dealing with trauma. The chapter on trauma healing skills will clarify the difference.

The overwhelm I am referring to here is a by-product of too much stress.

It can often feel insurmountable yet, one of the golden tools to deal with overwhelm is a technique using NLP called 'chunking things down'. Following are two client examples to demonstrate how it works.

CLIENT SESSION – KIRSTEN

Kirsten shares the feeling of overwhelm from work.

> **Me** *How is the feeling of overwhelm showing up?*

> **Kirsten** *It feels like pressure on me, touching my skin. I can feel it in the brain.*

I take Kirsten through an exercise to help with the overwhelm.

Step 1

> **Me** *Describe each aspect or element of the overwhelm by giving it a number, a name, a shape, a size ... even a colour and a location. Shape doesn't matter – it can be a storage unit, a garage – they just need to be clear shapes that can be separate from each other and be locked.*

Kirsten chooses boxes and ends up having nine different boxes, eight of them relating to aspects of her work – she works as a coordinator for a lot of people in her job.

Some of them are subdivided into smaller boxes.

The last one, box nine was related to herself, her inner dialogue, pressure through high expectations on herself, fear of disappointing people.

She eventually visualises all the nine boxes in one big area.

I repeat the names of all the boxes and have her breathe out the stress related to each area. Then, she locks each box.

Step 2

> **Me** *Move all the boxes further away from each other and further away from you.*

She starts taking a deeper breath and I can feel her relaxing more as this step generally brings more space.

Step 3

We choose one box to start working with. She chooses box nine with her inner stress.

At the end she feels much better. I encourage her to use this visualisation in the following week and assure her, we'd keep working with the different boxes in the next sessions.

CLIENT SESSION – BEN

Ben is overwhelmed by stress. Using visualisation, I invite him to divide the huge bulk of stress into different parts. He creates six different storage containers and in each he'll store a component of his stress – work stress, relationship stress, financial stress, etc.

He chooses a name, a size and colour for each container (the size symbolises the level of stress and pressure each issue creates). He might choose a big black container for work stress, a smaller orange container for relationship stress. Once created, he visualises all the stress around the specific issue, gathering and flowing into its container. Eventually each container has scooped up all the stress and gets locked. I ask him to move them further apart from each other to allow space to come back in his mind.

As the overwhelm starts settling, I guide him into how it feels without all that stress or tension. The anger and frustration he felt overwhelmed by changed into a true calm.

And, once he's calm, we can look at every issue from that place. We start with the easiest one and I guide him to understand what the contents of the containers are, as well as invite his practical insights to come through. One-by-one he gets clearer and stays calm till all six containers are addressed. In the end, he has clarity on how to move forward and out of the state of overwhelm.

Moving into or away from an emotion

I have wasted a lot of time not understanding the importance, the delicacy of knowing whether to go into the depths of an emotion or to move away from it.

When I started my therapy work in the late 70s, we made mistakes. It was considered courageous for therapists to invite their clients to jump into anything that was troubling them, head-on. Often it resulted in the client being overwhelmed, or experiencing shock, or not really processing what was going on. Today, as I worked with Bella, a client in her early 30s, who was grappling with the theme of disappointment, I understood how vital it was to tread sensitively, while still making progress with her issues and her understanding of how to heal.

Our overall theme for that session was the art of feeling. As we'd been working together for some time, she had skills in identifying and feeling different emotions.

Bella loves mountain climbing and had been invited to join a friend for a two-day climb. She is fit enough and willing to do the climb but wasn't able to commit to those dates.

She was disappointed she couldn't do it – an understandable and acceptable emotional response to the situation. Yet, she had a strong reaction to that and brought her feelings of disappointment into the session.

As we began peeling the layers of her emotional response, it became clear that disappointment is an old, charged theme for her. Bella has a vexed relationship with her mother that began in childhood and still exists.

There was a great deal of old stored disappointment in her and she's not yet addressed it. In that situation, her newly felt, healthy disappointment touched all the old, stored disappointment.

I can sense the enormity of these two doses of disappointment meeting. There needs to be a specific way of working with the resulting emotional crash. So, I teach Bella the difference between moving into an emotion and moving away. I am passionate about this tool now, particularly because of all the wasted time in my own journey when I didn't understand it.

We compare the state she is in, to climbing. For mountain climbing, you'd need to have the right equipment and know what weather is forecast and probably wouldn't climb in dangerous weather conditions. Then, when you're prepared and climbing in the right conditions, at your level of expertise, you can have an exhilarating experience.

That same process is appropriate with emotional work. Confronting overwhelming old emotions – in Bella's case the disappointment from her childhood – may feel like falling into an abyss. After which, you'd need to go to hospital, heal broken bones and take time to repair. Eventually, you climb again but soon, you fall again. A vicious cycle.

Without the right tools this can create unnecessary fear of the inner world. It creates shock and stress in the nervous system.

Follow step-by-step

The right way forward from this emotional impasse, is to follow specific steps.

The first step would be to move away from the intensity of what she's feeling. This is easier said than done.

I ask her to conjure a visual image for the disappointment. She comes up with a tall mountain with a pointed top and gloomy clouds hanging around.

The next step is to look at that image as if it were a still picture in the distance. I help her to ground herself in a safe place inside herself. Then we ask her deeper wisdom to give her an image of the transformed state once it is all healthily worked with.

She gets the image of a sunrise and the feeling of freedom. The work for her right now is simply acknowledging the emotion and agreeing that it's enormous and will remain overwhelming, till she has learnt to transform it with support. She is happy with that.

GOLDEN TOOL
MOVING AWAY IN OVERWHELM

When the feeling is overwhelming move away. Once resourced, when you feel grounded and safe enough in yourself – not overwhelmed – you approach it in the right way, well equipped. This way you can even start looking forward to difficult inner territory and not dread it as you did for a long time.

Teaching

If the emotion is manageable for you, move towards it and feel it. Follow the steps in *Chapter 5.1 The art of feeling*.

If the emotion is too big, move away from it first. Then, if you have a choice, move towards the emotion in the right way. Learn the steps of transformation and, always, do it gently.

You'll still need courage to do it at all. I'd call that appropriate courage.

TIPS FOR MY 21-YEAR-OLD SELF

- Get curious about what you're feeling; get to know your emotions.

- Learn to accept emotions, and how to allow and process each one, consciously.

- No emotion is bad; it is the repression of emotions that creates tension and suffering.

- Any challenging emotion can be transformed into something positive.

- There is a trustworthy voice in you – the voice of truth. That true voice creates expansion.

- There is, also, the untrustworthy voice that creates contraction (see *Part 7 Inner guidance* for a deeper analysis).

- Become suspicious of guilt, shame and unworthiness. They are artificial emotions; they don't exist in true nature.

- Shock is a form of overwhelm. If you're in shock, you'll experience a lot of mental pressure. The remedy for shock is love and kindness towards self, slowing down.

PART 6

DEEP HEALING

CHAPTER 6.1

HEALING THE
INNER CHILD

ONE OF THE MORE important aspects of any exploration of our inner world, is our visualising, and understanding the concept of the inner child. When we look at how we act and respond in the world, it's important and useful to discern what elements of it can be related to childhood. In fact, truly appreciating the concept of the inner child is the most efficient way I have discovered to relieve our adult struggles when we're dealing with an issue that goes back to childhood.

The inner child concept

> *In popular psychology and analytical psychology, the term inner child is an individual's childlike aspect. It includes what a person learned as a child before puberty ... often conceived as a semi-independent subpersonality subordinate to the waking conscious mind. The term has therapeutic applications in counselling and health settings.*
> —WIKIPEDIA

More than one child inside us

Whenever a client recalls a memory from their childhood, I ask, 'How old is the child in this specific memory?' Because, knowing the age, matters. We don't have just one inner child.

There can be many, and they can be different ages. Part of the healing of childhood wounds includes being able to visualise the younger self from the time of the particular wound and sense it being separate from the adult we are today. Seeing the separation allows the adult self to support the inner child.

One age can represent a span of time with a specific theme. The memories from age six to 10 can be covered by an eight-year-old who embodies that whole period.

If, for example, a client's parents have fought a lot during the client's childhood, then the client may pick just one age to represent that entire period. Once that particular aspect of the inner child is healed, it's felt through all the other relevant memories.

The crystallising event

These are moments in our childhood where an event can change us, dramatically. In the Journey Work of Brandon Bays such one-off moments are called 'core crystallising events' where, as a child, we might make decisions about ourselves, or life, that can have long-lasting, negative effects.

Experiencing one's parents' divorce, for example, can create a deep mistrust in love and marriage. From that, we might decide, 'I will never marry'. Experiencing the death of a loved parent, might create a belief to never open our hearts again. These mostly unconscious decisions we make in childhood can last an entire life.

If we live in accordance with a damaging belief from childhood, then healing the inner child is crucial if we want to go on to live a healthy life. Reparenting the inner child, replacing what was missing – finally giving the child what it always needed – is incredibly fulfilling for the conscious self. It is an important part of our journey towards becoming whole.

I went through a period in the early 80s, after first learning the concept of the inner child where, for about a year, I made regular contact with my inner child. I used a guided healing visualisation to meet my inner child and also learnt to trust myself and my capacity to respond to different aspects of the inner child.

Sometimes she was happy, sometimes sad, sometimes scared. I learnt to just be with her, to be present and let her know that I was there to love her and support her.

So, a favourite healing exercise I suggest to clients who first come across the inner child is simply taking the time to be present, feel the child in the moment.

In this exercise the client visualises and feels the inner child and intuitively senses what the child is experiencing. Sometimes the child might communicate it, but sometimes they might not yet be talking, so can't communicate directly. Still, the adult self can feel what's going on or visualise it in the child's facial or body expression.

It might go something like this:

Adult I can feel that you are mistrustful, and I am here with you. I can feel you're scared, and I am here now to love you and support you.

The adult self can repeat back to the child whatever they're feeling, moment by moment, as the adult perceives it, and this can be very reassuring. This simple technique of repeating an affirming statement, builds trust and rapport between ourselves as adults and our inner child. This is especially important with disconnected, abandoned, rejected or even dissociated inner parts of ourselves. Over time the connection will heal and this allows the child to connect with the conscious self.

This won't happen swiftly. Rebuilding trust is a slow process in any relationship. A wounded foster child might be brought into a loving home, but might take months or years to repair their fear or mistrust.

Sitting in the dark

A wounded, abandoned younger self will most probably have learnt to hide from the world. They might retreat, metaphorically, to their own hidden cave, or dark room, and not want to be seen. The wounded child doesn't trust grown-ups.

In such a case, I would ask the client to visualise sitting at the entrance of the cave or dark room, and simply being present, waiting, receptive, and not pushing or forcing contact. The conscious adult should not storm into the cave and drag the child out.

It is important to be sincere in our intentions and build trust. The inner child responds very well to that and the adult will need to wait till the child approaches them. If the child senses there is a genuine offer of healing, they will respond well.

Allowing not forcing

Displaying the patience required, on the part of the conscious adult, is what I call the yin approach – allowing not forcing. It can be a supremely positive and powerful feeling when reconnecting with lost parts and feeling childhood wounds heal.

The greatest thing in all of this, is to know that the adult, conscious being has all the inner resources to provide everything the wounded inner child needs to heal. Anything that has ever gone wrong, can be repaired. We become the medicine, the salve, for our own wounding.

Once, when I was healing from a broken relationship, I consciously spent time with my inner child, at home. I imagined talking to her, being with her. I have a vivid memory of the feeling of inner wholeness from that time. For me, a positive outcome, after connecting with my inner child repeatedly and persistently, was that I felt more whole.

Though it can be a difficult process to go through, it is truly worth doing inner child work. With the healing, so many of the qualities of the healthy inner child return – playfulness, spontaneity, creativity, boundless aliveness, laughter, joy, childlikeness, innocence, openness. It's an ongoing journey that gets easier over time. I know that healing the inner child is possible; I know it has a multitude of positive flow on effects.

'*I love you, mum*'

In 2013, I wrote a blog about the relationship with my mother and I thought I'd share it with you as an insight into the way mother–daughter relationships which had already been close, can deepen significantly.

> As I write this I am sitting in the same spot where I used to do my homework as a teenager. The window is facing the beautiful garden that has my mum's signature all over it.
>
> Being back home in Germany for my yearly family visit it felt appropriate to write about my relationship with my mother. As I have lived far away for most of my adult life, first in India, now for fourteen years in Australia, it is precious to have this time once a year with my parents.

Shared rituals

My Mum and I have many little rituals. One of them is drinking a coffee together midmorning and chatting. My Dad has stopped trying to join; he can feel the invisible wall protecting mum-daughter time. This morning, during those cherished moments, she stated with a cheeky look, 'I love nature' and I burst out laughing. It was absurd to state the obvious. She has put her love into this garden for a good 40 years and it is a piece of art.

My parents built this house when I was 15 and I always appreciated it. My Mum loves beauty and one of her many gifts, other than making great tasting food, is creating beautiful environments. It makes coming home a perfect holiday for me. I can appreciate it even more now as my husband and I just bought a place in Sydney. During the search I developed an eye for details and this, my old childhood home, I would buy in a flash.

I have always loved my Mum but in recent years more than ever. I had to work through different things to get to this very clean, undisturbed feeling of love and appreciation. It was tainted before, layers covering the real connection. My experience now is that nothing can be compared to it. It is unique.

One of the unforgettable moments with my Mum happened about six years ago. She used to work in a bank yet always had an openness to learning new things. Fortunately, she appreciated my alternative path.

At some point she learnt foot reflexology and offered to share that with me. I have had many reflexology sessions in my life, but nothing compares to what happened that time.

It was the special mother's touch, gentle, loving and full of feeling.

I could feel her pouring the most beautiful, exquisite love of a mother for her child into my feet and through my feet into my whole body and heart. My whole being was soaked in the sweetest feeling I ever had from her. I understood, in that moment, the essence of mother-daughter love. There was nothing in the way anymore, every pain or misunderstanding or grudge was dissolved. I was able to fully receive her love.

We both were stunned, transported into another realm. A mother completely giving the best she had to offer, a daughter completely receiving.

Welcome all emotions

I attribute being able to receive her love in that moment to all the inner work I have done. There were some difficult layers I had to face in healing my relationship with her.

I learnt to feel angry at her without feeling guilty, to have my own boundaries, to not merge with her struggles, and feel my own light.

I had to deal with the feeling of abandonment and inner deficiency, as she had to go to work when I was four weeks old. After many years of inner work, I learnt to recover the early baby feelings and felt how terribly I missed her, as a baby. We, like many others, had very little materially, and she had no choice but to help earn some money as soon as possible.

I am so grateful for the many honest talks we have had in the last 14 years. Times we cried together when it was, once again, time to leave. Both showing each other how much it hurts to be separated again. I was finally connected enough to myself to show how much it hurts to leave her, how much a young part still wants to cling to her and never let her go. And what a relief to be able to express that and feel deeply connected with her now.

I am grateful that I finally learnt to not always be the strong one but to share feelings of weakness and vulnerability. I have learnt to call from Sydney when I need her support. That was never possible before, as I was the strong and independent one who needed nobody.

I feel I got the gift of a second childhood, where everything that was difficult when I was young, is healed now. The drama of me being an unplanned pregnancy when my parents were very young and all the trouble that came with it, has now turned into a blessing. My parents are still fit and healthy.

I look forward to many more years where we can enjoy the beauty of our healed connection.

FIRST CONTACT WITH THE INNER CHILD – DENISE

A female client, Denise, is experiencing a lot of hurt feelings in her romantic relationship. As we start exploring, she identifies feeling abandoned, hurt and lonely. We start tracing it back to a time when she was five years old and her mother left the family.

I ask her to visualise or sense herself as a five-year-old and help Denise today, to dialogue with the child.

Me *What would you like to say to your five-year-old?*

Denise *Believe in yourself, never give up.*

Me *Do you have any idea how she might respond?*

Her inner child *I am scared.*

Me *How would you like to respond to her?*

Denise *How can I support you? What do you need from me?*

Her inner child *I would like a hug.*

Denise visualises hugging her inner child and can sense her relaxing. Being there for her now will heal the old wounding of abandonment in time. This won't be just a one-time fix and the process may need repeating but the connection has been made.

We allow the dialogue to unfold as it could with a real child in the outer world. This step is easier for parents as they can apply whatever they learnt in relationship to parenting their children, to working with the inner child. It's possible to use a relationship with a child in your extended family or children of friends as an example. In the process we learn to trust our intuition and the natural intelligence of our hearts as we would in the relationship with real children. You learn to listen, have compassion, understand and support them. The inner child responds the same way an outer child would.

MEDITATION: FIRST CONTACT WITH THE CHILD

It is crucial for this meditation to be centred in your heart. You need the capacity to be present, listen without judgment, be patient and accepting. If you're finding it difficult, start with a simple heart meditation.

Take about five minutes every day to connect
with your child in an imagined safe space.

Simply show up, with no expectation, exerting no
pressure. Perceive whatever is there in the child.

You can imagine the child approaching slowly from the
distance and you being as welcoming as you can be.

Take notice of the child.

What is she or he feeling? Are they happy to see you? Open?

Are they withdrawn, shy, mistrustful? Slow to warm up?

They might not want to share how they feel yet.

What is their facial expression?
What clothes are they wearing?

Don't think of changing them. Just observe and get to know them.

First contact: What happens?

The child might not be open at all in the beginning. If they are really hurt and have been hurt by adults, they will not trust you – you are an adult. You need to earn the trust of the child like you would in any other relationship.

My very first encounter with my inner child happened in a group in Pune in the 80s. I was probably 24.

We were instructed to sit on a cushion and have a second one close by – that means, one for the child, one for the adult self. I started by sitting in the adult cushion and said, 'Hello' to the child.

When we were guided into sitting on the pillow of the child, part of the instruction was to discern and trust whatever physical position the child wanted to sit in.

Mine turned around and sat with her back to me. She was maybe five or six years old. She didn't want to talk.

I didn't know how to respond as my adult self, but I turned my back to her, too. I hadn't done any work on opening my heart yet, so I had no clue about true acceptance, compassion, presence. We were off to a bad start.

When I started the exercise all those decades ago, it felt as if I was in the worst possible spot. We'd both turned away from each other, weren't talking, the child not trusting adults, and my adult self no clue how to take care of the child.

It took me many years before I healed that inner relationship and then, the adult self and child self became very good friends. The inner child learnt to trust me and my adult self began to understand the child and how to be with her.

I often share this as an encouragement when clients try their first encounter.

Safe space meditation

The definition of a safe space in this work is that you have something that is your space and yours only. It has solid boundaries that cannot be crossed. Nobody else can enter unless you invite them. You are in healthy control. (See *Chapter 6.1 Healing trauma*.)

Creating a safe space

We can learn to visually create a safe space. One of my clients calls it her parallel universe. I often describe it as your dream property in the perfect location.

You can choose any part of nature that you love. Mountains, trees, lakes, ocean, whatever works for you. It can be as big as you want it to be – a whole forest or a part of the forest. It can have buildings or not.

Draw boundaries

Once you've chosen what it looks like and how big it is, you create a safe boundary. That can just be a feeling or a big wall, a force field, a dome … whatever works for you. Once the safe space is created, imagine being there. You walk around, claim the place, become familiar with it. Look at the colours, breathe in the specific fragrances of fresh air or ocean or flowers.

Walk around noticing how safe you feel. Is your mind relaxing? Are you slowing down? What is happening in your body? Are you starting to feel safer?

You can create many different areas within the bigger space. The main character in this space is the present adult or conscious self. The next step is to find the **power spot** for the adult self. This is defined as a spot that has the best energy. It might be sitting under a tree, or close to the water, in a tree house or anything that suits you.

Rescuing the inner child

When we have been through trauma in childhood, it is valuable for the adult to rescue or save the child. This will help whomever – the child, the adult, the present self, the unconscious self – stop getting stuck in dark memories. Eventually, if the right healing steps are applied, it is even possible to retrain ourselves to not go back to these dark places at all as going back to them reawakens the feelings of that difficult time and perpetuates the trauma.

If you remove the child from the old memory and transport them into a safe space, you as a whole being start feeling safer, more resourceful and you can heal on a deep level.

If, when you are accessing the inner child, you discover another age that needs support and is wounded, bring it to this safe space. You can create a separate area for any part of the wounded inner child.

Let's say your inner six-year-old needs rescuing. You feel what you would have loved when you were six. Did you like to learn? To create? To play? You choose an area and set it up. A little house, a tent, a blanket, a tree house. It needs clear boundaries. This space will be just for that younger you. The same way parents set up rooms in their home for their children. Even you, the adult you, is not allowed in that area unless invited.

You might guess by now that assigning boundaries or repairing ones that have holes in them, is crucial to healing any wounding.

Once the space is created, you imagine the younger you is approaching. You can meet the younger self on the boundary and invite them in.

Walk around, introduce the safe space and eventually lead the younger you to the prepared area.

If this is your first meeting with a younger self introduce yourself as the future self.

Watch the response in the child till it understands that you are here to help.

Let them know that this space will be there for them for good. They can change things, add pieces, remove them, as they wish.

Area for deeper healing

When old wounding needs to heal it happens in a specifically set-up area. To be able to express old, stored emotions that could never be expressed before, we create an area that is there only for healing.

The purpose of this area is to empty out raw emotions till we feel free.

This area has – of course – a clear boundary that defines it. It can be a hut or an open space. I have clients use a sauna or a circle of stones. It is up to you and your intuition.

In this healing dialogue do as much as you can cope with at any given time. If either the present you or the younger you reaches a limit, you arrange a sign and stop. Then each of you can go to your prepared areas and rest.

Over time the inner child learns to express all of its emotions again in a safe and supported way.

There are more aspects you can add to your safe space meditation in time. This needs to be done with an experienced therapist in the beginning. Once understood and learnt you can do it on your own. You can visualise guardians, wise beings or nannies for different ages; create monuments that honour past survival strategies.

You can get creative with imagining an area for the superego to retire – like chilling in a spa – as it doesn't have to push so hard anymore.

There is no limit to what you can visually create here as you learn to trust your intuition: areas for play, sports, music or whatever your heart desires.

Feedback from a client

I can't tell you exactly what I was feeling because it would have been related to me feeling unsafe and my inner child feeling scared.

You guided me to build the outdoor type of fortress, with guardians that circle it, it had trees, water, all the natural elements and it had a space for my inner child and a space for me.

I loved it. Specifically because after the session I felt so connected and compassionate to my inner child and really felt that I could be the guardian for my inner child, that I could heal her and feel compassion for what she had to go through undeserving. It was a significant healing that helped me continue developing a sense of safety that was more expansive. And actually connect with my child self, rather than dissociate. —GEORGIA

GOLDEN TOOL
RERUNNING PAINFUL MEMORIES
TO A GOOD OUTCOME

Our brains are plastic; they can change, they can create new connections, at any age. The notion that once we have a trait or even, a pathology, then it's ours forever, has been dramatically challenged by research into neuroplasticity. It represents a great step forward in the freedom we have to believe we can change, we can heal.

One thing I learnt from The Journey work, is the idea that we can rerun old memories that feel painful and, each time, have a different response to them. Then, with enough repetition they can have a positive outcome. It's a powerful tool for inner transformation.

I was struck by its power when I first came across this technique. I watched and understood the changed memories in my own mind and felt the healing effects of it in my physical body, emotional body and mind. There was a new-found relaxation, aliveness, happiness, joy, hope and trust.

Running the rerun

How does the rerun work? Imagine you're the youngest, a girl, in a family of four children. Your siblings are boys, louder, older and stronger. Mum is stressed, Dad is working most of the time. You feel nobody is listening to you or taking you seriously, so you withdraw, more and more. You become the quiet one who doesn't want to stir the pot. You disappear into the background.

Later in life, you work as a secretary in a real estate office. All the agents are running trying to clinch deals. They're loud, busy, pushy. You feel like nobody sees you or listens to you. You are like background furniture. In the evening, you go home alone and watch TV. It's not very long before you are diagnosed with depression. You have shut down.

To work with rerunning these memories, it's good to free up all the old unfelt emotions, hurt, fear, anger, disappointment – whatever was not felt in the childhood home of the past, and the real estate office, now. Freeing up past emotions will bring back a lot of aliveness already. Then we would pick one typical scene: the boys are running around; you are somewhere quiet, not making a peep.

Resources

It's an interesting thing to realise here, that we each have inner and outer resources. A resource is useful; it adds value to your life and is anything that works for you, makes you feel better, improves your quality of life and supports you in a healthy way. Inner resources are qualities like the courage to deal with a difficult situation. Outer resources can be a cup of tea, reading a book, going for a walk, a great chat with a trusted friend.

In rerunning painful memories it's important to ask: What would you have needed to have a happy, satisfying outcome – speaking up, being listened to?

Seeking help is a way to get resourced and could mean seeing a good therapist. Other ways might be finding and using your voice, feeling respected, being noticed. With professional help, you can reframe or rewrite your early scene till you feel happy.

Once the healthy scene is ready, you rerun it, go over it in the next few weeks as often as possible to allow the brain to change. The secretary, for example, would rerun a typical childhood memory, where she disappeared in the background, by doing the opposite: finding her voice, speaking up and being heard.

Take time to remember the visualisation and feel the healing effect in your body. You can also share it with trusted friends or write it down, whatever works for you. With enough repetition we can reprogram ourselves. We can upgrade our brains to healthier thinking.

Rewriting the script

Every time we revisit a bad memory, we recreate not only the old emotions but also the physiological responses from that memory; it can lead to stress and illness. However, when we start rewriting the script we create a healthier mental and physical climate.

When I was able to rerun painful memories in this healed and empowered way, I trusted myself – more and more – to be resourceful and able to heal. I knew that with enough commitment, I could heal any wound.

Think about our real estate secretary being able to change her childhood story with the right therapeutic support. She might find her voice, feel more a part of the group, join conversations in the breakroom, join in for after work drinks. With enough time and reinforcement of her own resources, she may well discover her natural fun-loving nature and feel happier. Her depression may become a memory.

Working with projections

Part of healing the inner child is understanding projections. In psychology, projection describes the process of projecting a person from our past, from a memory onto someone in our present life. The term transference is also used to describe this activity. Projections are a normal mechanism in our brains that happens when we remember something from our past.

What is a projection?

Imagine you are in a relationship and something is troubling you. Perhaps, your romantic partner reminds you of one of your parents.

So, if you have positive associations, that's unlikely to be a problem. In fact, you might feel really warm towards someone because they remind you of someone you love, a favourite aunt or grandmother.

But negative projections can become major obstacles to building healthy relationships. If your girlfriend reminds you of your Mum and your Mum was very demanding and controlling, you might rush to end the relationship because of those suggestions of similar behaviour without giving the relationship a chance.

Is there a way to know if we're projecting? Is there a way to change our behaviour if we are? Working with our projections involves ongoing honest inner explorations and generally needs therapeutic support. The following technique is a powerful tool that I find intensely useful in my work.

GOLDEN TOOL
MOVING THE PROJECTION SCREEN

Gerry, a client of mine, projects his ideas and feelings about his mother onto a present girlfriend who would like to move in to his place. He loves her but, as he felt emotionally manipulated by his Mum, is scared he'll feel suffocated by his girlfriend.

Gerry's mother was very protective, and he never felt he had enough space to be adventurous. She wanted to know what he did, who he was spending time with, all the time. She was always scared that something bad would happen to him.

So, the idea for Gerry of his girlfriend moving in, is overwhelming.

In order to change his projection, Gerry can change the angle of the projection screen. I ask him to:

Visualise your girlfriend in front of you.

*Now, visualise your mother in front
or behind your girlfriend.*

Feel the feelings you are experiencing in this moment.
(In his case shock, overwhelm, defensiveness.)

Now imagine moving your mother away from your
girlfriend, to the right or left, but at least a few metres away
(this allows Gerry to change the angle of the projection).

Now, feel as if you're in front of your girlfriend
again. Gerry feels relieved, can feel more
space, can feel his love for her again.

Then, turn towards your mother. What do you feel?
Gerry mentions that the overwhelm returns.

Once he sat with the understandings and feelings of this exercise, Gerry could see that the negative feelings he has are from his past. He can choose to do more healing on the inner child in relationship to his mother. He now has more mental clarity and can make the right decision for himself in the present time. He decides to move in with his girlfriend.

A good question to ask yourself whenever someone in your present life triggers you strongly or you become very reactive around them is this:

'How much of my reaction/emotion/inner turmoil
is related to this person in the present time and
how much might belong to the past?'

You will be surprised at times. In my own experience I remember situations where my intuitive answer to this question was that 10 percent was related to my present life, 90 percent came from the past.

CHAPTER 6.2

HEALING TRAUMA: RESTORING SAFETY

HAVE YOU EVER WOKEN up in the middle of a nightmare? Do you feel wound-up all the time? Does your mind race a lot? Do you have panic attacks? Are you always on the run, can you ever relax? Do you feel unsafe in perfectly safe environments? Do you have an unexpectedly strong and out of place response to something others see as normal? All of these can be symptoms of unhealed trauma.

The word trauma has entered the current lexicon; it's bandied about quite regularly when talking about psychological events, damage, and distress. Trauma is the nervous system's response to an event and, it's not necessarily the event itself. Trauma can affect each of us differently.

What is psychological trauma?

*Psychological trauma is often the result of an overwhelming amount of stress that exceeds one's ability to cope, or integrate the emotions involved with that experience...not all people who experience a potentially traumatic event will actually become psychologically traumatised. However, it is possible for some people to develop post-traumatic stress disorder (PTSD) after being exposed to a major traumatic event —*WIKIPEDIA

243

Trauma can be a one-off event – a parent dying in early childhood – or it can be cumulative as might happen when a child grows up in a household with parents continually fighting.

In my training, trauma is defined as *'too much, too soon, too fast'*. When we experience any form of trauma our sense of survival feels threatened, we are in danger.

So, one of the biggest gifts of engaging in any work to understand and deal with trauma is the surety that we can restore a sense of safety in the nervous system through healing the old trauma in the right way.

The territory: An iceberg

I'm introducing basic trauma healing skills as it's likely each person will experience trauma at some time in their lives. To understand the territory when you start working with old, stored memories, like trauma, is to imagine an iceberg.

An iceberg is made up of frozen layers of ice, which are laid down early (as our memories might be in our childhood) and, as difficult experiences happen later in life, these are layered on top of the base layer. Yet, within the frozen layers there are individual capsules, or shells, that enclose a specific painful memory.

When the trauma work, or trauma healing work begins and emotions begin to be seen and freed, it helps to think of a delicate but tough capsule, say a porcelain capsule in one of the frozen layers. The iceberg melts from the outside freeing up the information stored in that layer. Stored inside the capsule are the memories of what happened, the pictures, emotions, sensations and beliefs formed at the time.

A common experience for those experiencing and recalling trauma is that we tend to blame ourselves for the pain. If anything goes wrong in childhood – the family environment, mistreatment, abuse, neglect, death of a family member, illness, financial stress, it is common for a child to blame themself for whatever is going wrong. If their parent is stressed and not available, the child might believe they are not loveable, or that something is wrong with them. Such feelings can be a foundation for feelings of unworthiness.

What are we to do? The iceberg needs to be melted and, with consciousness about the event, out comes the sun to melt the ice.

Thankfully, our deeper wisdom regulates what is ready to surface and when.

Symptoms of trauma

One of the effects of exposure to trauma is that the nervous system becomes alert and remains prepared for it. Trauma can lead to either chronic hyper- or hypoarousal, also called activation. The effect is an overcharge or undercharge in the nervous system – just like the voltage going through electrical circuits and being either too high or too low. If that's the case, the electrical appliances will not work.

Common signs of chronic hyperarousal are emotional overwhelm, panic, hypervigilance, defensiveness, feeling unsafe, being reactive, being angry, racing thoughts.

Hypervigilance is a reaction where part of the brain looks out for danger every moment of your waking state. When you're hyper-vigilant, it doesn't feel safe to relax at all, in any form – relaxation means letting the guard down.

Common signs of chronic hypoarousal are feeling numb, passive, having no energy, an inability to think, feeling disconnected, shut down. It can lead to depression and lethargy.

Both states are very uncomfortable and indicate the loss of safety. In therapeutic situations, and from my own experience, I am more familiar with hyperarousal.

Restoring safety

When we deal with trauma and are learning to restore a sense of safety again, it is crucial to exercise compassion for ourselves and what happened to us. That's why the heart needs to be open. (See *Chapter 4.2 Qualities of the heart.*)

Safety scale

When a client comes with any form of trauma or overwhelm, I begin to get an idea of the intensity of the trauma using a safety scale. I ask clients to imagine they are using a thermometer with a range from one to 10. Nominating 10 is the safest they can feel and one the least safe.

An inner sense of feeling unsafe as a result of trauma or overwhelm can present as anxiety, nervousness, racing heart, racing thoughts or a shutting down in the mind. It can also show up as nausea or dizziness. We can identify our personal signals. Early trauma leaves a stagnant response in the nervous system and, later in life, despite no repetition of the traumatic event, still triggers the trauma response. This ongoing, debilitating and often inexplicable set of feelings is what needs healing.

When we feel unsafe, we can be in a subjectively safe outer situation, like being alone at home in a secure building yet still feeling unsafe. The inner sense of unsafety has nothing to do with the outer situation.

Oasis of safety

The first step in working with trauma in the sessions is establishing an oasis of safety. Once established, it's the place the client can return to, when working with the trauma triggers overwhelm.

Part of the oasis of safety can be the relationship with the therapist, the safe atmosphere in the therapeutic space, an object in the room, the visualisation of a safe space or a place in the body that feels comfortable in the moment, for example, relaxed hands.

One of my favourite exercises to establish an oasis of safety is to invite the client to think of things they naturally love. I go through all the five senses so they can find something that fits each of their senses. This can also be used as a heart-meditation to open the heart.

GOLDEN TOOL
WHAT DO YOU LOVE?

What is one of the favourite things you love to look at? A colour, an object, a vast stretch of green?

What is your favourite feeling? Love, joy, satisfaction?

What do you love to touch? A silk scarf, stroking your dog's hair, feeling your bed cover on your skin?

What sounds do you like to listen to? The ocean, music, silence?

What smell do you like? Fresh air, fragrance of a flower, the smell of the ocean?

What gives you pleasure when you taste it? Fresh water, your favourite meal, ice cream, fresh orange juice in summer?

If you answered the questions in your own mind, check how it makes you feel right now?

There are many possible examples from sessions – the sight, sound and smell of the ocean; walking along the beach with a fresh juice, feeling the sun on your skin.

After I find out what works for a specific client, I do a short, guided meditation visualising everything they mentioned as if they were experiencing it in the present moment.

I let them use the safety scale to measure their sense of safety before we start creating the oasis. I let them check the rating, after every question and again at the end when all the senses have relaxed. It is generally an effective way of bringing the safety scale up anywhere from seven to 10.

Once this is achieved, I let them connect to a safe place in their body. When we feel safer the heart softens, anxiety lessens, and the client is in the position to look with loving eyes on their inner child's trauma.

Window of tolerance

A term used in trauma work to describe our capacity to bounce back from trauma, to cope or recover is the 'window of tolerance'. Within this area, this window, our feelings and reactions are tolerable, we can think and feel simultaneously, we can react appropriately to specific situations.

A lot of the trauma work aims to teach the affected to return to the window of tolerance when they are remembering trauma, or, if they are in that window, to stay in it for longer. It represents a measure of healing. Within the window we feel good; we're in a balanced state that's also called **resilience**.

Resourcing

Once we are in activation or hypervigilance, or hyperarousal, shock, a state of 'can't handle this right now', one of the main tools used to restore balance is called 'resourcing'. It is related to the concept of resources that I have introduced earlier. It reestablishes a subjective sense of safety.

Resourcing, in the trauma healing context, means *becoming conscious of everything that makes you feel **safe***. The main categories we can draw on are people, places and activities in our lives.

It's very useful to begin to gather resources and make a resource list. You might like to keep it in your phone or in a notebook.

Begin by listing **people** who make, or made, you feel safe. That includes people who have passed away – it could be your favourite grandmother, a family member, a friend.

Or an imagined wise being, angel, guardian or mentor.

Then, include **places** you love, either in nature or a country you've travelled to. For some people it's their bed. Their couch. A forest, the beach, the mountains. If there is no physical space it can be imagined.

Next, include **activities**. Drinking a cup of tea or coffee. Playing sport, reading, watching TV, talking to a friend, going for a walk, exercising.

Nothing is either right or wrong; your resources are selected by you and, therefore, utterly personal. For an introvert it can be being silent, for an extrovert sitting in a busy coffee shop.

TIME TO STOP: WHAT MAKES YOU FEEL SAFE?

Take a moment and ask yourself, 'What makes me feel safe and allows me to relax?'

Returning to the window of tolerance

Once you come out of overdrive, that's been propelled by experiencing or remembering trauma, you will begin to slow down. But, the return to the window of tolerance is not immediate.

Generally, coming back to normal is a slow process and starts with small sensations:

- the speed of thinking slows down
- a fog lifts in the brain
- the breath deepens slightly
- relaxation anywhere in the body begins and increases
- a part of the body that felt vacant comes back into awareness
- there's a feeling of tiredness
- the digestive organs gurgle
- you feel hungry.

The key to healing after reexperiencing trauma, in order to clear it, is to bring attention to the first changes and keep noticing them. It's one of the best ways to reverse a negative spiral and turn it into a positive one.

Typical symptoms indicating the release of activation or discharging the nervous system include:

- trembling: releases stored fear
- crying: releases old stored pain and tension
- laughing: always a good way to discharge
- yawning: I always encourage a client when they start yawning to really allow it. Yawning can feel so relaxing. It is also a heart opening meditation
- running: releases the flight impulse, can be done visually or physically
- fighting: discharges the fight impulse; can also be visualised.

Trauma spiral

A trauma spiral is a state where we might feel like our ship has been swallowed up by a whirlpool and sunk to the bottom of the ocean. It might be that while working with your trauma healing you get too close to a significant trauma which you are not yet prepared for, much like a storm chaser that's come too close to a hurricane and gets sucked into it.

The trauma spiral is one of the most uncomfortable experiences in the inner world. It feels like a natural catastrophe. It is an extreme experience of trauma.

When we come too close to a trauma spiral, symptoms of hyper-vigilance or hyperarousal escalate, and we feel completely out of control. In time, we can learn to recognise the symptoms before it is too late, and we really do lose control. We learn to move away or find safety early enough to avoid being sucked in completely.

Healthy and unhealthy control

The concept of healthy control is very important in healing trauma. The technique I used with Alison, a female client in her 30s, was how to resource herself through feeling a safe sensation in her body, which is an aspect of healthy control. This is how Alison recalled an aspect of her session.

> I was sitting with my eyes closed, emphasising the good warm and snuggly feeling in my legs and as I concentrated on it and let myself feel it even more, I noticed how hopeful I was about controlling/ being able to choose which emotions to feel. How great that I could choose to feel something good, deeply and put aside anything ... not good?
>
> So, I can control how I feel just by choosing to feel something good. I can feel even better, by choosing to feel that good feeling even more strongly.
>
> It feels very different to unhealthy control like someone trying to manipulate me.

Healthy regulation: Slowly turning on a tap in overwhelm

When we experience an overwhelming emotion, for example, lots of old sadness, it is possible to regulate the feeling in a number of ways.

Visualising turning a tap slowly, for example, so we can truly feel the relevant emotion. This is related to the control we might have if we turned a tap slowly to fill a glass of water knowing we can turn it off any time we want. We choose how much water we want in the glass.

Trauma – 'Too much, too soon, too fast', makes us feel out of control. But we can learn to healthily control old, stored emotions.

The antidote to trauma is, naturally, the opposite: healthy regulation. We still feel emotions, but they come in little bits, at a pace we can handle which allows us to feel in healthy control. We don't want old pain to flood us and recreate the traumatic sense of overwhelm. We want the pain to transform into something positive.

In time, the capacity to safely feel strong emotions which would previously have triggered a trauma response grows. Think of it as learning to surf and gradually, with practice, being able to ride larger and larger waves without falling off your surfboard.

Pendulation

Another technique for healthy control is beginning to be able to identify positive sensations in your body – by finding and feeling a part of your body that feels good and easeful. Then imagine a boundary around any difficult sensation, for example, a tight stomach. Then move your awareness between the easeful area of your body and the tight area. This swapping, from positive to difficult can at times dissolve tensions without even working directly on their cause.

In one client session, I used the pendulation technique, with a very positive and swift result.

> One of my faves was the pendulation. When I came in, I was very on edge, very stressed, all over the place. Because of that I had different sensations of pain and tightness over my body. You then guided me to find a good sensation in my body which I remember was the palm of my hand, instructing me to move from the good sensation to what wasn't feeling great which was my tense forehead and back and forth. The tension dissolved so quickly.
>
> I valued it so much because that is one specific thing that I have continued to use and it led me to feeling freedom in knowing I don't always have to dive into what causes discomfort but can still have release. —GEORGIA

Fight, flight or freeze and 'thawing'

As part of trauma work it is important to understand the three main survival impulses intrinsic to all humans and animals: fight, flight or freeze. These trauma responses come from an instinctual part of the nervous system.

The three Fs

Every human has a main tendency when it comes to their instinctual response to danger.

Some personality types fight as their first response. They get angry, red, hot, irritated and externalise. They might shout, scream or blame.

For some people, the main impulse is to run or get away. For example, they might leave a relationship when they fear confrontation.

Some people's main response is to freeze. Freezing can be experienced in the body as coldness, like a block of ice or rigidity like legs turning into wood. It can feel like parts of the body turning into stone, metal covering the chest, or the belly filled with plastic or glass.

When we freeze, we stop the natural impulse to fight or get away from danger.

One of my girlfriends has the flight impulse as her first response. She is in a good supportive romantic relationship now, but regularly has moments when she wants to run, which comes from her specific history in childhood. She started making things lighter for herself and her partner and she now labels it – with the road runner emoji – when she sends me a message about feeling that.

By knowing our tendency, we have more choice, in the moment, to stop and ask ourselves, for example:

'Do I really want to leave this good relationship and hurt my partner and then come back and do all the repair work to build trust again?'

Or, 'Can I feel the impulse to run, but choose to stay, talk about how scared I am right now and talk about the bad memories surfacing from my childhood?'

My training in trauma work was with teachers trained by Peter Levine – founder of a school of trauma work called Somatic Experiencing. In trauma work a lot has been learnt from observing animal behaviour.

A simple scenario helped me understand fight and flight.

Imagine a cat walking down the road. She reaches the corner and, on turning round it, sees a dog.

Scenario 1 The dog is smaller than her (which means no danger); she starts hissing, her hair stands up and the dog runs away. She knows she can win.

Scenario 2 The dog is much bigger than her (which means possible danger), she turns around and runs away as quickly as possible.

Both these responses are survival instincts. The cat will do whatever is needed to survive. If she can win, she will fight, if she can't she'll run. These are deeply engrained survival impulses in the instinctual part of the nervous system.

A typical example of the freeze response in animals is demonstrated in the following examples:

An animal in the wild is being attacked by another, stronger animal that could kill it. It will pretend to be dead to avoid being killed.

A little bird flying into a window will shake it off after the first time it happens. In case this happens repeatedly the bird will eventually be disoriented and fall to the ground. It won't shake it off or release the shock. Its energy freezes.

When we as humans can't run or fight, the energy of those two basic impulses freezes. These experiences get locked into our body, muscles, tissues and thinking.

Mental freezing can be experienced as confusion, shock, not knowing what's going on.

Trauma and stagnant energy

The energy that stagnates when we experience any form of trauma is often compared to ice. When it starts thawing and becomes fluid again, whatever has been frozen, memories, emotions and body sensations from the traumatic experience, start resurfacing.

These need to be dealt with or 'digested' with the right trauma healing skills or with the support of a trained trauma counsellor. The unfreezing can also turn into a physical experience.

A typical example is the experience of a client expressing a traumatic incident and suddenly feeling cold all over. Despite no change in outer temperature the client can feel an invisible chill in the air. It can be felt all over or can affect only some parts of the body. It makes a lot of sense – we are truly melting an inner iceberg, or frozen energy and that cold has to be felt somewhere.

When clients experience this sudden drop in body temperature, I usually offer a blanket during the session. I also suggest warming the physical body after the session. They might use a hot water bottle, take a warm bath, sit in the sun, have a hot drink or a sauna, whatever works to warm them up again.

Direct experience of an inner thawing

The inner experience of a frozen iceberg can be very real, and the thawing of that iceberg can produce dramatic results.

A client, Eloise, in her 50s, Australian, presents with hypervigilance, anxiety, difficulty sleeping, waking up in the night with fear, confusion. Her physical symptoms are a very contracted diaphragm, that doesn't let go even when we practise conscious breathing together. The tightness seems to have a life of its own.

We start exploring by her lying on her back, breathing gently into the diaphragm, with her hands softly touching under the ribcage. As she does this, she sees an image: a massive frozen iceberg with rough edges and murky colours. It looks dirty, brownish like frozen slush in winter.

It fills up most of her body – from her feet to the top of the chest. The only parts spared are her head and arms.

Eloise begins to delve deeper into the iceberg. It's a relief to her to identify what is going on. She has a memory of herself around four years of age at a time when she felt very alone in her family. Her parents were going through a change of jobs, and very stressed. Her mother was pregnant with a second child; she felt nobody had time and space for her.

What unfolds is fascinating. Eloise sees the visual of a saucepan in the iceberg. At first, it makes no sense to us. But I've learnt to trust being receptive to what the unconscious presents. Very quickly, she has the impulse to bang the saucepan loudly with another object like a hammer. She starts visualising banging the steel pan with a hammer and making lots of noise. She wants to be noticed. 'Is there anybody out there who can hear me? See me?'

She starts to come alive. Her body starts moving, her voice gets clear. The younger part in Eloise is saying: 'Wake up people, something is so wrong at home! Doesn't anybody notice anything?'

Her body feels alive now, she can feel energy flowing in her legs.

Eloise had learnt to survive in childhood, by being quiet and invisible. She didn't want to provoke her mother who was already very stressed. Making any loud noise to be noticed was a very unsafe prospect; it had to be frozen.

She had felt other layers before, the terror of nobody being there to help, and deep pain. But in this case, it was her anger that was the most repressed and hidden aspect. Eventually her body starts moving and rocking, her knees move in and out and her natural aliveness returns.

After the physical body has recovered, we then support the child and have the conscious adult talk to her. 'It is safe now to be alive, to be visible, to make noise. You can show up. It is safe to be noticed.'

Eloise describes a new sense of aliveness and inner strength at the end of the session and we are both curious to see how she will experience this change in her life in the next two weeks till I see her again.

The power of visualisation

Visualisations are useful in so many ways in therapy. This specific example will help to release a person's flight impulse, in a healthy way. It is quite a revolutionary technique as most of us learn to freeze the flight impulse. Here you learn to express it healthily.

In this chapter, we build on the technique to release fear safely. (See *Chapter 5.4 Transforming fear.*)

CLIENT SESSION – BEN

My client, Ben, is in his 50s, married, with two children aged eight and ten. He grew up in South Africa.

At the beginning of the session, Ben says he's experiencing a lot of fear. When he first started seeing me, the most obvious emotion he was experiencing was frustration and anger. We worked with that and eventually got in touch with a lot of sadness, which he has been working with for a while.

Now he is getting in touch with the fear, which is usually more hidden. So, it makes sense to me and sounds like an organic progression of the issues he's dealing with.

GOLDEN TOOL
RUNNING FROM DANGER
TOWARDS SAFETY

I introduce a new tool to Ben. I ask him to visualise running away from danger towards safety.

I explain the basic survival impulses of fight or flight or freeze to him. When, in childhood, we can't run away from a frightening situation, because we wouldn't survive, we freeze that impulse. It gets stored in the body – especially in the muscles. Survival fear keeps us from running. That is a difficult mix to feel and heal. There is fear, which is real, and you can't run. So, to survive you lock it all in psychologically and physically. This locking in makes us tense and makes the body sick.

Run for your life
To heal this trapped energy, it's possible to start visualising yourself running, and with that, stored frozen energy starts moving again. If there is a lot stored, the running might last for a very long time. One client felt like he could run around the world! Three times.

I usually ask a client to keep visualising till they start feeling some relief or the running slows down, naturally. A vital element in this technique is that we run towards safety.

This is one of the golden tools and your muscles, your nervous system and even your bones, will thank you for learning it.

There are different options that you can explore, to release the overcharged energy in the body:

- visualising the running
- visualising and running gently on the spot while sitting, moving legs up and down or knees towards each other
- physical running (for as long as it takes to feel a release).

The recipe for health and wellbeing – on all levels – is balance.

Back to Ben and how it applies to him. He felt relieved to finally be allowed to feel fear and run away. Ben is a strong man but having grown up in Johannesburg – where there is a lot of crime – he had to learn to repress his fear about being in a very unsafe environment. The repression could mean his fear is even more hidden than in other people that grew up in a safer environment.

I also introduced another tool to him to release fear through shaking and trembling.

Me *If you could learn to feel your fear again directly, where would your body shake and tremble? Check your hands, jaws, legs, or even under your skin.*

Ben notices a trembling in his breath, on the exhale. I invite him to feel the quivering gently, to meet the fear with compassion, to be kind to it and slow down. I don't want the fear to overwhelm him in this moment. This will help him to befriend his fear.

Me *Be with the fear like you would be with your child when it is scared.*

As he is a father, he understands that approach. If fear is met with love, it transforms.

I invite him to exaggerate the trembling and bring it into his jaws the same way we shiver when we are cold. He slowly finds out how to release more of the trembling through trembling in his arms and legs. It is a new skill to him and somewhat foreign, but he understands that this is a healthy way to release fear.

He has already learnt how to release anger in a cathartic way, so trying this makes sense to him. Finding an outlet through the body is a shortcut; it's one of the fastest ways to release old, stored energy. Still, it needs to happen in digestible portions.

Clearing fear on your own

Sometimes when we have bad dreams and wake up during the dream, the fear might be close to the surface. That moment is a good time to practise the techniques I'm mentioning. For more understanding I recommend further research on Trauma release exercises (TRE).

TRAUMA HEALING TOOLS IN ACTION

Corinne, mid-30s, Australian, single, has a full-time corporate job. When she comes for her session, she's feeling awful and worried about ending up depressed. Again. She's overwhelmed by the demands of her job and she is on an intense schedule. She has suffered from depression and is scared it might swallow her up again.

I suggest that she imagines her conscious self holding hands with the part that fears the depression. I remind her that she has come out of it before; whatever helped her before can be a resource now.

It's important, I tell her, to not go into the darkness she is experiencing but rather, to witness the frightening space and that she's holding hands with the fear.

She knows some trauma healing tools already and so she has those – **healthy control and regulation** – at her disposal.

I remind her that I am with her and that I always use my feeling sense and inner guidance system in sessions. When a client gets stressed, for example, I feel that in my body. Symptoms in the client can be dizziness, overactivation, not feeling grounded, laboured breath, coldness in any part of the body. Any of these are warning signs for me that we have left the zone of safety, the window of tolerance and need to create more safety again.

I invite her to describe whatever she is experiencing, any visuals or sensations in the body, from a safe distance.

Corinne *It looks like a black hole, and it's very close to me.*

Me *Can you move further away from it or move it further away from you?*

She manages to do that, and I check in after some time: *How does it feel to have a bit more distance between your conscious self and the black hole?*

She starts feeling calmer, which indicates that the technique is working.

Me *You can learn to be in healthy control of certain aspects in your inner world. If a black hole is too big, you can learn to move away from it. You can keep increasing the distance, if you want to.*

What does overwhelm feel like?

Overwhelm is an emergency state that needs to be attended to because, when we are overwhelmed, we are not equipped to work with whatever is arising.

Overwhelm is having too much going on at the same time compounded by the feeling we don't feel capable to deal with it. It might be too many feelings simultaneously, so they all form one big chaotic mess.

Once we feel grounded and safe enough, we can deal with a challenge. When your car is in the ditch, you need to first get it out of the ditch. You can only drive once you are on the road again. In the ditch you can't drive.

I invite her to describe anything that is starting to feel better now. She feels calmer, less emotional, more centred. These are effects of knowing that she can be in healthy control again.

This is the diagnostic stage of the work where we are 'mapping out' what she is experiencing: the black hole, the fear of it, a safe distance.

I suggest to move even further away towards a **safe space**. We have worked with a safe space before. (See *Chapter 6.1 Healing the inner child*.)

She remembers hers and describes it.

> **Me** *Visualise your safe space and imagine walking towards it, even feeling the movement in your muscles as you are moving towards safety. As you do that, feelings, like sadness, can come up. This is a good sign as it indicates the overwhelm is breaking down into its components.*

As she comes closer to her safe space the black hole starts sucking her in again and lots of sadness wells up. I encourage her to allow the feeling, to breathe into the sensations and she lets herself cry. I stay with her and wait till the wave of tears starts settling.

A lightbulb moment

As we talked, we discovered an old belief of hers: 'Whenever I feel joyous, happy, excited, relaxed, not on guard, something bad will happen.'

Negative beliefs come from past experiences and eventually become deeply engrained in our thinking. The strength of a belief is directly related to how often something negative happened to us or how traumatic the event was. Like one terrible car accident can create a fear of driving for the rest of our life. Or if something that is only a little bit traumatic happens repeatedly, it can have a similar effect. The same way water dripping on a stone eventually creates a dent.

If a belief is a 10 on a one to 10 scale, we think it is the truth. She rates this one a nine.

As we recall the time and place for where this belief got created, she doesn't remember a specific event, but she feels little, younger, a child.

This is a deeply engrained belief from past experiences and the belief now has a life of its own. The belief tells her 'Don't relax! If you do, something bad will happen.'

Nothing bad is happening in this present moment. She's sitting with me in a very safe outer space, she trusts me as we have worked together for a while. I help her to understand what is happening.

> **Me** *The old belief is there as a background program in your mind. Every time you start relaxing it gets triggered. Once activated, it creates the visual of a black hole. Which brings*

up memories of past experiences when you drowned in the feeling of depression.

Then the feelings come back and are overwhelming. All this is happening in the head while everything is perfectly safe on the outside. The good news is that old beliefs can change even if they have become automatic.

We are planning to do a basic belief change (*see page 74*) in the next session.

Dissociation

This is the description from a client of their direct experience of loneliness in their childhood.

Why can a school yard feel so cruel?

Groups of people have their heads together. A blanket of togetherness lies over each group. Snippets of sounds float through the air teasing my ears, tempting them for more, desperate to make sense of these incongruent sounds.

The air feels misty, it's hard to breathe.

They are together. I am alone with my head down and my shoulders drooping.

What would I give to know what they are talking about? I am sure they're talking about me, but what are they saying?

I feel weird, different. Not like Aldi's slogan: GOOD. DIFFERENT.

Bad different, strange different, isolated different.

I have no idea how to bridge the massive gap between me and them. The idea of walking over feels impossible. It's like those moments in bad dreams, when I try to move forward but some invisible force presses itself against me making the next step nearly impossible.

In this vacuum sounds get swallowed. Everything feels distorted, muffled, muted. No sense of belonging. A floating piece that wants to land but any maps are lost. Where is home? Lost in another universe, with planet earth gone.

Working with trauma is delicate work. There are mechanisms that get triggered, or retriggered, when we revisit a traumatic memory. Dissociation is one of those mechanisms and is usually associated with traumatic experiences early in life. It is not the easiest mechanism to understand. It is a protective mechanism that can be activated by memories or strong emotions. For the client noted about something in their experience was too much for their nervous system.

CLIENT SESSION – EMILY

A feeling of dissociation comes up for my client. She feels as if her awareness is not in her body; it's moved a few metres behind her, which leads her to feel – even though nothing has changed in our room or surroundings – that there's a vast distance between her and me.

I explain the mechanism of dissociation to her so she can deal with it better in the future.

I always make sure that the client is safe and knows they are safe. Sometimes, though, the conscious mind knows that they are safe, but the unconscious mind doesn't.

I invite Emily to describe what she is experiencing. We trace back to what was happening or being spoken about when that sense of dissociation started in the session. I also ask where she went. Dissociation can move in many directions: upward, sideward or backwards. I am yet to encounter a client who moves forward.

The different elements of the mechanism

Dissociation is an automatic pattern and in the beginning of exploring it, it can feel like we have no control over it. It happens to us and we have no choice. In time we can develop the capacity to stay present with the underlying emotions or traumatic memories which means eventually we don't need to dissociate anymore. As one element of the defence mechanism is the direction in which those experiencing it go, it's useful to ask where Emily goes when she dissociates? We need to find the trigger: what was too much? Was the emotion too strong? The memory too painful? Sometimes it's so automatic that it takes a while to truly understand the mechanism, in order to change it.

Emily, it seems, moves behind herself. The trigger was her feeling very vulnerable when her heart opened at some point in the session. I explain to her why being vulnerable can be perceived as dangerous to an old protective part in her.

'If being vulnerable had been a blissful experience in your childhood and growing up, if it was respected, you felt loved and had beautiful experiences being vulnerable you would not dissociate right now. What that means is that being vulnerable triggers a chain reaction of memories that were not good. It triggers a protective mechanism that says, 'Let's not go there, enough. Let's switch off.'

The memories of what was bad in the past, have triggered the dissociation.

Emily uncovers an issue – it has to do with anger and is the next puzzle piece. To help her I ask different questions. 'What might the memories around anger be, that you had to dissociate from? What made you angry? Was it your anger or somebody else's anger? How was anger thought of in your childhood? What happened when you were misunderstood? How did that feel?'

Eventually, she recalls a memory of her father being angry and screaming at her, when she was vulnerable. It was too much for her as a child; she coped by learning to shut down. As she understands more about when and why the feeling was created, she recognises the intelligence in the mechanism to dissociate, step away, move out of the body and go behind itself.

Me *Because you were not supported lovingly to stay with these strong, confusing emotions, you had to shut them down. There was nothing wrong with that mechanism, it's just automatic, ingrained and was necessary then. It is still automatic now but will slowly become less automatic. If you had overwhelming,* *emotional, confusing experiences as a child and nobody vali-dated what you were feeling or supported you to process them, you did the safest thing a child can do – you shut down, you checked out.*

Today the feeling of deep appreciation and gratitude in your heart towards your sister triggered the old fear of someone being angry with you. And your old protection said: 'Too much, let's check out.' And that is okay.

As she understands and validates the old mechanism, I ask,

Is it really dangerous right now to feel what you're feeling? In the past you dissociated because, otherwise, you would not have coped. And now, when strong emotions come up, it's the go-to mechanism. 'Switch off, enough, could get dangerous.' For you deep appreciation, gratitude and missing of your sister are big emotions. You could feel them for a while and then it became too much.

With practise you can learn to stay present in strong emotions longer. A helpful question is: 'Can I hang out in this a little longer, maybe a minute more, two minutes more? I am actually still okay, nothing dangerous is happening right now.' Eventually you get more and more courageous. And you are building a muscle, the 'emotional feeling muscle' gets stronger.

I encourage her to start befriending this mechanism, as her homework exercise, to see it as an old companion, a bodyguard, that means well. Also, I encourage her to become more aware of, and dialogue with it.

CLIENT SESSION – LEAH

My next client, Leah, is a female in her early 20s, who is working in an adventure company. Her boss was killed in an accident recently, and she is dealing with overwhelming grief. She loves her job, the company and really liked her boss. She describes to me that she feels like she has 'checked out' and doesn't know how to cope at work.

I explain to her that she is experiencing dissociation and that it is a valuable protection that is appropriate in certain situations.

Me *It is a mechanism to leave the body and go to another place when things get too much. It gets created in childhood when a situation is too overwhelming, and the feelings are too strong. Eventually that mechanism becomes unconscious and automatic. We will gently bring consciousness to it and understand it. We won't force or push, instead we will bring more acceptance to it.*

We discover that for her dissociation is like taking an elevator up above her head to escape the overwhelming emotion. Up there it is quiet and comfortable, protected and sunny. The visual is of a grassy paddock like a farm.

I ask, 'How intelligent is that for an unconscious protection?' As she understands that she stops judging herself for 'checking out' and not being present enough. She had just learnt to be more present to herself and her emotions through the recent sessions and was experiencing more happiness because of it. When she found herself checking out, she thought she was losing all the progress she had made to stay present with herself.

Unconsciously she went to a safe space outside of her body to soothe the part that couldn't cope with the grief. It is important to understand our places of protection and learn to feel grateful for them, to open our heart to them and treat them like a friend.

Once we can feel gratitude for an old protective mechanism it usually starts transforming on its own. It is like a computer program that updates itself to the latest version. One that suits the present time and our circumstances.

Leah understands that her mechanism is related to shock and overwhelm. I use the session to restore a sense of safety for her, in the now. At the end of the session she can relax back into her body, able to face the reality of her loss and work progressively with the grief over the next few weeks.

INNER HOLES AND WORKING WITH THEM

The Theory of Holes is a fundamental idea used in the Diamond Approach. Under usual circumstances, people are full of what we call 'holes', which refer to any parts of you that have been lost, meaning any parts of you that you have lost consciousness of. —ALMAAS

Navigating inner holes is one of the most difficult things to achieve in inner transformation. Having holes is part of everyone's inner landscape. An important step in transformation is regaining the consciousness for a certain part of ourselves that got lost in a hole. The part may be love, or value ... or ability to connect to others. Those parts are aspects of true nature. And they can be reclaimed. Understanding inner holes is one of the routes to opening the inner treasure chest.

We don't believe that there is anything good to be found in holes. We all learn to get away from and avoid them. I did too till I learnt and understood this.

One of the indicators of a hole is loneliness, which I felt a lot growing up.

When I started my inner work, I was certain that the one emotion I was happy to never encounter again, was loneliness. Yet, as I describe my journey with loneliness (see *Chapter 5.1 The art of feeling*) I wasted years because I avoided dealing with this specific feeling. Whenever

I did deeper work, I came across it. And all I did was turn away from it, into the mind or outer activities, I would comfort myself with all the great friends I had or distract myself by being busy.

When I was finally introduced to the theory of holes from The Diamond Approach, it was a revelation. One of the main teachings that I use and pass on to my clients is the understanding, that in every hole there is an aspect of true nature.

I first didn't believe it. For me loneliness felt endless, a roadblock that meant, 'turn around and go back. Nothing worthwhile here.'

And in the vast empty smog of loneliness, anything good was erased and I felt cut off from love. Why would someone choose to spend one more minute in it? That sounded delusional.

Would there be any use in delving more deeply? I found there was. There is. I saw that in the core of loneliness are abundant qualities. A few of them from my experience are sweet self-love, healthy aloneness, freedom, deep relaxation, spaciousness, peacefulness. These are definitely worth having.

What are holes and why are they there?

When we are born, we are born complete and in contact with true nature. Through our upbringing we learn to disconnect from ourselves and look for appreciation from the outside. We get value or love from our environment, parents, surrogate parents, caretakers, school.

Because we learn to look for validation and confirmation from the outside from early childhood on, we lose the ability to connect to original qualities like love or joy till we have forgotten who we truly are and can be. Every disconnection from a specific quality creates a hole or place of deficiency. This is how we end up with many holes. We develop the conditioned self and start replacing the lost qualities with imitations. Real strength becomes rigid strength, essential joy turns into trying to experience joy through outer achievements or activities. Most psychological traditions that I am aware of, talk about that disconnection being fully established between the ages of four to seven. Some people never remember their true self/ true nature once they are grown-ups. Some – who some call spiritual seekers – start the search for, and manage to remember, themselves.

Some people are motivated to remember through a dramatic occurrence – a life-threatening illness, loss of a loved one, the break-down of a business, betrayal. Those drastic life-challenges can be the wake-up call to eventually reclaim their true self.

Courage to travel in dangerous territory

It takes a lot of courage and consciousness to navigate inner holes with awareness. It is similar to travelling in dangerous territory. In *The Lord of the Rings*, for example, those seeking find monsters, demons or strange forests full of life-threatening plants to confront. Not territory for the meek.

In the Catholic religion, my understanding is that inner holes are nominated as Hell. In Hell, we are disconnected from our true nature, which, in that tradition is seen as Heaven.

Identifying a hole

There are different indications that we are in a hole. Understanding them can help recognising the fact that you are in a hole.

Mental identification

When a thought pops up about how you are – an experience, or idea, or behaviour – it can be positive, and it can be negative. Beliefs and thinking patterns are negative when we're in the hole, and they generally seem real, true. It's because we are identified with the hole. They sound like this:

> *I am unlovable; I am weak; I can't do it; I don't have what it takes; truth is an illusion; the universe hates me; I am cursed;*

> *I am shameful; I am guilty and a horrible person; I should be punished*

It truly is inner hell. Being in a hole can lead to depression. It can also lead to us making bad decisions when we are in a hole. I now remember, 'Do not make decisions when in a hole'. We have a distorted perception of reality and ourselves in a hole. It can feel like we're wearing darkened glasses and cannot see the light.

It can be experienced as an abyss, a vast space of nothingness.

Emotional identification

Typical emotions arising from an energetic hole are hopelessness, despair, loneliness, confusion, lostness, rejection, collapse, weakness and more.

We could say that the most uncomfortable emotions we experience as humans are those forming the emotional side effect of being in an energetic hole. It's a common experience to feel like you are drowning, or the world is crumbling, when you're in a hole. Yet, once out of the hole, and I'll tell you what you need to do to make that happen, the emotional climate changes completely.

When the emotional climate changes, then positive aspects – trust, optimism, clarity, belonging, love, strength, freedom, determination and more are available again.

Physical identification

When you are in a hole it can feel as if a part of your body is disappearing, like you have a hole in your chest or in your belly, in your sexual organs. It can feel like your legs have been cut off or are jelly, you have no stamina and want to collapse. Holes usually feel cold and empty in the body.

Navigating holes safely

The darkness and, often, confusion of being in a hole is something that needs exploring. In the beginning it is safer to do any exploration with a skilled therapist. Together, you identify and navigate a specific hole and then, when explored enough times, you can learn to navigate your way out of it, yourself.

After decades of experience I can now say with confidence that I can help most people in one session to get to the other side of a specific hole if they are open to letting me help them and be the tour guide. I feel like a safari guide, helping a client to not be eaten by a lion or crocodile. Or if I was a climbing instructor, I'd be instructing people how to not fall into an abyss.

There are steps that can be learnt and once applied rightly, it gets easier and easier.

Recipe for navigating holes

Step 1 – **Recognition** of a hole, knowing the symptoms, either mentally, emotionally or physically: 'I am in a hole'

Step 2 – **Meeting the hole**: describing it, turning towards it, not rejecting it

Step 3 – Learning to **relax and navigate** into and through the hole
- just by staying present or mindful with the symptoms
- slowly navigating into a hole with enough safety measures

Learning to relax into the hole

This is a main key and it's easy to say, relax! It's so hard to do. Everything in our conditioned self is designed to get us away from a hole. Holes are experienced as dangerous to the conditioned mind. They contain difficult history, memories, emotions – it's not easy to stay present with these in the beginning. We get tense, busy, distracted, speedy, resistant to avoid them.

One of my important teachers, when talking about holes said, 'It is very difficult, if not impossible, for anybody on this path of truth to navigate into or through a hole on their own in the beginning. You need someone experienced to facilitate this a few times. Eventually we can do it alone.'

Navigating this 'no-go zone' requires us to create new pathways in our inner world; we are, almost, cutting a way through a jungle or building a road in new territory. Eventually, this previously unknown territory becomes familiar.

Example: A hole shows up like a dark black abyss. The fear is to fall and crash and die like in the outer world. I always use a safety scale from one to 10 (see *Chapter 6.1 Healing trauma*) to monitor the client's subjective sense of safety. If they go below five, we stop and move back. I like to work where the safety rating is above six. Best is seven or more.

Once the client has described what they are experiencing, we come closer. If there is a fear of falling, we can use creative visualisation to have a safety harness. Or to go down on a ladder or in a floating balloon. You work it out with your client what works best for them.

This way we also activate their inner resources. They will learn to trust more and more that they can do it. I affirm that if they climbed down, they can climb up again and it follows then that they can reverse anything, any feeling they contact when they are in the hole, at any given time.

I often let them test going into the darkness and coming back. Once they know about reversing, they are usually less scared.

Then we enter the darkness of the abyss slowly, they describe everything they are experiencing. Most of the time this makes it very safe for them and they go deeper.

Sometimes, when they go into the abyss, it might appear endless yet, they eventually end up on some solid ground.

A typical experience is them saying, 'I suddenly feel like I am on a green meadow with flowers or I see light coming through the dark.' Or they feel something positive coming in, a warmth or a relaxation. Some might hear a comforting message like: 'It will be ok,' or 'It is all ok now'.

When that change towards something positive starts, I give that as much attention as possible.

In that moment I know that they are coming out on the other side of the hole and reconnecting with the lost quality, that original quality from true nature, that was originally lost.

True nature holds deep wisdom

There is a deeper wisdom in true nature that always gives us what we need most at any given time. Let's look at an example where the issue is unlovableness. Later in this chapter, I will present specific examples of how it all works, this is just the overview. So once through the hole the person will experience some form of love. They might feel love for somebody or themselves. They might feel loved by something bigger. They might even feel as if they are love, itself. It will be whatever they are ready for.

If the issue was unworthiness, they will feel a sense of value or worth just by being themselves and feeling connected.

If the issue was uncertainty, they will find clarity.

Dropping through and reconnecting

Once the first contact with the feeling of emerging is made, it is crucial to stay patient and keep bringing awareness to what feels good.

Somewhat like staying on the beach in the first rays of sun light and waiting for full day light.

It usually takes time for a very tense physical body and nervous system to slowly unwind. There might have been a deep contraction in the chest and ribcage at the beginning of exploring the hole of not feeling lovable after being rejected. When the dropping through the hole has happened and the person has reconnected with a sense of love in their hearts, the tension in the ribcage will start softening. When that starts happening, we can learn to bring awareness to the softening and not focus at this stage on the main tension.

By focussing on the first signs of relaxation we can support that process which I call a positive spiral. We all know negative spirals, where our situation gets worse and worse. In a positive spiral one good sensation leads to the next good sensation and, eventually, our whole system has recovered.

Then, when we can feel we're fully out on the other side of the hole, it's useful to spend time recognising what the essential quality is that we had lost and are now reconnecting with.

Coming back and integrating the experience

I like to give clients time to slowly come back to their awareness of being in the room, and then we talk about how the whole experience of meeting a hole consciously was for them.

An important part of the process is for them to grasp, in their conscious rational minds, what happened. This way they create their own maps for their inner world. In time, they learn to travel or navigate the inner territory with more and more confidence.

It usually is a revelation for new clients to discover that their inner territory is not, in fact, terrifying.

My main role is to help clients understand that there truly is something good to be found in the core of everything, even in the places we fear most. Even where we believe there is nothing good to be found.

I've developed a deep trust in true nature through direct experience and know that it is intrinsically good, very wise and always wants the best for us. For me true nature is what is called God in religion. Unfortunately, religion externalises it, yet it is in all of us. My truth and deep understanding today is that god is in you, in me, and in everybody.

MONICA NAVIGATING THROUGH A HOLE

My client, Monica, Australian born, late-30s, works in a corporate job, is single, and has recently returned from a four-week holiday travelling through Asia. She tells me that she feels overwhelmed being back at work and misses the connections with others she had on her trip. She feels alone, empty.

When we start exploring, I ask her to describe the sensations she is experiencing in her body.

Monica *I feel constriction in my throat and pressure in my chest.*

Monica is a newer client and we haven't explored the territory of holes yet. But I can identify what she is describing as a hole. So, I begin with basic teachings on how to navigate through a hole as explained in the previous chapter.

Me *In every hole there is an essential quality to be found. When you learn to navigate through a hole safely a new perspective and way of thinking will arise eventually, like: 'Ok, there is another hole, another void, let's find out what's on the other side. What have I been disconnected from? What will I find here?' It will replace the old way of thinking: 'Oh my god, this is horrible, I will die, there will be no end to this suffering. I will never come out once I go into this.'*

I invite Monica to feel into her inner experience of this specific void. She discovers fear of rejection and loneliness. Fear of putting herself out and finding a partner and it not working out.

Me *The way through is identifying, describing, mapping it out, understanding all its components. It is a treasure hunt. If we didn't expect to find a treasure, why would we do the work?*

There is something good in the core of this terrible place and by learning to relax with this we will find a reward.

I help her to stay present as much as possible. But it is only on the other side of the hole, that true relaxation comes.

Me *Not running away from it can feel impossible in the beginning. Learn to stay present with the discomfort by describing it – that's the inquiry part. Describe the uncomfortable sensations, tensions, thoughts, struggle or resistance.*

All her sensations are in the upper chest and arms. Her arms feel heavy and disconnected.

Me *Perhaps a natural impulse in your arms got stopped at some point? Keep describing whatever you are experiencing.*

Her legs feel rigid, her belly feels like stone – another crucial puzzle piece.

At this stage none of it makes sense to her, yet it starts making sense to me.

Me *Let yourself feel all these difficult sensations with curiosity and kindness: lead in your arms, a stone in your belly, rigidity in your calves, I know it is not an easy experience.*

I explain to her that she's describing a specific state that she needed to develop in her specific circumstances. It's a survival state. I also explain the freeze state.

We start exploring the impulse in her arms.

Me *What would they want to hold or grip?*

Monica *I want to grip onto something to steady myself.*

Me *What would it feel like if this could happen successfully?*

Monica *That would feel very good.*

Dive into the history

All holes have a history to tell. Monica and I are now able to uncover that history and in this case it's the feeling of unsteadiness as a child, where everything felt chaotic, so she needed to hold onto something. As that safe, stable part wasn't available, she froze the impulse to reach out.

> **Me** *The impulse you are feeling is natural. The need to feel steadied, to hold onto something, to feel supported, to have some ground is absolutely right. If that is not available, it feels horrible. And that's how you learnt to shut down.*

> I give an example, *If you were on a swinging bridge in the rainforest in Queensland with strong winds, and the bridge was swinging, wouldn't it make sense to hold onto the railing with all your strength to not fall?*

It all starts making sense to Monica. The need to reach out for the right support got stopped and now creates the leaden feeling in her arms. The natural impulse in her arms is still there even if it got frozen for decades. She understands that she's allowed – when in chaos – to look for something to steady her.

For homework, I ask her to practise holding onto something and explore the feelings that come up.

> **Me** *What material could you practise with?*

> **Monica** *I could visualise holding onto a metal railing.*

> **Me** *Could you physically hold on to something around your home?*

> **Monica** *I can practise holding onto the solid top of one of my dining chairs, to feel how good it feels to grip and hold onto something.*

I like that suggestion and we agree for her to experiment with that. At the end of the session she feels more grounded than she did coming in. We decide to explore more in her next session.

MAYA RELAXING INTO THE CASTRATION HOLE

This next example demonstrates how easy it can be to navigate through a hole when there is no resistance to the process. What took a few minutes for her could take a few sessions for someone else.

Specific holes have their own characteristics, like their location in the body, related thought patterns and emotions. For example, the disconnection from love can make you feel unlovable, feel rejected, hurt and unable to believe in love anymore and will most likely show up in the chest area.

One of the holes that we work with in the Diamond Approach is called 'the castration hole'. It's not gender specific but comes from the idea that when we directly experience this, it feels as if we are saying, 'I don't have what it takes'. One central aspect of the castration hole is the experience of the loss of our will. It can show up in the lower part of the body around the genital or pelvic area and/or our legs. Being in this hole can feel like the rug has been pulled out from under our feet, we have wobbly unreliable legs or no legs at all – like our strength and grounding has been cut off or castrated. It often results from not feeling supported enough by our parents or care givers in our childhood during times where we truly needed support. As an adult it can get activated when we don't feel supported. And because we are disconnected from our will, steadfastness and endurance we cannot keep going or continue with a task.

My client, Maya, has been having a great deal of trouble in her marriage. She feels unsupported by her husband and they are considering separation.

Maya is able, having done previous work with me, to feel and identify her emotions. So, I propose the next step in our work together is to learn to navigate into – and through – a hole in her inner world.

I invite her to relax her body, her breath and her attention as much as possible. We start identifying how the hole shows up. She feels it in the lower part of her body. She starts experiencing something that is very common when confronting inner holes:

the feeling of falling. I encourage her to gently let that happen, while reassuring her she is safe.

Me *I am here with you and you don't have to do this alone.*

She trusts me enough to not be frightened of the sensation of falling and to let go into it more and more. She is practising what's called '**Relaxing into a hole**'. It doesn't take very long for her to come out on the other side.

The first positive change is a sense that she can feel sunlight on her face. (The room is not filled with sunlight.)

Me *Keep allowing that.*

Eventually she feels like she is floating on water. She relaxes more and more, and I can feel that sense of relaxation with her. What she has done is to conquer a part of her inner territory.

Maya didn't fight with the feeling of falling and dropped through very quickly. Other people could struggle the whole session with resisting the falling sensation.

Conquering inner territory

The biggest challenge when considering going into, and through, a hole, is the misunderstanding that holes are 'the end of the world as we know it'.

So, quite predictably, our conditioned self is designed to avoid holes; to develop strategies to feel better by not delving too deep; by avoiding feelings or distracting ourselves.

Maya reframed that conditioning and found support within, not outside of, herself.

There is a deep sense of support inside of us, available to us if we dare to reconnect. If we dare to encounter our inner holes. Eventually holes disappear because they are simply a symptom of disconnection. Once we reconnect with the lost quality there is no more hole.

When we are reconnected to inner support we have a sense of our inner ground. We can say, 'I have what it takes'.

TIPS FOR MY 21-YEAR-OLD SELF

- You will learn to meet your inner child and become great friends. It will make you feel more whole.

- The inner loneliness you are feeling will become a great teacher and a doorway to unimaginable treasures.

- You can look forward to discovering trauma healing skills. All those tools are gentle, easy and efficient. They can heal even the worst memories.

- You will confront some frightening, empty and deficient places in your inner world but with the right guidance you will learn to navigate them.

PART 7

INNER GUIDANCE

INNER GUIDANCE SYSTEMS: WHY THEY MATTER

So always remember, whatsoever I say to you, you can take it in two ways. You can simply take it on my authority – Osho says so; it must be true. Then you will suffer, then you will not grow. Whatsoever I say, listen to it, try to understand it, implement it in your life, see how it works, and then come to your own conclusions. They may be the same, they may not be.

They can never be exactly the same because you have a different personality, a unique being. Whatsoever I am saying is my own. It is bound to be in deep ways rooted in me. You may come to similar conclusions, but they cannot be exactly the same. So, my conclusions should not be made your conclusions. —OSHO

This quote is meaningful to me and is the essence of this chapter. Another favourite Osho saying, 'If you follow your own understanding, you follow me' confirms that he was a true Master. False Masters create fear in their disciples, and dependency. Osho wanted us to be free, to be ourselves and drop the shackles of limiting conditioning.

Reconnecting with inner guidance is the foundation for living a conscious life and for taking right actions in harmony with ourselves and the environment. I am passionate about the development and use of inner guidance systems – for many reasons.

One is that I dream of a conscious world where people live with an open heart, where mindfulness, kindness and compassion are not something we 'try' to find but they become, indeed, normal attributes. Where the mind understands the transformative power of the heart and uses it to create a better world.

In my vision of a conscious world we all feel and understand our emotions and find constructive ways to release emotional baggage; to transform emotional energy into positivity. Right living includes respect for our physical body and needs. In such a world, communication will strive for mutual, healthy respect and solutions to opposition and hostility.

Healing intergenerational trauma

I was born in Germany, twelve years after the end of World War II into a country that had suffered the complex trauma of defeat, physical and psychological damage to the country, and damage to its sense of nationality.

I was exposed to the desperate and convoluted suffering for so many individuals from the protracted hostilities. Both sets of grandparents, and my parents, were deeply affected by the War. It was a very different place to the world that I see as my ideal – a conscious world, of right-living people.

At times, when I did deep inner work, I felt as if I was there at the time. Of course, I wasn't yet born, but the more I study and learn about human psychology, the more convinced I am of the existence of intergenerational trauma.

It is the idea that a legacy of trauma exists and it is transmitted from one generation to another in multiple ways. I carry the responsibilities I feel as a result of my history in the writing of this book. I feel I'm the one in my family who's waking up. That with this chance for healing myself, I can pass on healing to my parents, my grandparents. Perhaps, too, I can lose, or at least, loosen, the German trauma from World War II that I carry in my bones.

In my adult years, I realised I carried guilt for just being German, particularly among my Jewish friends. The feelings were unexpected yet seemed to be surfacing from the depths of my unconscious. I am committed to healing intergenerational trauma in myself and not pass it on any further.

My father's family

My father's family lived in East Prussia on a big property in the grounds of the school where my grandfather taught and was headmaster. In their large garden, close to a small river, they grew vegetables and raised chickens – a setting my father described as paradise.

When my paternal grandparents' property was seized by Russians in 1945, they left their belongings behind and travelled by foot – parents and five children – to eventual safety in Germany. It took many years before they felt secure and safe again.

When I was a baby, I was cared for by my paternal grandparents – both my parents had to work outside the home. Having a screaming new baby, along with what was probably PTSD from the War, was, I think, the last thing they needed to contend with. Though devoted grandparents providing shelter and food, I imagine they were overwhelmed with their tasks and, probably, mostly unavailable emotionally.

My mother's family

My maternal grandparents had, by then, already suffered through a terrible accident. My grandfather had been on a freight ship bringing German soldiers and war refugees home from the East coast when, at the end of World War II in 1945, the ship was bombed.

Only 334 of the 7000 people onboard survived. My grandfather was one of them. People were crammed into chambers like cattle but he was lucky enough to be on the upper deck when a bomb hit. He grabbed a wooden ladder and survived hours in ice cold water before he was saved. When he returned home, he buried his trauma deep inside. I don't believe he ever got any professional help to deal with it. At 76, he died of a 'weak heart'. Despite having experienced this War trauma, the Opa I remember was a very loving man with a heart of gold.

My maternal grandmother, alone with two young children during the War, had only infrequent visits from my grandfather as he was out at sea. She had depression and ongoing stomach problems, which I believe were a result of the War. It's hard to know how the War affected my parents – young children at the time.

Still, everybody suffered. And that suffering was passed on, either consciously or unconsciously. I believe that because of that I always dreamt of a world without war and I am committed to making this world a better place.

Relevance to inner guidance systems

The deepest question I still have about that time, those events, is how a whole nation followed a character like Hitler; how millions supported and enacted such horrific policies. The vile propaganda, the anti-Semitic hate speech, the inconceivable cruelties of systematic eradication not just for Jews but for gypsies, and homosexuals and people with disabilities... unthinkable atrocities occurred. As I grew up, I was astounded that any person with any level of open heart and normally functioning mind could have colluded with, believed, or agreed to such devastating, criminal policies.

My understanding and deep belief is that had everybody listened to their inner guidance system, World War II could not have happened. To have a functioning inner guidance system, the heart needs to be open. With an open heart you feel others, you simply cannot do harm. The crimes that were executed could not have happened.

My deeply held belief about this, fuels my passion for finding truth, for being in contact with our true voice – the voice of the heart and/ or gut.

Tools for making better decisions

Listening to our heart, our gut, using the compass of joy, trusting that we have an in-built truth detector are all aspects of a functioning inner guidance system. The tools in this chapter are all extremely useful for accessing, understanding and beginning to use your inner guidance.

When I use inner guidance, I pick the pieces that resonate with me in anything I read, learn or study and discard the rest. As no one recipe suits all, I encourage you to find those elements of a specific approach that are right, revise and hone them and keep them in your toolkit.

Head, heart and belly: Differences

Learning to discern where an inner voice or message comes from is crucial in making the right decisions. Head, heart, gut/belly: what are each of these centres and their voices?

The voice(s) of the head

Ever hear the voices in your head? Or, put it another way, who doesn't know the craziness or madness of the mind? Sometimes, the mind can sound like a busy marketplace, with lots of voices talking over each other, arguing even, as in a heated discussion.

One of the main voices you'll hear is that of the superego – an aspect of our inner dialogue that's generally negative and judgmental and can be very sharp, very critical. The superego is such an important aspect that it's covered in some detail in *Chapter 2.1 Opening to the mental territory.*

Voices in opposition

The head lives in the realm of polarity and opposites. The to and fro happens in the climate of fear, doubt, worry and judgment. Generally, you will find the mind has opposing voices vying for supremacy. It can sometimes feel as if we're stuck in the city in rush hour traffic, horns tooting, drivers impatient, pushy, scared, exhausted. It's a busy place.

Understand the madness

When dealing with the cacophony of opposing voices, it's useful to have a technique to counter it. One such way is meditation and it's useful to have a regular meditation schedule. It is a very positive step to finding some peace and calm in your life. However, when you begin meditating, you won't find peace first up! You'll encounter the madness of the mind. I've heard it said that if we wrote down every thought we had for just one day, we'd all be candidates for institutionalisation. The mind is mad.

Persevering with a meditation practice will bring the head/mind into alignment with the heart and the belly. It then is able to serve us; it becomes a personal assistant to the real bosses – the heart and the gut.

Meditation is not easy. It's hard to witness the madness of the mind. It's brave to not jump up and run away. Fortunately, it is possible to persevere but we need patience, commitment and an understanding of what to expect.

Let's begin by saying that you may not find peace 'just like that' when you begin meditating.

The voice of the heart

The heart is compassionate, loving, supportive and always wants the best for you. It takes practice to listen to it. It can be quiet, even hidden by the louder voices coming from the mind. By learning to open your heart and developing your feeling sense more and more, your heart voice will get clearer. Your true heart works towards greater fulfilment of your life's purpose. *Chapter 4.1 Meeting your heart* will hopefully have given you a deeper insight into the voice of the heart.

....

GUIDANCE OF THE HEART: A MEDITATION

Whenever we have a decision to make, whether it's big or small, it is immensely useful to consult our inner guidance. Using our own heart as a feedback system is very powerful, and this heart meditation is something I've used – since I was introduced to it some 30 years ago – for all my important decisions.

It works to clarify the yes and no of your heart.

Think of something you know you love and feel the response in your heart. It will be through visuals – a colour or bright light; a sensation – feeling of expansion, opening, uplift, warmth; or through a sound – you may hear a resounding 'Yes'.

Now think of something you know you don't like at all. A place, a person, a food that doesn't agree with you, a bad smell. Now connect with the response in your heart. It may appear as a dark colour or clouded visual, feel like a contraction, withdrawal, sinking feeling, coldness. It might arrive as sound – a 'No' or warning.

Once you're clear what those yes and no signals are, you can start delving more into the specifics of the particular decision. You're practising making a true decision for yourself. To do that you need to ask the right questions.

Start each question with: 'Will I love myself, if —?'

*Practise with smaller decisions, which food to eat,
whether to go out or stay home one night.*

*Once you're more comfortable and trust the signal
of your heart, apply it to bigger decisions till you
expand it to life-changing decisions.*

My yes signal is a feeling of warmth expanding in my chest. A very strong yes can feel like a happy child jumping up and down in excitement. My no signal is a feeling of contraction deep inside my chest and a sinking feeling.

....

The heart always means well

One of the qualities of an open heart is that it creates and welcomes connection; connection from us to everything around us, people, animals, the environment. An open heart is not capable of exploiting anybody or anything. It invariably thinks of a situation in terms of win/win.

I've found that the heart will always guide us, signal the right direction according to our true path and purpose. The head leads us to take practical steps.

Once our head understands the nature and capability of the heart and respects it, it can come into alignment with our heart. The head follows up on the decisions made by the heart – like a good personal assistant.

Who's talking? The gut or belly voice

The deepest truth we can hear or get in touch with is that from our being centre.

The terms gut or belly voice, gut instinct, voice of being or being voice are interchangeable and describe guidance from the being centre. The being centre's nature is to be present with precisely what is happening at any moment, and to always be relevant. It focusses on one thing at the time and has the authority of a wise being.

The being centre makes decisions that are crucial for our growth and in our highest interests. It can tell you to leave a relationship, perhaps one that might look good to others, of which others are, even, jealous. Still, your deepest guidance is telling you to leave because this relationship is not aligned with your deepest truth.

Your being might tell you to stay in a difficult relationship because you are growing from the experiences. Messages we hear from being are often not what the mind wants to hear.

The being centre will only 'speak' when needed and when it does, my recommendation is to trust it.

When I heard the voice in my belly talking to me for the first time, it honestly felt like I had swallowed somebody who was lodged in my belly and speaking to me, as if it were a separate person.

One morning, in the ashram in India, I was walking in our Multiversity plaza to make a booking for a training. Suddenly I heard a voice from inside myself. It was clear; it was loud, but it wasn't anywhere in the outside world.

'Be as if you are not!' the voice said. Wham, that's it.

There was no introduction, no explanation. I certainly had no idea what that statement meant but it started me exploring. This was more than 25 years ago. Since then, I have had lots of insights and experiences in relationship to that statement.

There isn't a black and white answer to this guidance. It is an invitation to deeper states of consciousness. Simply put, it means get out of your head and follow the truth of your being. It's advice is to not follow the conditioned voice in my head.

As I had been listening to Osho for more than 10 years by that time I recognised the quality of that voice. I have learnt to listen to it since.

What I know about the belly/gut voice

I've learnt that I can't manipulate it. The voice will speak when it is important for me to know something, but it can't be forced. Once I was better at listening and trusting its authority, I tried to have a conversation, a dialogue, as I would with a friend.

For example, when I had stayed in India for four-and-a-half years, I knew that it wouldn't be forever. So, every season I tried to get an idea from my gut voice about how long I would stay. And each time, for years, the answer was the same.

'You are not meant to know! Once it is time you will know. Everything will fall into place once the time has come. You will know when to go, where to go and what to do! Everything will unfold.'

This damn voice could not be bent or manipulated or forced into obedience. I tried it every half year when a new season started, and I had to commit to being on the new program. As I was running groups I wanted to know if I should still go on our group schedule or not. But the belly voice didn't care, didn't listen, wasn't interested in the practicalities of it all. I ended up staying from Oct 1993 to March 1998.

My inner voice was also right in the end. Three months before I left it spoke to me again. One evening, in the stillness of our Buddha Hall, where we did our evening meditation, I heard the voice again. This time, the instruction was different.

'It is time to leave,' the voice said.

My reply: 'What? Now? No. I don't want to go.'

Timing is everything

For years, the answer had been that I didn't need to know, yet! Then when I'd stopped being interested in when I should leave or even, if I should leave, the voice spoke. I went into a very big sulk. The inconvenience of such stupid timing! It was so wrong. My friends, who agreed with me, tried to convince me to stay.

I tried the question once again, part of me wanting to hear that I had a weird astrological transit and should wait it out. But the gut voice repeated the instruction. And the gut voice has an authority. It was wise, convincing and I couldn't argue against it.

I had different images over the years when I try to imagine what my gut voice could look like. One was of a traditional Zen master. Someone quiet, stern, yet compassionate, wise and knowing, who speaks only when appropriate. He would never gossip or chitchat; would rather sit or stand in silence than say just anything. Another image was of a Native American medicine woman, who was very wise and compassionate. My understanding today is that these are images that help us connect with inner wisdom the same way tarot cards can do till we learn to trust ourselves fully again.

When I think of the voice now, I realise something in me had always recognised its intrinsic authority. Was it a commitment in my soul for this lifetime to listen to the gut voice? It is certainly what's guided my specific path. Against all odds, again and again.

Timing and circumstances: All is true
Everything my gut voice said would happen, came true. Things fell into place after I stopped resisting. So, I announced that I'd leave, passed my job on to someone trained to do it, and got ready to leave the ashram.

I had only ever left the ashram once a week, if at all, for a dinner outside and via a 10-minute rickshaw drive. There had been no life outside the confines of the ashram, no internet or television or outside news. Effectively, I rarely left my small village and now I was leaving the whole country and a way of life.

Ongoing work
I was invited to offer the groups I'd been running in the ashram in other countries. I travelled through Russia and Finland back to Germany. This meant I had the chance to earn some money on the way back to Europe. My plan was to settle somewhere in or near Germany – maybe France. I thought it would make sense to be closer to my family of origin again.

Little did I know that other plans where in the making once again. This time, those plans involved me going far away from Europe and not to India. These new plans were to take me to the furthest point away from Germany to the then 'foreign country' of Australia.

Negative emotions and gut instinct

Are those emotions that we have labelled negative useful to us? Are anger, rage, disgust, repulsion, for example, worth understanding? Well, yes, they can become the fuel or raw material for us to develop a stronger gut instinct. This, in turn, helps us make good decisions.

Think about how disgust, for example, might be a useful emotion. When we are disgusted by the smell or taste of a food, we reject it. It is a strong no to ingesting the food and it often means we're saved from a case of food poisoning! This is a healthy impulse and protects us.

The same is the case with emotions. Someone's behaviour or

energy can make us feel disgusted – a good warning sign if we pay attention to it. In situations of manipulation, for example, where someone talks sweetly but perhaps too sweetly, can you feel something is off? Can you tell when someone is lying, or pretending, when it's not truly obvious?

Many of us become disconnected from certain emotions because they have been labelled as bad. A sickened feeling, for example, is a natural response in our guts to something that we then recognise as simply not ok for us. This is as real a feeling as a positive, affirming, bubbly feeling is a 'Yes' to what is happening to us. Feeling sickened or being happy are both expressions of the capacity to feel.

When we repress 'bad' emotions all the alive energy contained in them is not available to us. When we allow these so-called bad emotions, we become more alive, grounded, stronger in ourselves, empowered. We have a deeper trust in ourselves.

Through allowing ourselves to be in touch with all emotions we reconnect to a deep knowing and inner wisdom that can otherwise get blocked.

Learning the art of feeling and understanding how to defend from the superego are important stepping stones to developing a functional guidance system. That's why this chapter is at this point of the book. All the other chapters are elemental to developing healthy inner guidance.

TRUSTING YOURSELF: A MEDITATION

This meditation allows you to connect with your inner wisdom.

Imagine you are sitting on a rock or patch of earth and you feel supported by it. Feel the solid ground under you. Know that whatever you're feeling is supported and allowed. No emotion is wrong or unacceptable. All judgment on any emotion dissolves. Any emotion can surface, open and be there with you. It expands in the body and moves naturally.

Then, imagine the rock is filled with deep existential wisdom. Imagine you can hear it, listen to it. What would

the wisdom of the rock say to you? How would you feel
if you were totally trusted and trusted yourself?

Another simple yet powerful way to practise this is to ask:

If I trust myself right now, I know that ...

You can repeat it out loud to yourself or start a special journal,
your own book of wisdom. In my experience starting a question
in this way connects me directly to my belly and deeper knowing.
I regularly share this technique with clients with great success.

Compass of joy

This is such a beautiful tool and I learnt the term for it from the late Barbara Marx Hubbard, a great teacher.

Imagine you are trying to find your way in uncharted territory? Imagine you're making decisions about which way to head? You'd be well served if you had a compass. This tool – the compass of joy – is a way to find direction in life based on your truth.

The measure, the 'true north' is a sense of joy that manifests as a happy emotion or a good feeling in the body, or both, in relationship to life choices. It will always signal to you the right direction.

The more joy you feel around any choice or decision the more you are on the right track in the moment as well as for your general wellbeing.

Superego – opponent to truth

The purpose of the compass of joy is to help you become more you. The aspect of the mind that does the opposite of that is the superego. It's directed towards protecting you from possible, or imagined, pain and that keeping the status quo is the way to do that. The superego always uses memories from the past as warnings, that create worry, doubt and fear – always aimed at stopping you from expansion, growth. The superego wants to prevent you moving towards your full potential as that might mean taking risks and facing uncertainty.

The superego is not malicious, but it is interested in functioning, and prevailing. It is not interested in joy or truth or wellbeing and can ignore the fact you may be miserable in your present situation. The superego will try to survive and guide your behaviour.

Truth detector; Crap detector

We all have an in-built truth detector as well as a crap detector. However, we may not have developed the capacity to use those detectors. We might receive the feedback on a very subtle level. If we don't train ourselves to listen to these finer signals, the feedback is easy to ignore. Prerequisites for both – having the capacity and recognising the signals – are an open heart and the capacity to feel.

It's also vital to have the courage to be honest with yourself. How do you know when you are being honest; that something feels really true to you? Or, how do you know when something feels false, or you hear a subtle or full-blown lie? How do you notice if someone is pretending?

The more you notice and listen to these signals, the more you develop your capacity to differentiate truth from its opposite.

One of my signals of my truth detector is a sensation of subtle to very strong goose bumps in different parts of my body. Sometimes it is just a deep knowing in my belly.

GOLDEN TOOL
RELIEF AS A TOOL OF GUIDANCE

Our being, our true nature has a signal for us, to let us know we're on the right track. That signal is the feeling of relief. Each time we think of something that is right for us, a decision we need to make, something we need to say to somebody, something we need to do, we feel relief. This signal of inner guidance is one I trust completely.

Whenever a client starts feeling relief in a session, I make them aware of the feeling so they recognise what it means, and learn to trust it more.

EXERCISE

ANY TIME YOU FEEL RELIEF, STOP AND:

Become aware of the feeling of relief itself.

Notice what the relief is about.

Choose to trust whatever the relief was about.

Let's say, for example, you're thinking about changing your job and each time you consider doing it, you feel relief. Consciously choose to trust your decision. Then let the head – the personal assistant – take the necessary steps to set the job change in motion.

In order to trust relief as a tool for inner guidance it's important to get to know the feeling itself. Use all the tools from *Chapter 5.1 The art of feeling* to turn towards it and notice how it shows up in the body. In time you'll learn to recognise it faster.

CHAPTER 7.2

ADVANCED GUIDANCE TOOLS

NOW YOU HAVE THE foundations to start making good decisions, here are more complex tools that can deepen your clarity.

Two doors: Deep decision making

This technique is a superb method for getting clear about a decision when you/your mind can see both sides and you're pulled in opposing directions. If you have three different options you can do the same exercise with three doors.

Begin by visualising an open space in nature. Stand at a fork between two pathways leading away from you towards two separate doors, which are five to 10 metres down the paths. Each door represents one choice. Then, see and feel yourself walking up to one of the doors.

Door 1

As you walk towards it, allow your consciousness to shift and put you into the world where you have made one of the choices in question. You are making this choice.

When you reach it, put your hand on the door handle and open the door. As you step inside, know you'll be stepping into the consciousness of that specific choice. Once inside, allow yourself to observe and take in what you perceive through all your senses – there may be an image, a colour, a sound, a message, a word, a song. You might feel a sensation or emotion in your body.

Does the place feel comfortable or uncomfortable? Expanded or contracted? Light or heavy?

Sometimes it's clear, as soon as you enter, whether it feels good or not. If you're unclear step a little deeper into the space behind the door. You're walking on a timeline into the future behind that choice.

This is a way to access the deeper knowing that some part of us, our inner wisdom, has. Unless there is a specific psychiatric condition that is active in a person, we do know what's good for us and what isn't.

Stay behind Door 1 till you have enough information. Then, step out and walk back to the starting point. Clear your mind and, starting afresh, walk towards Door 2.

Door 2

Follow the same process. Once your Door 2 time is complete, walk back to where you started.

Here, spend some time feeling and thinking about the insights that arise as you compare the experiences behind both doors. Most of the time, this process will clarify the question you began with. If you're not yet clear, you can add another door.

In a session with my client, Gina, it was necessary for her to open one further door. This is how she described the process.

Opening a new door to inner guidance

I have always desired to live with passion and purpose. It often got in the way of enjoying my present reality – I tended to dwell in possibilities, in the future. It led me down paths that filled me up, momentarily, when I thought I had perhaps discovered my purpose. Then, shook me to the ground when it came not to be. The hardest part of this was the pressure I put on myself, and my sense of being lost.

Then, I had a breakthrough in a session. It was about exploring whether a slight change in my current work situation would reveal my long-desired dose of passion and purpose. Karima posed that I visualise two doors, behind each were the two different scenarios.

In each situation Karima guided me to see not just the present, but the future – one month ahead, six months, a year ahead. Unsurprisingly, neither of the doors held thrilling options, nor varied much. For a flicker of a moment, I thought maybe this idea of finding your true path, living with passion was made for just a small percentage of people.

That thought evaporated as quickly as Karima said, 'Now I want you to open one last door'.

I didn't know what to expect but what was inside that final door has led me – to this day – to live both my passion and purpose with a knowing I had never experienced before. As soon as I opened the door a visual immediately unravelled. Me studying Traditional Chinese Medicine. The vision was in massive detail. I could see the university, I could see my life and each future timeline – from one, to six months to a year – expanded without any effort. It came so clearly and surprisingly with such certainty, it almost involved no sensation at all. Until that time I have always been both visual and sensory; every visual was created with equally as much sensation. Yet this time, the message was so clear it seemed beyond needing either. No other potential existed and so, no reassurance through sensation was needed.

While knowing this was my path, it didn't prevent the trepidation when I applied to do the course. However, like no other time in my life, I was driven by a knowing that was more powerful than any worries or fears. Making this decision at 26 to start a four-year degree, continue living at home, alter the way I live to make space for it all was the greatest decision of my life to date.

Sacrifice is no longer sacrifice as it simply makes way for passion and purpose – more fulfilling than anything else. Being guided to listen to my deepest truth has shown me how the universe is aligned with your truth, allowing it to be fulfilled in so many ways. As much as I want to say the experience is like being surrounded by perpetual fireworks and celebrations, it is simpler than that, it is grounded in knowing without reassurance.

Now, even after a long hard day, my mind can't coax me out of this knowing. If I get troubled by thoughts, I simply remind myself of what I am doing and a peace like no other, arises.

Sitting in inner council: Making conscious decisions

As we are complex human beings with thoughts, emotions, memories, conditioning and lots of different parts that can be contradictory, making a life-changing decision can take a long time. Renee, a female client in her mid-50s came to see me when she had a momentous decision to make.

A good marriage for 30 years and then …

Renee wanted to leave her marriage after 30 years. She and her husband had two children and Renee waited till her youngest child was married to act on her decision. It had been a good marriage, but she had grown out of it and wanted to explore more freedom, learn more about her spirituality through travelling, and be open to other relationships.

Renee wanted to make a conscious decision and look at it from every aspect. She wasn't suffering before she left. It took about two years till she was ready to leave and, in that time, we looked at many elements of the relationship, mainly her opposing needs for security and for freedom.

We used a technique – talking to an inner council – that is part of voice dialogue, Gestalt work and likely other modalities. We explored the question through inviting different parts and voices of Renee to speak via an inner council – a process built on the understanding that every part in us has a right to be there, to speak and be listened to.

In the end, awareness itself – such as the director of a company listening to the opinions of employees might have – is what helps make the choice. The awareness would lead to an informed decision about what's best for all involved.

Renee fluctuated between two essential human needs: security and stability and freedom, adventure and exploration. Many people make a strong decision to choose one over the other. For those who choose security it's inevitable that the freedom wing gets crippled. And with freedom chosen, the security element is threatened. Yet to live healthily and consciously, we need to learn to allow the expression of both needs.

Renee allowed different parts to have their voice, listened, took her time till she knew what the right decision was for her and till the letting go was easy – like a dry leaf falling off a tree. She and her partner had a conscious separation and stayed friends.

Future selves

Connecting with a future self is another great tool in making the right decisions. The following quotes from two clients talk of the benefits of a technique called Future Integration.

> When I came into the session, I believe that I was feeling very lost and not sure what I was doing/where I was going in life. During the session you had me stand up and visualise my future self standing ahead of me, making me see and feel all the aspects of my future self including the energy.
>
> Then in my own time you told me to begin walking towards my future self until I stepped into her and I was her. I remember feeling so light and all fears and confusion dissipated, and I was so certain I was on my path and that I was the same person that my future self is and there was just the sense of wholeness and completeness. That feeling that everything is great, and everything will be ok, you just have to trust. —GEORGIA

> In one of our early sessions I was struggling to communicate effectively with my husband. We went through a visualisation of me and how I see myself in 12 months' time and how that vision of me would hold my hand during the talks I had with my husband. The session gave me a visual representation of where I wanted to be, how I wanted to feel and, realistically, how long it would take to get there – it's never going to be an overnight process.
>
> Feeling the presence of this version of me made me open to the possibilities of change and feel safe as well as giving me the confidence to talk to my husband, knowing I must make changes within myself rather than try and change him. —JULIA

I use this technique – called Future Integration – in a lot of sessions. It comes from NLP and I learnt it through my Journey Practitioner Training. When a change has happened, either from one or many sessions, it's vital that we get a chance, as well as a way, to anchor that and, effectively rewire our brain to consolidate the healing of an issue.

Future integration

If, for example, a client has worked with their sense of unworthiness in a session and the outcome has been a healthy feeling of self-worth. I'd want to take the opportunity to anchor that positive feeling.

At the end of their session I'd take them through a guided visualisation, a future integration, where they imagine themselves in the future. It doesn't usually take more than five to seven minutes.

My questions would be, 'Who will you be in a week/month from today with the issue healed? Who are you when you are feeling confident? How would you think, act, behave?'

I'd invite them to describe themselves in one month, three, six months and then a year.

Once the future self – one year from today – is imagined I ask the client to visualise a timeline with 12 lines, one for each month. Their present self can see the future self at the end of that timeline. Then, they are to imagine that the future self turns towards them, gets very excited to see the present self and starts waving.

Then the future self walks towards the present self until they are face-to-face. Sometimes I'll do the countdown from 12 to one.

At this point they might hug (in imagination) or they might talk. The future self might offer guidance, for the next few days, about how to integrate the learning.

When that exchange is complete, there's one more step.

I ask the client a question.

Me Where would you like your future self to be? Merged and inside your heart right now? Or outside of you? If outside, where is the most supportive position? On your right? Left? In front? Behind?

I let the client test each position and choose the one that feels most supportive.

CLIENT SESSION – EMMA MEETING HER FUTURE SELF

> **Me** *She's joining you in the now and she's right in front of you. She has travelled down the timeline to be there as a support, a companion; someone to discuss what is good for you and what isn't. She's that extra buddy, a best friend who can help you make the right decisions because she knows that you can become her. She is you in the future. How do you feel with her there?*

> **Emma** *My future self has a golden glow around her and, well, she's radiating happiness. So, I feel calmer, now, in my present self.*

> **Me** *Can you imagine her becoming an internal great friend? You know, when we do this inner work, going back into difficult aspects of our childhood, healing old wounding, learning to feel emotions that were too big originally, we need all the support we can get. The future self can become a great support as she knows you.*

Emma is looking forward to having that extra support, to feeling comforted by the close presence of her future self. It makes it easier for her to stay with the pain that she's confronting in her sessions at the moment.

> **Me** *Is it easier to consider letting go of the pain in time knowing who you can become?*

After this imagining, after we included the future self, Emma was less scared of meeting the pain. Because of that, she was able to face more and more of the pain and, at the end of that session, felt relaxed and trusting.

INNER GUIDANCE IN ACTION – CLIENT SESSION LISA

I am working with Lisa, a client, on how best to make decisions. I let her know that we'll include the head, the heart and the being in the process culminating in a Future Integration.

When I use all three, I call it the **head – heart – being structure**.

Lisa is choosing a specific question for our work on decision making. 'Shall I move in with my present partner?'

Me *The mind chatters and offers options. It's the researcher, it lives in duality, presents opposing sides and can argue for both. This is the nature of the mind – to give input through thought processes. So, here, we'll retrain the mind to become the best personal assistant to your heart and gut. Let's start with the for and the against, for your question.*

Lisa elaborates arguments for and against moving in with her present partner. This part is more an emptying out and exhausting of the mind.

Me *The answer is not always right there. Sometimes you stay with a question till you get a deeper clarity. All of that will get clearer as you start experimenting with listening to your inner guidance.*

Connect with the heart: Clarifying yes and no

Me *Bring your attention to the chest area and we'll connect with the heart chakra. Think of something you know you love – a thing, person, activity, place or food.*

Lisa chooses resting on the couch, on the weekend, reading a book and having a cup of tea.

After teaching her how to identify the yes signal in her heart (See *page 286, Guidance of the heart*) she describes her yes signal as a feeling of warmth spreading in her chest.

Her no signal is a coldness and a contraction in her chest.

I share a story with her of a friend where the signal of the heart possibly saved her life.

Me *My friend was in Mumbai and planned to walk some- where, when she suddenly got a big no signal from her heart, warning her to not go the way she was planning. She listened and walked another way. Later she learnt that there had* *been dangerous riots in that part of town, and she would have walked into the middle of it. People were killed in the riots. Rationally she couldn't have known the danger, yet the wisdom of her heart protected her.*

Me *So, Lisa, let's use the yes and no signal for your question. Ask your heart to help you. 'Heart, help me make the right decision.' Feel the response in your heart.*

Lisa felt a yes in her heart in relationship to moving in with her partner. Her signal was the visual of yellow sun light radiating from the centre of the heart and a sense of happiness spreading in her chest.

Connecting with being

In her session, we listened to the arguments in Lisa's mind – some were for, some against moving in together. We did, though get the yes in her heart. So, I now teach her how to connect with the voice of being.

Me *The voice of being, unlike that of the chattering mind, only speaks or gives guidance when it's essential. The signal can come through as a deep knowing.*

Physically the being centre is located five centimetres below the navel and, the more present you are, the stronger this centre becomes. It can start pulsing and be experienced as a gateway into some vaster dimension. It can help you feel solid and grounded.

While the heart functions in the vibration of love, the being centre is pure isness, beingness. It, like the heart, always acts in your highest interest. The messages may come in poetic or symbolic ways. You might be really stressed, full of questions, for example. The answer, from being, when you ask for guidance about what to do, might be, 'Just sit down and look at the sky for a while'.

Lisa is able to connect to her being centre. When she thinks of moving in with her boyfriend the yes in her heart is supported by a deeply grounded and relaxing feeling in her belly.

Me *What would the guidance from your belly, your deeper knowing, tell you if it could speak?*

Lisa *Give it a go, moving in with your partner is the right choice.*

After evaluating the arguments in her head, the clear yes in her heart and the yes in her belly, she decides to move in with her partner.

Future integration

Lisa now understands how the head – heart – being structure works in decision making, so I take her through a future integration to help her mind become more familiar with the new technique.

Me *Imagine doing this questioning process each day, for a week. Then, try for four weeks. You will get more and more insight into how it works, how you and the process will work.*

Now imagine doing it for three months. What could be the benefit for you of doing this?

Lisa *Sharing it with others.*

Me *Now think six months into the future with this as part of your toolkit for life. What is the benefit you can sense at that time?*

Lisa *More clarity.*

Me *Imagine a year from today. It is normal by then. How will it feel a year from today?*

Now see the future you one year from today on a timeline and let her turn around and see you. Let her walk towards you with a lot of love and appreciation.

Wait till she's standing right in front of you. What does she look like? Feel like?

She is another puzzle piece of your inner guidance system. Does she have any message for you? What would she say to you?

Listen to her. Allow any other contact. Maybe a hug. You can keep her with you. Ask her to stay with you. It's you in your future. She can show you your potential, point you in the right direction.

The future world?

I believe anybody should learn the head – heart – being structure. Imagine a world where everybody listens to their inner guidance. I believe very strongly that this movement towards knowing our true centre and acting out of that, would make for a harmonious future for … well, the world!

But we can start with us.

EXERCISE

HEAD – HEART – BEING STRUCTURE

Make a list of questions that are relevant to your life.

Find a quiet place and ask yourself one question at a time.

First tune in and listen to the mind and note its answer or answers.

Then bring the question into the heart. If you get a visual answer note how the visual makes you feel. If it feels good, it is a yes.

If you need more clarity about a question, take it down into your gut.

Eventually this process will be so familiar and successful for you, that it will become your established way to make decisions. It will be a safety zone for you and something you can trust more than outer advice.

Talking to wise beings

Connecting with wise beings is another tool for getting the right guidance for our specific path. I will keep this as simple as possible. The easiest way to make sense of the technique of finding that guidance, is to see it as another very helpful visualisation. I have my own beliefs about wise beings and so I'm sharing my direct experience. But it doesn't mean this is right for you.

An incident with my mum comes to mind in relationship to this. In recent years our talks have become deep and all inclusive – I speak my spiritual language, talk about energy, inner child, emotions. One day, I wanted to talk about past lives, and I asked her, 'Are you open to the concept of past lives?' When she said no, that the idea was a stretch for her, I accepted that, and we talked about something else.

I do the same in sessions. If a client doesn't want to use a technique that I recommend – any of them – then I respect that. I was trained to doubt till I found my own truth and understanding. It's what I want to encourage you to do with anything in this book. Of course, if a technique doesn't resonate with you, please skip it. I am mentioning this particular one because it is something I use a lot for myself and in sessions.

Woo-woo disclaimer: You're about to read of communication with beings who are not on or of this earth. My experiences with this left me in no doubt of those events. I can understand, though, how this might seem rather outlandish to some readers. So, in the interests of 'full disclosure' I alert you to this. You'll read about people being in touch with other-worldly beings. It's interesting, and, for those in the sessions, was transformative.

My experience with wise beings

I have come to believe, over decades, that there is a realm of raised consciousness around or close to the earth and within that realm there are beings that we can make contact with. That realm is benevolent, evolved, caring, and it prays for us – as individuals and as humanity in general. Wise beings are available in that realm, and their participation is always in response to an invitation from us, they never impose themselves on us or demand anything. That is my understanding through direct experience.

Wise beings are also called guides, guardians or mentors in different modalities I am trained in. I will use the term wise beings. The best definition of a wise being I have come across is this: *it is someone whose wisdom you trust and in whose presence you feel safe, supported and loved.*

I have seen and felt angelic presences, gods or goddesses, guides and wise beings around me for the past thirty years. I feel the presence of three, with whom I speak regularly. I can ask them questions and I can get their feedback. I have made contact with a guide called Galadriel during the Hoffmann Process. He was an interesting one as he looked like a strong bodyguard or gladiator. He made me feel very protected. Since then I know that wise beings can appear in any shape or form. Some clients perceive them as fairies.

For some people their wise being will be the God of their religion or faith. It can be an ancestor or family member who's died.

The wise being can be a character from a movie like Gandalf, from 'Lord of the Rings' or Yoda from 'Star Wars'. It doesn't matter what size or shape the wise being takes; it is the consciousness behind it that matters.

I believe that, when we are in need and would like intervention or help of some sort, it is possible to reach out to a wise being. That's where prayer comes in. Prayer in my world is defined as 'asking for help'. I have done what I can, and I don't know what else to do, please come and help me.

I enjoy reaching out to my spirit guides in our sessions, and this is something I've incorporated into my days when I don't have time for meditation or reflection. Just a quick 'can you help me out here?' while I'm on the go is sometimes all that is needed. —ALICE

CLIENT SESSION – DREW MEETING HIS GUIDES

Drew, a single Australian successful businessman in his mid-forties, is a client who I have seen for more than 10 years. Drew is committed to the work and his pursuit of truth. When sessions have been challenging, or revealed confronting ideas, Drew's stayed the path and, even though it was difficult territory at times, has not run away.

In this session he mentions wanting to connect more with his guides. He has two, that he is aware of, a male and a female guardian. Drew participated in a seven-day transformative process a few years earlier and connecting to a guide was an intrinsic part of the process. His male guide was the one he connected with at that retreat. The female was further away and the connection not yet as conscious.

I was thrilled – connecting to guides has become normal for me. When we connect to our inner world, we use the same five senses as we do when we are connecting to the outer world: looking, sensing, listening, smelling and tasting.

To build on what has already become normal for him, I ask him how he connects to them and find out that he feels them and sees them, somehow – inner vision is not necessarily like outer vision. It can be very clear or blurry or just puzzle pieces like seeing the hair or a garment. Whatever puzzle pieces are available to the conscious mind, you build on that.

I ask Drew if he already talks to them or has conversations with them – what I call 'dialoguing'. He says no and, as I know from my experience how much talking to your guides deepens the connection, I feel excited about the prospects for Drew.

Drew had two core questions. 'What have I come here to do? Who have I come here to be?'

I teach him that dialoguing with his male guide is the same as talking to a friend. The dynamic is one of asking questions and then listening to the answer. If an answer doesn't make sense yet, then ask more questions, till it does.

Drew says hello to his male guide and asks if it is ok to talk to him. 'Ed' is excited and responds, 'Finally'. The dialogue unfolds easily, and Drew receives helpful guidance.

The female guide, whom Drew had felt was far more distant, is also happy to come closer and have a conversation with him. Both give him insights about different areas of his life. The dialogue with the male guide is about work, how to become a better boss, how to talk to a difficult employee, how to set healthy boundaries. The female guide talks to him about his mother and how to heal and improve the relationship with her.

In my experience, guides always come from compassion and wisdom, they never judge, push or force. They invite, suggest, activate our creativity, intuition and allow us to become our best self.

They support opening our hearts, learning to feel, understand, forgive. They want us to evolve and be well. In Drew's case, the guides encourage him to have more fun and laugh more. They note that he can get very serious and give him permission to enjoy life more.

Guides are always encouraging, supportive and kind, in direct contrast with our internal judge or critic, the superego, which will create a contraction within us. Guides create expansion in us, an uplifted feeling. They're in direct relationship to our internal true nature and have the same beneficial influence on us as listening to our inner guidance system.

This is the end of the overview of all the tools that are helpful in connecting with inner guidance. When you do your inner work though, finding the right therapist or a combination of therapists and healers to work with, is crucial.

Look for the right teacher

The therapist/client relationship is unique. For me the therapist–client dynamic becomes a co-creation. The relationship can be compared to a friendship or, even, a romantic relationship in that in order for it to be healthy, you need to have the right fit. Though, of course, the therapist doesn't come to the client for help. They are in a supporting, helping, facilitating position and so the term 'asymmetrical' is useful if we're comparing it with a love relationship.

The client receives the support and the agreed exchange (essential part) is the payment from client to therapist. What a therapist has to offer needs to meet the needs of the client.

If someone who is dealing with a strong drug or alcohol addiction might come to me as a client, I would not be the appropriate therapist. For the integrity of the relationship, I'd say that I am neither trained nor have personal experience in those areas. So, in that regard, what the client brings to the session needs to fit the skills of the therapist.

My training ensures that whatever I offer by way of direction or insight has come from my own direct experience. I never teach a theory or anything I haven't tested myself. If I can relate to what is being presented to me, I am naturally better able to help.

My role is to empower clients and help them find their own understanding. I teach them the same tools that I'm sharing with you in this book. Once their inner guidance system is activated, they are on their right path and their life can unfold in the right way for them. In the words of Osho, 'Create your path while walking'.

Besides individual sessions I highly recommend participating in longer transformative group processes like Path of Love or The Hoffman Process. These generally week-long processes with group and individual work allow an acceleration in our transformation or personal growth.

Whatever the process, it is possible (and likely, with a good therapist or group) to make significant progress, by attending to our mind, heart and being, towards feeling good in the world, happy to be alive and true to one's self. This client's answer to a question about the process was very significant for me; it made me laugh and feel proud.

The most important tool used I find is actually that I'm doing all the 'work' myself in the sessions, there really is very little work done by Karima. This sounds negative but in fact is the most empowering thing to learn, that we all have the power and knowledge within us at all times. —ALINE

TIPS FOR MY 21-YEAR-OLD SELF

- Know that you are wise. Trust that all the guidance and wisdom you need is available deep inside you. Once you listen to that your life will move in the right direction for you.

- There is an intrinsic plan to live your life at its best. There is only one version of you, and it is unique. Just like each flower is different from another, so are our life plans just for us.

- No one can know exactly what is right for you, but you. This applies to food, lifestyle, life choices, job, friends. Everything.

- Only follow outer guidance, tips, advice if it resonates with you.

- Trust your own feedback mechanisms. Your mood can guide you. For example, if you start feeling grumpy, inquire whether you've overstepped your own boundaries and need to say, 'No'? If your body starts aching, maybe you need to slow down and rest? If you feel restless and anxious maybe you need to listen to your heart and not your head?

- Choose the **right friends**. Friends that nurture you, where you feel seen, met and understood. Never follow people that create fear in you or make you feel smaller or 'less than' in any way. Being with the right people will make you feel better or bring the best out in you.

- You have your mind, your body, your emotions and your deeper spirit. They are all equally important.

- **Balance** is the answer to everything. Everything is important in the bigger picture; nothing is not important.

- Find a **good therapist** that you can trust.

PART 8

FROM BECOMING TO BEING WHOLE

THE MOVEMENT

THIS IS THE END of us travelling together to understand the process of *becoming whole*. I hope you have a solid tool kit now for your ongoing journey of inner transformation.

What have you learnt?

- to understand and befriend the mind
- the right attitude for inner exploration
- to identify the superego and how to protect yourself from its judgments
- to develop a healthy relationship with your physical body
- awareness of your breath
- to connect with your heart and use its intrinsic qualities for inner transformation
- to understand and transform your emotions
- to disengage from guilt, shame and unworthiness
- to heal the inner child
- the basics of trauma work
- to navigate inner holes and deficiencies
- to start trusting your inner guidance systems.

You are well set up now to continue, and deepen, your journey of becoming whole. This is the part we *can* do to come out of fragmentation, separation and disconnection.

The journey continues and unfolds. In the following pages there will be those elements of wholeness that all of this has been preparation for. This is the most important discovery of inner work: knowing that we are already whole. Being whole.

True nature is always whole, undisturbed and indestructible. But all the steps to becoming whole are prerequisites to discovering and enjoying the truth of being whole.

True self

At the beginning of the book in Chapter 2.4, I introduced a basic map for the inner world with four layers: conditioned self, shadow, true self and true nature. Now, I want to highlight the true self (also called the pearl or personal essence in the Diamond Approach) as it is this true self that's our personal expression of the universal aspects of true nature.

Consider, for example, how we express the universal qualities of peace and love. When I experience either of them in myself, they become my personal experience. I know how love feels in my physical body, how it makes me think and feel. All of that is unique and personal to me. It might be similar to your experience, but it will have my personal flavour. It might make me think of my Mum, my husband or friends I love.

In my experience, the development of the true self is one of the most beautiful aspects of inner transformation as it symbolises growth in such an appealing way. We become, as a 'pearl', more and more mature, integrated and content. The inner pearl, like an outer pearl, keeps growing. Every life experience – easy or difficult – is part of the ongoing development of the true self. When you are in contact with the true self you will feel, 'This is really me'.

Fluidity of selves as an aspect of wholeness

Today I had a client whose issue was how to combine all the different parts of herself. She is a businesswoman, a mother, a wife, homemaker, a friend, a daughter ... and more.

Her struggle how to bring these parts together easily led to over-whelm. It made me think of my own learning around having so many different parts.

One of my greatest teachings while living in the commune, was

Osho's dedication to teach us many practices to dissolve the old beliefs about hierarchies, superiority and inferiority, with which most of us entered the ashram.

He insisted we were all equal; he helped us see that money or status, degrees, social background, nationality weren't criteria by which to value a person. We are all human beings on planet earth. I loved those teachings and the way I imbibed a sense of equality. My heart's name for him is 'the Master of dissolving separations on all levels', internally and externally.

In the ashram I learnt about fluidity of selves. In any day, I would flow from being a cleaner in my apartment in the morning to being a therapist or group leader during work hours to being a friend during mealtimes.

I had, at some point, also been the person checking entry passes at the ashram gate, seating people in the evening meditation, running an office.

I was looking for love, dating, finding love, girlfriends.

I had fun with friends in the evening after dinner with a drink and music.

Some days, I might be crying from heartbreak at lunchtime, then dropping into stillness in the evening meditations. All of that created a sense of fluidity between my inner selves. I had a very strong sense of being able to be all of it and everything. Nothing was higher or lower than anything else. All these different parts coexist in me and create a bigger whole. Like many puzzle pieces can make one big, beautiful picture. Some parts are bigger, some smaller but they are all valuable.

In my life now, I flow from cleaning our place in the morning, getting it ready for work, being wife to my husband and housewife in the kitchen. I am a therapist giving sessions, gardener on my balcony, secretary to my business, bookkeeper, girlfriend to my friends, daughter to my mother, sister to my brother. Renovator.

I am meditator, carer of my body, recipient in my own healing in sessions or trainings, student in the Diamond Approach Australia.

I love the feeling of it all coexisting in me, and everybody.

I enjoy flowing between all these parts, these different expressions of my personality. I love them all. I also experience fluidity in my emotions now. They can come and go.

The feeling of fluidity is part of my experience of wholeness. It is something that has grown over decades of inner work and keeps unfolding.

Psychology of the Buddhas

In the Mystery School we used a technique called the 'Psychology of the Buddhas' to identify the many different parts of our inner world. We would make a card for each part, like Tarot cards, choose a picture from a magazine or paint something, and write a description as well as give the part a name.

It was a great way to understand and accept all the different aspects of our whole being. One part could be the pusher and another, the lazy one; one the adult and one the child, the efficient part and the relaxed part, the meditator and the romantic. I loved being curious and discovering more and more aspects or parts of my inner world.

Wholeness as an all-inclusive state

A map of the inner world that I use a lot is that of comparing it to the ocean. The ocean has a surface and depth and many layers in between. You can swim on the surface with your head above the water or dive to the bottom. It is the same on the inner, we can stay on the surface or dive into our core. There are many layers in the inner world. We can be operating from either layer at any given time. As we learn to travel from one to the other – the surface to the core, for example – the pathway becomes more and more flexible and open.

When you have done inner work for some time, a very interesting state can emerge. For me it started a few years ago when, on an eight-day retreat, I became simultaneously aware of all my layers – I could identify thoughts in my head, emotions, body sensations, and the stillness of true nature deep inside.

It was a vertical experience – from surface to depth – like feeling all the layers in the ocean simultaneously. Before that I lived in one layer or another. I believe experiencing this is a natural evolution and part of expanding consciousness. It feels great because no part of us has to be excluded. There is no judgment or division and only a beautiful sense of wholeness.

It has since become a term I use a lot to describe a specific perception or way of experiencing myself. During and after that transformative retreat, I experienced the least resistance I have ever had to *what is*.

I simply met each experience with the same level of presence and openness; I didn't reject anything. This understanding deepened beautiful states and transformed disconnected states quickly. I assume that will continue to deepen.

Objective awareness

Deep in our belly there is an objective awareness of the nature of life or presence that doesn't judge anything. What is *is*. Once any resistance to what is dissolves more and more, an awareness can arise, where every expression of human behaviour – good or bad, creative or destructive – coexists simultaneously. The awareness is not a judge. It is like a solid and immutable rock. The landscape around it changes, seasons come and go, people and situations come and go. The rock lies, in the same spot, unaffected, undisturbed. It just is.

The ongoing journey is organic, natural, never ending and never boring.

On top of our internal awareness are all the other dimensions of us. There's the physical body with whatever is going on in there at any given time; the emotional body with its ongoing changes and the mind with its ever-changing thoughts.

These processes occur simultaneously. Deep in our core we can experience objective presence, and at the same time, the mind can have an opinion of what it likes or doesn't like, what it is for or against; what it labels as good or bad, right or wrong.

True freedom

What I have understood since is that I can be aware of different layers at the same time. I have depth and a surface and everything in between. Everything coexists at any given moment. Each level can be. For example, I can be peaceful in my core, my body could have aches and pains, emotionally I might be affected by a conversation I had, and my mind can be planning what I will have for lunch. It all coexists and instead of only being aware of either the mind, the body, the emotions or my being, I am aware of all the levels simultaneously. And there is no conflict, a still centre and a busy mind can coexist. The more we open our hearts, the more we are able to be aware of opposites.

It is like an ever-expanding awareness that includes more and more aspects of our experience.

And this understanding has grown organically, I didn't have a goal to experience this kind of awareness. It grew, developed and unfolded naturally. Once you commit to your own journey it starts taking you on a ride.

It is guided by a deeper wisdom that we connect and reconnect with, as we go along. The more we commit to it the stronger it gets. Like a good relationship. Trust and connection deepen and grow the longer you are together.

Like a healthy tree growing deeper and deeper roots, the trunk getting bigger and stronger, its branches solid. Roots and trunk supporting the changes on the surface. Leaves growing and falling, fruit ripening and falling off, flowers appearing and disappearing.

Wholeness as vertical alignment – The Inner Pillar

The concept of vertical alignment is important and helpful. When all the chakras are open and connected with each other, they start aligning. The inner experience of that can be of a channel of light or uprightness. When all chakras are aligned it feels whole, peaceful, harmonious, empowered.

The chakras have different colours. Imagine the inner pillar as a wooden stick on a base and onto it you place coloured balls that each have a hole in them. The order of placement is the order of the chakras. From red at the base, then orange, yellow, green, blue, purple and white. The lower pillar are chakras one to four, the upper pillar four to seven.

The inner pillar can also be experienced when head, heart and being are in alignment.

Energy in the inner pillar flows in two directions: up and down or *ascending* energy and *descending* energy.

The easiest image to understand this is the image of a tree.

The roots represent the base chakra, the trunk represents the inner pillar. Branches, leaves or fruit represent the crown chakra, our connection to something bigger.

Another image I often use is an elevator that connects seven floors in a building.

Wholeness as balance

When I studied metaphysics, I was interested in the concept of each chakra having its own 'breath'. The same way our physical body breathes in and out all the time, so every chakra has a movement or polarity.

Let's take the heart-chakra as an example. A movement or polarity in the heart is giving and receiving love. Giving is the in breath or the movement towards another. Receiving is the out breath or the movement towards ourselves. **Both need to be in balance in order to provide a feeling of health.** Just as the physical body cannot just breathe in or just breathe out.

Second chakra in and out breath: Liking and not liking

The second chakra or feeling centre in the belly, is linked to the movement from being together to being alone. The in breath is saying, 'I love being together' and the out breath – 'I want to be alone, I need my own space right now'. This is also called 'liking' and 'not liking'.

I didn't understand the need for movement between both poles until I was in my metaphysics training. When we think about relationships, most people tend to be locked into one state. Some people always want to be with others, cannot be alone. Some people prefer being on their own; can't handle being with others (this is represented by the 'hermit' archetype).

But the healthy measure of it is that our need for togetherness, or aloneness, is like a spectrum and we are all somewhere on that range. Where we live on this spectrum comes from our conditioning or indeed, perhaps a mental illness. We learn to identify with one position and lose our flexibility to allow both.

Balance is the answer to wellbeing

The same way the physical body needs to both breathe in as well as breathe out, we need the movement and flexibility to express both needs. Sometimes we love to be together, to share, talk and engage.

At other times our idea of heaven is going to bed early or crashing in front of the TV with a blanket, alone. Both these needs and behaviours are real and important if we are to be emotionally healthy.

Yet, we are likely to have one side more dominant at different times. A way to find out which one is dominant at any given time is by asking, 'Would being together right now give me joy or would being alone be preferable?'

There is a freedom in having the answer to what state we prefer. And, there is no set time for our specific in or out breath. Each can last for hours or days. Some people who never 'breathe out' in a relationship, might suddenly, after months or years, leave their partner to finally have their own space again.

What happens when we don't listen well

It's important to recognise the symptoms that occur when you are not listening to your need for balance. You can feel grumpy or irritated, depressed, negative, angry, claustrophobic. The solution is, though, that you will know what your signal is once you start listening and learning to trust yourself more.

In a healthy relationship both partners have the space to allow both needs. It is always easy when both are in an in breath. That's when we really love being together, it is super yummy, you can't spend enough time together, which is very common in the beginning of a new relationship. Or both need space, which is easy again.

The obvious challenge happens when both parties in a relationship are in different polarities. Yet, when each party understands this, there is no suffering anymore, as you know the other just needs some space. It is not a rejection and it doesn't mean they are going to leave you or don't love you anymore.

Everybody has an in and out breath in each chakra.

I was so relieved when I learnt this. It gave me permission to listen more to myself and express a need to be alone sometimes to my love partner; it didn't mean that I don't love him anymore.

Direct experience of the balance

There were about 50 people in my metaphysics study group and the massive group room was divided into halves and a line was drawn in the middle. One end of the room symbolised the in breath, the other the out breath. We were invited to walk around the room and explore different positions and then be conscious of what feeling came up; taking account of whether there were judgments and objections or memories in any location.

Eventually, we were asked to find a spot that symbolised our preference, the place that is most familiar, our conditioned status quo.

I felt comfortable with the area of being together. At that stage of my journey I was not yet familiar with being alone or taking my own space, saying no to the other, having healthy boundaries.

Now, 28 years later I am happy to say that all of that is integrated and familiar. I love my own space, quiet time, unplanned time or what I call 'doodling' – spending time seemingly aimless. I know when I need it and can ask for it. It is a non-issue now. My husband and I both respect that in each other.

In traditional upbringing we learn to identify with one position and believe that is who we are.

Reclaiming flexibility

Towards the end of the group exercise we kept walking around, from one end of the spectrum to the other in order to experience it all and reclaim lost flexibility.

Applying this ability to reclaim each segment in our life is a slow process. Once we understand how to listen, we identify when our need for an in breath or out breath changes from one to the other. Then, we slowly learn to communicate it. Eventually, it becomes second nature.

Learning this was a revolution for me in the beginning and I have shared this with many clients over the years.

One New Year's Eve in India I experimented with this. I wanted to be alone and not go to the big party. I listened to myself and very much enjoyed being alone on the roof top under the beautiful, smooth Indian night sky. I felt a happiness that I hadn't known before. Until then, my conditioning had been to think that I had to be with people.

The feeling sense becomes our biggest teacher, it will always give us feedback.

Recently one of my clients felt claustrophobic in her relationship and needed more space. After I taught her this tool and she understood it, she decided to give herself time alone as a birthday gift. It truly was a gift.

This is how another client describes her understanding of the in and out breath of the belly.

I had an AHA moment while discussing my change in attitude towards my boyfriend. We had only been together three months, but I was so incredibly happy with this person on the whole.

Then, I began to notice something very worrying. I started to pull away and react negatively towards affection. I didn't know what was different between us, but my changed behaviour just didn't make any sense.

Due to a rostered work schedule my boyfriend was home for a month at a time and then away for a month. The last month he was home we spent the first two weeks together every night and day that I could, when I was off work.

But soon, though I realised I needed to have at least some time to myself following those two weeks, I couldn't understand why I had had such a strong physical reaction.

What I came to understand was that during those two weeks I was 'breathing in' so much that I never had a chance to 'breathe out'.

The concept of the in and out breath made so much sense. My inner wisdom was trying to tell me that I needed space to be alone after two extreme weeks of togetherness.

I understood that my reaction was a healthy one; one that would allow my relationship to progress in the right direction. I need to figure out how much 'breathing space' I need to balance myself and schedule that regularly, so we didn't arrive at the place where I couldn't take any more affection. —AYLA

Wholeness as male/female balance

I have done a lot of training around the idea of Inner Man/Inner Woman. What is important to say in this book is that each of us has a male and a female aspect – also called yang and yin – inside, these need to come into balance. When this 'inner relationship' is healed, we experience more wholeness and come out of fragmentation. See more detail in *Chapter 2.4 The power of yin for inner transformation.*

One of the original definitions that I learnt in India was that enlightenment was achieved when male and female aspects are in complete balance. And it makes sense to me.

There are many different ways to experience wholeness. Trust yourself and notice how you experience it.

Connecting with true nature

I am sure true nature won't stop surprising and fascinating me. A favourite way to strengthen my connection to true nature is to be alert to my inner states. I notice any moment I experience a positive state of mind or body, emotion or energy. I try to deepen my connection with it by becoming aware of it and staying present with it. I focus on what is already good inside.

It is possible to cultivate our connection with true nature by spending more time with it – in spiritual traditions this is termed embodiment. Once certain states, like love, are already familiar, our experience of them deepens over time.

So, I recognise essential states as they arise. If I feel a moment of peace, I turn towards it and consciously allow it to develop. I liken that to having a good friend come and visit. If they did, I'd sit with them and share a cup of tea. If, however, I ignored the guest, they might visit less often. If they felt welcome, they'd drop in more.

True nature is the gift that keeps giving. I believe I'll be marvelling at the beauty of true nature till I die.

The more we learn to connect to true nature, the more we start to experience the benefits of different universal laws intrinsic to true nature. One of these laws is called the optimising force. What that means is that in contact with true nature we get guided through impulses, intuition or knowing how to live our life in accordance with our true potential. True nature supports us in a gradual and patient way, never judging, always encouraging. We can make as many mistakes as we need to, till something is learnt.

Four stages in our relationship with true nature

There are distinct stages that we can experience in our relationship with true nature.

A client recently mentioned he was feeling very flat so we explored what lay behind the feeling.

We discovered that he needs time out; his job has been very stressful. When he describes the flatness, it is a very soft energy in front of him – it's ivory coloured. The more we explore, however, this flatness is not a negative state at all. It becomes clear that it's an essential state, part of true nature that he experiences as joy. Without the extra delving, he might have missed a great opportunity to discover a new quality in him.

When aspects of true nature arise, I let clients choose their own word for it. It's such a strong personal experience and part of creating a map in our mind, of our inner world. It's vital to find our own names for inner experiences.

As we keep exploring, the client deepens into the feeling of joy and goes through different stages.

Stage 1 'I am aware of it,' he says. *There is joy.*
Joy starts wrapping itself around him; he can feel it gently pouring into his body and fills him more and more. It is a calm relaxing joy that makes him feel he is on the right track and that everything is, and will be, ok. His experience is different to a common inner experience of joy as a golden bubbly champagne-like quality.

Stage 2 'It is in me, I am it,' he says. *Joy is in you, you are joy.*
We stay present with this beautiful quality and it keeps expanding more and more to all parts of his body. We explore how it makes him feel in the physical body, the emotional body and the mind. As the joy expands, his physical body is relaxing more and more and his mind changes from stressed to optimistic.

Stage 3 'It is,' he says. *Joy is all there is.*
In many spiritual traditions this state is also called beingness or isness. My client starts feeling formless and all he experiences is an exquisite sense of presence. His awareness of the body moves to the background. He is completely one with the experience of joy.

A Japanese haiku, a short form poetry in three lines, makes sense to him: *Sitting silently, doing nothing, and the grass grows by itself.*

Stage 4 'It is me,' he says. *Joy expresses itself through you.*
This state is the true self or pearl, where true nature expresses itself through us.

We are deeply connected to who we truly are and our expression in life comes from that place. I wrote a poem, many years ago to express my experience of this stage.
Walk me, talk me, look through my eyes.

Misunderstanding darkness – positive and negative darkness

I am mentioning this now as it is one of the most common misunderstandings in relationship to true nature that I have ever come across in myself and my clients. Misunderstood, you can miss an incredible treasure.

I will never forget how excited I was when I discovered the difference between positive and negative darkness.

Until then, I believed darkness was bad. Growing up I feared the darkness of the night and projected negative things onto darkness. One of the projections came from the Catholic Church, the belief that 'darkness is the devil' and experiencing it makes you 'evil'.

My first conscious explorations of darkness happened in Pune. At some point, I participated in a 'darkness meditation' which took place in a completely dark room. We all looked into black space for one hour being sure to allow each and every projection till everything settled and deep peace descended.

I was also introduced to darkness as part of teachings in the Mystery School on the nature of the heart. I learnt to experience positive darkness in the centre of my heart. It felt strange when – for the first time – I walked around on a sunny day in the ashram with an awareness of darkness as deep restfulness in my heart.

Positive darkness – also called black essence – is peaceful, free and empowering. It is a gem of true nature. It helps us to discriminate the false from the real. I like to call it the 'truth essence'. It is also meant to balance the endocrine system, all the glands and hormonal system. And that makes sense to me. It is one of the best natural sleep remedies to visualise black.

When clients come across inner darkness, I always ask, 'What is the feeling quality?'

Our feeling sense shows us the difference: positive black generally feels comfortable, friendly, smooth and silky, it doesn't create fear. Negative darkness – often a symptom of a hole, inner deficiency or disconnection – can feel cold, scary, contracted and empty.

GOLDEN TOOL
MEETING THE BLACK

When you come across black on the inner, don't approach it with a judgmental mind. Be neutral, find out freshly. Ask, 'How does it feel?' When it feels positive or comfortable, it is worth exploring more. If it feels negative, only explore it if it doesn't overwhelm you. If you need help, reach out to a trained therapist.

I am a fan of black essence. The following meditation has become one of my favourites.

MEDITATION:
FALLING AND DISSOLVING INTO DARKNESS

Lying down on your back, relax your body, mind and breath as much as possible. Imagine falling and dissolving into an ocean of black energy below you. Allow it to get vaster and vaster the longer you relax into it. Stay in that experience till there is a calming or settling in your mind, body and/or emotions.

True nature: How do I live from there?

Once we are in contact with true nature we can learn to live from that level of consciousness.

The shift from the conditioned self to our true self is commonly described as the movement from doing to being. In true nature, we are. Being is enough, there is no doing needed to prove anything or get anywhere.

Living in connection with true nature means we move from reacting to responding, two dynamics with which we humans interact with the world.

Reacting, which comes from the conditioned mind, is the way we operate when we're on automatic, act the way we are programmed to act.

Responding is a gradual process that enables us to be in touch with our true nature. It involves behaving in a conscious way in the present moment or situation.

With practise we learn to recognise the difference between an automatic reaction and a conscious response. So, it's helpful, if we want to get closer to the dimension of true nature, to ask ourselves, 'What is my conscious response to this situation? What is my truth here?'

A conscious response would come via a check in with the wisdom of our heart, or our inner guidance system.

A concrete way to understand where this might happen, for example, is if someone says something that hurts you or you felt misunderstood by those around you, and you have an automatic reaction. That could be to shut down, to withdraw, to decide to never talk to this person again, to lash out and hit back, to defend yourself ... There are many options.

However, the wisdom of your heart – which is connected to true nature – might guide you to ask the other what they meant by their hurtful comment or further explore why they didn't understand you. In doing this, you might expose your vulnerability, saying you felt hurt, or risk not getting clarification.

While those actions might be risky, there are alternatives. Listening to your heart would lead you to knowing what the right step is. It might lead to the other person apologising or clarifying. It could, possibly, deepen the relationship and bring the two of you closer.

Your heart *will* tell you what the right action is.

Benefits of doing the work

How do I now see personal growth?

Well, a healthy vision to work towards for any personal growth is to be able to **like or love your life**. To be in a place where you look forward to planning and designing your week, making things work for you while you also ensure the right balance – of work and free time, social and alone time, exercise, fun, creativity, food, sleep.

Plan for your normal regular week to be attractive so you look forward to your life as it is.

Ask yourself what balance means to you. Start with the pieces that are already working and make that your **baseline**. Think about where you relax and where you feel well. Then, add other elements and tweak your week; do it step-by-step.

One of my clients says that more time outside in nature, walking, spending time on the beach would create more balance. She likes to feel grass under her feet or the sand between her toes. Can you relate to that? Is it in your week's list?

Once you have realised what's important, you need to want it. Then, to schedule all you've chosen to do till healthy habits are established.

My client decided to spend some time outside of her office every lunch time and to schedule a walk with a friend. This small and simple addition to her weekly activities made a large difference to how she felt about herself.

When you start experimenting, don't feel pressured. It doesn't matter how long it takes to identify and incorporate those elements you really want into your life. With sustained effort and enough leeway, you're bound to find the balance and enjoy your life.

When we don't need to escape our lives anymore, that is presence in action.

EPILOGUE

THIS MORNING I WAS reflecting on my journey of writing this book, as the completion of the manuscript approaches. I remembered my intention as described in the prologue.

Writing was new to me when I started. In my work as a holistic therapist I felt very experienced, mature and confident; yet, like a baby as a writer. For the first two years I worked with a writing mentor to bridge that gap and find my writing voice. I loved the moments where something was birthed, words emerged on the screen describing what I was trying to convey. I felt proud when I had my first experience of 'writers block'. It felt like an initiation, I became part of the tribe of writers. At the end of those two years most of the content and overall structure of the chapters had become clear to me. I understood why I am writing this book and who my readers are.

I'd collected many different documents filed under chapter titles. It was a conglomeration of pieces that were never written in any specific order.

And then the journey into editing started. I was looking for a midwife for my 'baby' to be born and found one. We had discussions about content, shape and intentions and worked step-by-step on making the chapters coherent in themselves, joining all the separate pieces and resolving repetitions, allowing each chapter to 'become whole'. We decided on formatting issues along the way, headings, subheadings, working towards a coherent manuscript.

For the past three years I have witnessed myself in sessions. The writer in me watched what I did, named the tools and made sure they were in the book. In the gathering process – the first two years – I would take notes at the end of the session about what needs to be in the book. And write a piece about it later. In this final year of writing, the inner witness was more like a secretary going through a checklist making sure all the important tools were mentioned.

This week I walked a sacred labyrinth with a friend in a beautiful park close to where I live. It was symbolic of my writing journey. You start and have an idea of the end – your published book. And during your journey you find yourself in twists and turns, sometimes not knowing if you are moving forward at all, or possibly even going backwards. Moments of impatience arise. 'Damn, I just want to reach the centre, can't I cheat and find a shortcut?'

And then back to the next loop, fully absorbed in the experience of that moment putting one foot in front of the other or seeing the trees.

And when you least expect it, you are in the centre.

I am not there yet, the manuscript is not quite complete even if chapters are starting to 'hum', but there's no more jolting or stumbling in reading through, everything seems to flow.

I have compared writing the book to friends with climbing Mount Everest. There were times I felt out of breath, lost my mojo, the process appeared endless. I thought, 'I will never reach the top'. Other moments where I enjoyed the 'climb/walk' while writing or reading a chapter, like revelling in the view of a beautiful landscape from a mountain path.

I understand the creative process more than ever. What painters must feel creating a complex painting like a mandala, or a composer creating a piece for an orchestra with many different instruments that need to harmonise with each other.

I have tried to put 42 years of learning and experience into words.

I hope I succeeded in creating a piece of art, instilling a fascination with your inner world and a confidence that you can find your way in the inner labyrinth. Knowing that there you can marvel at the beauty of true nature at the core.

I hope you feel inspired to activate your inner guidance system, discover your true self and learn to trust it. So it can guide you, from hereon, to bring harmony, fulfilment and purpose into your life.

My wish for you is to become your own best friend or in the words of the Buddha **Be a light unto yourself.**

MEDITATIONS, EXERCISES AND GOLDEN TOOLS

Time to stop

- Be present now 2.1
- Remember a message 2.1
- Basic sensing meditation 3.1
- Finding the right breath 3.1
- Meditation for connection 4.2
- Name an emotion 5.1
- What makes you feel safe? 6.2

Meditations

- Making the shift to sensing/feeling 2.1
- Releasing tension on the out breath 3.1
- Four calming techniques 3.1
- Simple heart meditation 4.1
- Self-forgiveness meditation 4.2
- Anger release meditation 5.3
- First contact with the child 6.1
- Guidance of the heart 7.1
- Trusting yourself 7.1
- Falling and dissolving into darkness 8.1

Exercises

- Basic belief change visualisation 2.3
- Dialogue with tiredness 3.1
- Connection between emotions and breath 3.1
- Awareness of shame 5.7
- Any time you feel relief, stop 7.1
- Head – heart – being structure 7.2

Golden tools

- Worst and best exercise 2.1
- Smiling at the unknown 2.2
- Easing tension 3.1
- Bubble of light 4.1
- Appreciation exercise for couples 4.2
- Overwhelm and chunking things down 5.9
- Moving away in overwhelm 5.9
- Rerunning painful memories to a good outcome 6.1
- Moving the projection screen 6.1
- What do you love? 6.2
- Running from danger towards safety 6.2
- Relief as a tool of guidance 7.1
- Meeting the black 8.1

FURTHER RESOURCES

Barbara Marx Hubbard https://en.wikipedia.org/wiki/Barbara_Marx_Hubbard

Brandon Bays, Founder of **The Journey**, World Leading Speaker on Cellular Healing and International bestselling Author of *The Journey, Freedom Is* and *Light in the Heart of Darkness* www.the journey.com
- **Journey Practitioner Program** https://www.thejourney.com/journey-practitioner-program/

Byron Brown *Soul Without Shame* https://www.diamondapproach.org/public-page/soul-without-shame

The **Diamond Approach** is a modern day teaching of inner realisation developed by **A. H. Almaas**, author of 20 books about this spiritual path and director of the **Ridhwan School**, from where the Diamond Approach is taught to students around the world
- **Diamond Approach Australia** https://diamondapproachaustralia.com
- **Ridhwan School** https://www.diamondapproach.org
- Their brilliant spiritual online library https://www.diamondapproach.org/glossary
- **Theory of holes** https://www.diamondapproach.org/public-page/theory-holes

Eckart Tolle *The Power of Now* https://eckharttolle.com/books/

Elaine Aron https://hsperson.com/test/highly-sensitive-test/

Enneagram: https://www.diamondapproach.org/glossary/refinery_phrases/enneagram-and-diamond-approach

HeartMath Institute https://www.heartmath.org

Krishnanada and Amana Trobe *Face-to-Face with Fear* https://www.learningloveinstitute.com/downloads/face-to-face-with-fear/

Optimum Health Clinic England
https://www.theoptimumhealthclinic.com

Osho homepage https://www.osho.com

Osho online library https://www.osho.com/osho-online-library/the-books
- **iOSHO** app https://apps.apple.com/au/app/iosho/id1528372736

Path of Love https://pathretreats.com
- Two of my original trainers, **Rafia Morgan** and **Turiya Hanover**, from my first counselling training are the founders of Path of Love. They are also offering the following training https://www.workingwithpeopletrainings.com

Peter Levine https://www.somaticexperiencing.com/about-peter
- His books: https://www.somaticexperiencing.com/se-books

The Hoffmann Process https://www.hoffmanprocess.com.au

The Shift Network https://theshiftnetwork.com

Thomas A. Harris *I'm ok, you're ok*

Trauma healing https://www.somaticexperiencing.com/home

TRE – Trauma Release Exercises https://traumaprevention.com/what-is-tre/

Yoga Fire Breath https://www.healthline.com/health/breath-of-fire-yoga#definition